# Introducing

## Microsoft®

# FrontPage™ 97

## Kerry A. Lehto and W. Brett Polonsky
with a foreword by FrontPage
co-creator Randy Forgaard

PUBLISHED BY
Microsoft Press
A Division of Microsoft Corporation
One Microsoft Way
Redmond, Washington 98052-6399

Library of Congress Cataloging-in-Publication Data
Lehto, Kerry A., 1966-
    Introducing Microsoft FrontPage 97/ Kerry A. Lehto, W. Brett
Polonsky.
        p.        cm.
    Includes index.
    ISBN 1-57231-571-7
    1. Web sites.      2. FrontPage (Computer file)    3. Web publishing.
I. Polonsky, W. Brett, 1965-   .   II. Title.
TK5105.888.L443    1996
005.7'2–dc21                                                    96-40955
                                                               CIP

Printed and bound in the United States of America.

1 2 3 4 5 6 7 8 9   QMQM   2 1 0 9 8 7

Distributed to the book trade in Canada by Macmillan of Canada, a division of Canada
Publishing Corporation.

A CIP catalogue record for this book is available from the British Library.

Microsoft Press books are available through booksellers and distributors worldwide. For further
information about international editions, contact your local Microsoft Corporation office. Or
contact Microsoft Press International directly at fax (206) 936-7329.

Macintosh is a registered trademark of Apple Computer, Inc. Microsoft, Microsoft Press,
PowerPoint, Visual Basic, Visual C++, Windows, and Windows NT are registered trademarks and
ActiveX, FrontPage, IntelliMouse, Visual SourceSafe, and WebBot are trademarks of Microsoft
Corporation. Java is a trademark of Sun Microsystems, Inc.

Other products and company names mentioned herein may be the trademarks of their respective owners.

**Acquisitions Editor:** Casey Doyle
**Project Editor:** Stuart J. Stuple
**Manuscript Editor:** Ina Chang
**Technical Editor:** Robert Lyon

*For Janell, Gage, and Emma,*
*the three reasons I do any of this,*
*&*
*Mom and Dad,*
*for more reasons than I can count.*
*I love you all very much.*
*—WBP*


*To all the wonderful people in my life who have shared*
*my path, even for a little while, and who have helped me to learn*
*something more along the way. Thank you for the beauty, the laughs,*
*and the challenges, and please remember that my love is with you.*
*If you've chosen to fly away, may our paths cross again on sunnier days.*
*—KAL*

# Contents

# PART 2 Creating and Managing Your Site

## Chapter 3 Inside the FrontPage Explorer                27

## Chapter 4 Templates and Wizards                63

# Chapter 5  Managing Your Web Site

# PART 3  Building Your Pages

# Chapter 6  Creating Your Pages

## Chapter 7  Fine-Tuning Your Pages  177

# Chapter 8  Getting into Graphics  221

# Chapter 9  WebBot Components and Forms  243

## PART 4  Finishing Touches

## Chapter 10  Advanced Features                          301

## Chapter 11  Web Servers                                325

## Appendix  Installing FrontPage                          343

# Acknowledgments

Just when we thought we broke the sound barrier in producing the first edition of this book, *Introducing Microsoft FrontPage*, Microsoft Press said, "Hey, we'll bet you can do that again in half the time!" And believe it or not, we did—but not without the loss of some prime sleep hours and the help of several key people:

Microsoft's Randy Forgaard, for help each and every step of the way. We truly appreciate the input and time you gave us, especially considering how busy you are.

The great folks at Microsoft Press: Casey Doyle, for helping to put the project together; Stuart Stuple, Project Editor Extraordinaire; The Wonderful Bill Teel, the Screen Shot Wizard; Robert Lyon, our tech editor, for checking all the fine details; and our manuscript editor, Ina Chang. And as always, we appreciate the help and support of Mary DeJong, Jim Fuchs, and Jack Litewka.

Tremendous thanks go to all others who helped make this project a success: Jean Trenary and Katherine Erickson at Frog Mountain Productions, for page layout and production; and The Lovely and Talented David Holter, "Mr. Cool," the best illustrator we know.

We'd also like to recognize the support of Mary Arnold, Shelly Thorn, Danna Gatti, and Steve Edwards.

"Nine Ball, anyone? Rack 'em up!"

# Foreword

On the afternoon of Thursday, April 7, 1994, my wife took an urgent phone call from a man on a car phone. He had gotten my name from my MIT master's thesis adviser, and was calling to offer me a job. Thinking he was a headhunter, my wife declined to give him my work phone number, but said he could phone back that evening. He was worried about the delay, but nonetheless phoned back at 7:00 p.m. and we chatted. The man was Charles H. Ferguson, a well-known computer industry consultant and author on technology policy and corporate strategy. We met and talked several times over that weekend. Four days after the first phone call, I quit my job and became cofounder of Vermeer Technologies, Inc., named after Charles's favorite 17th-century Dutch painter. As it turns out, Charles's general sense of urgency was extraordinarily justified.

In the beginning, Charles was the idea and business person, and I was the technical person charged with transforming the ideas into concrete product features that could be implemented by a small group of talented engineers within a reasonable time frame. When we began, we actually had not heard of the Web. Charles's original notion was that it was wasteful for companies like CompuServe, Dow Jones, Bloomberg, and Apple to have each spent millions of dollars building proprietary online services with incompatible client software and based on outmoded mainframe server technology. Our goal was to build inexpensive, standardized, and interoperable client, server, and authoring software that any company could buy to set up a dial-up online service for information dissemination and commerce. End-users could run the same client software to access all online services built using our technology.

This idea changed dramatically a month after the company was formed. In May 1994, we got wind that the Internet was starting to be adopted by businesses, and that a new infrastructure called the World Wide Web provided online service functionality on top of Internet protocols. Mosaic, the first graphical user interface for the Web, had been released five months earlier by the National Center for Supercomputing Applications (NCSA). Netscape Communications Corp. (then called Mosaic Communications) had been founded in April (the same time as Vermeer), and would release their famous commercial Web browser toward the end of that year.

It occurred to us that the Web provided much of what we were trying to achieve: standardized protocols (HTTP), server software that supported those protocols (various Web servers), universal client software that supported those protocols (various Web browsers), and even a communications infrastructure (the Internet) that was more robust and convenient than we were planning (dial-up to each online service). The major missing piece, with respect to our original plans, was a complete, visual authoring tool for non-programmers to create, maintain, and administer whole Web sites (online services), including the individual pages that make up such sites. The creation of such a Web authoring tool became the focus of Vermeer.

We were extraordinarily fortunate to attract the most talented group of individuals I have ever met, despite the fact that we had no funding yet (except for direct expenses, covered by Charles), and asked everyone to take no salary for many months. Andy Schulert and Peter Amstein, both seasoned professionals, were our first two engineering hires and became our two technical team leaders. We were joined by many other first-rate engineers, plus excellent marketing, sales, administrative, and executive personnel. Every one of them was a consummate professional, driven and focused on the task at hand.

The name "Vermeer" turned out to be an interesting choice. Many thought we were a Dutch company, and we got e-mail from strangers in Holland. Early on, we were contacted by Vermeer Manufacturing Co., a maker of construction equipment in Iowa, asking if we were interested in giving them our registered Internet domain name, *vermeer.com*. (We weren't.) During the big exhibition of Vermeer paintings in Washington, D.C., art-lovers visited our Web site expecting…well…art. But the nontraditional company name also helped us stand out a bit from the sea of other high-tech companies.

For the first eight months, everyone at Vermeer worked out of their homes, with e-mail and fax machines keeping all of us in touch. We had weekly get-togethers at the Cambridge, Mass., offices of Andy Kerr, our part-time CFO. Charles, Andy Kerr, and I shopped around for venture capital financing, toting a Visual Basic mock-up of our software written by Peter

Amstein, while the engineers worked hard on a functional prototype. At that time, it was still not completely clear that the Web would be an unqualified success. Our business plan forecasted sales of 500 units in the first year, and it explained how our software could be ported to Lotus Notes or our own infrastructure if the Internet failed to catch on.

Vermeer closed its first round of $4 million funding in January 1995, with Sigma Partners and Matrix Partners as lead investors, and Atlas Venture as an additional investor. This cash let us lease some office space in Cambridge, start paying modest salaries, purchase needed computer equipment, move beyond the prototype, and start writing the actual software in earnest.

While Vermeer was building its first product, the Web became an unprecedented success. There were only an estimated 10,000 Web sites in existence when Vermeer was formed, but one year later there were approximately 500,000 such sites, including both external sites on the Internet and intranet sites within organizations. By just about any measure—communications traffic, new Web sites going up, downloads of Web browsers and servers, new Internet accounts—the Web was growing at 20 percent per month, the fastest-growing phenomenon in economic history.

Vermeer shipped version 1.0 of its product in October 1995, just one week behind schedule. The name of the product, FrontPage, was suggested by Mitch Kapor, the founder of Lotus. On the one hand, FrontPage was a great success, winning many industry awards and praise from customers. On the other hand, during the brief life of Vermeer, Web authoring had advanced from a curious backwater to a major focus of some of the largest players in the software industry. Tiny Vermeer, with just 35 employees, suddenly found itself in the hot seat.

At around this time, Microsoft Corp. became interested in Web authoring tools. Steven Sinofsky, group program manager for the Microsoft Office product line, discovered the 30-day evaluation version of FrontPage 1.0 posted on the Vermeer Web site. Steven showed it to Mike Mathieu, program manager for Microsoft Word, who wrote up a 10-page review. Mike showed it to Chris Peters, vice president of the Office Product Unit and a 15-year veteran of Microsoft. Chris gave it to Bill Gates to try out during his annual "think week." At Vermeer, we watched our Web server logs as 25 different Microsoft people downloaded FrontPage 1.0 over a two-week period.

In early November 1995, Chris Peters called us. They really liked the product. They felt we had just the right idea—focusing on building a whole

Web site, and not just creating individual pages. They liked the fact that FrontPage looked just like a Microsoft Office application. They were impressed that we seemed to be 9 to 12 months ahead of the industry. They wanted to know if we were interested in some sort of relationship, anywhere from co-marketing to technology licensing to the "full meal deal," as Chris called it—being acquired by Microsoft.

We took a hard look at Microsoft and were extremely impressed. They had recently transformed themselves into a highly Internet-focused company. They were extraordinarily good at shipping products. Chris Peters himself would resign from his highly visible role as head of the Microsoft Office product unit to take command of tiny FrontPage. And we realized that our efforts would be multiplied a thousandfold by joining Microsoft. So, on January 16, 1996, we did.

I got my first taste of Life in Redmond when I visited Microsoft head-quarters together with Vermeer's president, John Mandile, to participate in the announcement of the acquisition. We found a huge, professionally de-signed vinyl banner hanging in Building 18, welcoming Vermeer to Microsoft (still in place today, as no one has yet determined how to remove it). The Associated Press leaked the story of the acquisition a day early, keeping busy a small army from Microsoft's public relations firm. Literally overnight, Microsoft graphic artists created a complete mock-up of a new Microsoft FrontPage box (wrapped around an Excel box—who would know?) for Bill Gates to hold during the photo session later that day. Microsoft Studios zipped around campus, shooting 20 minutes of "B-roll" video segments (Gates being interviewed, Sinofsky using FrontPage, Peters/Mandile/Forgaard pretending to talk earnestly about something, Microsoft flag waving in the breeze) to be shown behind newscasters nationwide as they reported the story. Microsoft Webmasters moved Vermeer's Web site to Redmond by the next morning. John and I participated with Microsoft officials in a giant con-ference call announcing the deal to 350 journalists. I did FrontPage demos for hundreds of Microsoft employees. Using a Redmond-to-Atlanta satellite link-up, Chris Peters was interviewed live on CNN.

Virtually the entire Vermeer engineering, quality assurance, and documen-tation teams moved to Microsoft headquarters in Redmond. Twenty-five families said good-bye to everything in Boston, and hello to the trees and lattes and grunge bands of the Pacific Northwest. You could almost see the roots dangling from beneath the airplane. FrontPage 1.1 shipped in early May 1996, just three weeks after everyone arrived in Seattle.

None of us was really prepared for the magnitude of what happened next. In June 1996, the first month of retail availability, FrontPage 1.1 hit *PC Week*'s list of best-selling software in the #22 slot. By July, we were #7. In August, FrontPage was the third best-selling software package in the country, outselling even Microsoft Office itself. Whereas Vermeer had sold a total of 275 copies of FrontPage in the company's short life, Microsoft sold 150,000 copies of FrontPage in the first four months.

As I write this, we are just a few days away from releasing our new version, Microsoft FrontPage 97, to manufacturing. It is the third release of FrontPage in just one year. In response to customer requests and trends of the Web, we have packed this release with new capabilities, ease-of-use features, and a healthy smattering of polish. Our goal has been to take the best of the latest Web technologies and make them accessible to everyone, with a special emphasis on Microsoft Office users. We hope you will enjoy using it as much as we have enjoyed creating it.

Kerry Lehto and W. Brett Polonsky, the authors of this book, share our vision for FrontPage. We gave them access to some of the earliest builds of FrontPage 97, and it shows in the depth and insight of their coverage here, with clear descriptions, tips, and advice on all of the new and existing FrontPage features. I read through each chapter, and the three of us consulted extensively on FrontPage features and plans. I found this book to be thoroughly accessible, informative, and fun, and I believe you will, too.

With time comes change. Today, if you visit www.vermeer.com, you'll find out about construction equipment rather than Web authoring. The large photographic reproduction of Jan Vermeer's *The Concert* now hangs in Redmond instead of Cambridge. But the Vermeer "star" logo still pulses on-screen when FrontPage is busy working. As the months pass and the future of the Web unfolds before us, I know that there will always be a spark of tiny Vermeer at Microsoft...and in FrontPage.

**Randy Forgaard**
Senior Program Manager, FrontPage
Microsoft Corporation
November 1996

# Introduction

## Welcome to FrontPage

The Internet and the World Wide Web are fast becoming mainstays of the business and home computing arenas. The vast array of technologies that have taken hold alongside them have become a part of our everyday lives, and will continue to change the way we live and work. Intranets, which use Internet technologies within a business or across an enterprise, are the wave of the late 1990s; businesses worldwide are expected to spend nearly $40 billion on them by the turn of the century.

Similar to other booms the computing world has witnessed, thousands of companies have formed to search for a piece of the Internet pie. Scores of good Internet-related products are available, but most of us don't have the time or the expertise required to sort through them, learn their pros and cons, and put them to use, whether at work or at home.

Microsoft FrontPage makes it easy for you to establish a presence on the World Wide Web or create a Web site for your organization's intranet. Designed to fit seamlessly into the Microsoft Office suite of applications, FrontPage is the first easy-to-use Internet client *and* server product that allows you to develop an entire Web site and connect it to many kinds of servers. If you want to set up a Web site but you're not a programming whiz, don't worry—FrontPage can do the programming for you. But FrontPage is also robust enough for amateur and professional developers who want to toy with the code.

FrontPage comes with several additional elements, collectively called the FrontPage Bonus Pack:

◆ Microsoft Image Composer, which allows you to create and manipulate images for your Web site, and comes with image effects and more than 200 MB of sample photos that you can use.

◆ Microsoft Personal Web Server, a version of Microsoft's Internet Information Server (IIS) that runs on Windows 95 and Windows NT Workstation. The Microsoft Personal Web Server has improved performance and additional features over the FrontPage Personal Web Server, which is included as a part of FrontPage.

◆ Web Publishing Wizard, which allows you to publish your FrontPage Web sites to any Internet service provider that you have an account for, or to online services such as America Online and CompuServe. You typically use this wizard for servers that are not running the FrontPage Server Extensions.

◆ Microsoft Internet Explorer 3.0, which is Microsoft's Web browser.

# Talk About Easy!

*Introducing Microsoft FrontPage 97* is your in-depth, one-stop shop for learning the ins and outs of FrontPage. You'll learn how to develop and maintain a Web site with the FrontPage Explorer, develop high-quality Web pages with the FrontPage Editor, and run your Web site with one of the Personal Web Servers for Windows 95 or another server of your choice. You'll also learn how to incorporate material from Microsoft Office files into your site, and link to, from, and within those files. You'll learn about some exciting new additions in FrontPage 97, such as working with ActiveX controls, Java applets, and VBScript and JavaScript; adding sound, video, and marquees to a site; and previewing your site in a browser directly from the Editor, to name just a few.

Because some of you like to lift the hood and tinker with the controls, this book also includes information about more advanced topics, such as Secure Sockets Layer (SSL) security, connecting to ODBC-compliant databases using the Internet Database Connector (IDC), editing the source code of your Web pages, and FrontPage's server administration tools and Server Extensions.

## A Look at the Book

Part 1, "The Beginning Stages," introduces you to FrontPage; talks about the birth of the Internet, the World Wide Web, and intranets; and explains how FrontPage fits into all three scenes. You'll learn some great tips on producing sites for the Web and for your organization's intranet, and you'll learn about the exciting new ways that FrontPage works in conjunction with Microsoft Office.

Part 2, "Creating and Managing Your Site," tells you everything you need to know about creating and administering Web sites in the FrontPage Explorer. In the Explorer you can view your site in different ways—in Hyperlink view and in the new Folder view. In Part 2 you'll also learn how to use the FrontPage templates and wizards, as well as the To Do List, an inventory of elements that need to be completed in your site. Web-site management, including changing passwords, access privileges, and much more, is also explained in detail in this part.

Part 3, "Building Your Pages," looks into the FrontPage Editor, which you'll use to create and edit your Web pages. Here you'll find in-depth instructions for creating terrific-looking Web pages that include video, audio, marquees, colored text, tables, frames, character formatting, font styles, and much more. You'll find the Editor as easy to use as a word processor. Part 3 also contains some hearty content on Web-site graphics, how FrontPage uses them, and ways to make them appear faster in a browser. A detailed look at FrontPage's WebBot components and forms is also presented in this part, along with a brief look at more advanced topics.

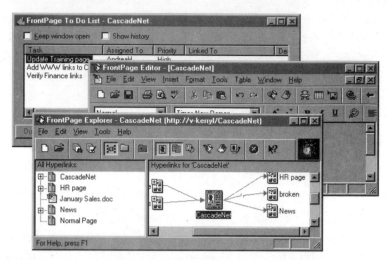

**The FrontPage client: You create and manage Web sites in the Explorer, craft Web pages in the Editor, and keep track of tasks with the To Do List.**

Part 4, "The Finishing Touches," introduces you to using servers with FrontPage. Here you'll learn about the Microsoft Personal Web Server and the FrontPage Personal Web Server, which allow you to test Web pages and set up an intranet on your local computer or network. You'll also learn about the FrontPage Server Extensions, which extend a server's ability to take advantage of features available in FrontPage. These extensions are available for a wide variety of servers that use platforms such as Microsoft Windows 95, Microsoft Windows NT, and various flavors of UNIX.

The Appendix shows you how to install FrontPage on a computer with Windows 95 or Windows NT.

## Tips and Terms

The book also includes Shortcut, Tip, and Warning boxes that provide more details about the subject at hand. Shortcuts show you ways to save time, such as clicking a toolbar button or using a keyboard shortcut instead of using a menu command. Just as there's more than one way to get from Cairo to Cooperstown, Tips offer alternative ways to carry out tasks, and they give you additional information on a topic. Warnings caution you against performing actions that can lead to trouble.

In the back of the book is a glossary of terms relating to the Internet and FrontPage; a similar glossary is provided in FrontPage's online help. Glossary terms used in this book appear in boldface—when you come across a boldface term in the text, just look to the glossary in the back to find its definition.

## Who Should Read This Book?

*Introducing Microsoft FrontPage 97* is designed for both beginning and advanced FrontPage users. Just as FrontPage is designed for nonprogrammers, so is this book. It's ideal for those who want to learn how to use FrontPage to create a Web site for the World Wide Web or for an intranet.

This book picks up where the product's online help leaves off; within these pages you'll find in-depth descriptions and scenarios about possible uses of FrontPage that draw on our experience in Web-site creation, design, and management. We hope this book will help you fill in the holes and answer your questions as you make your FrontPage sites "sights to see."

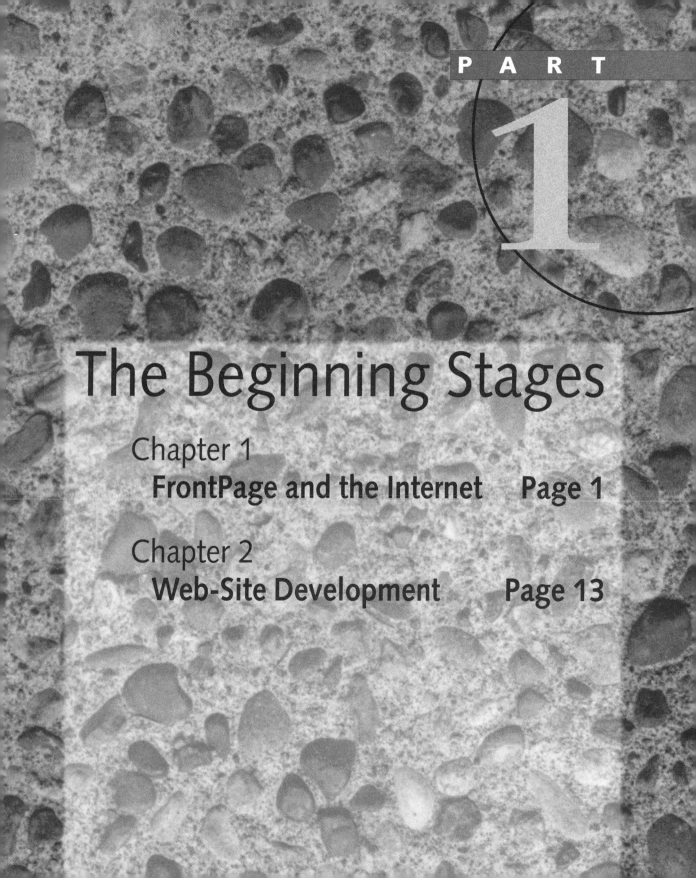

# The Beginning Stages

# Chapter 1

# FrontPage and the Internet

## It's Here, It's Now

There's no escaping the **Internet;** it's become almost as essential as the fax machine. Businesses large and small are using it to tap information sources worldwide, communicate via e-mail, and post their **World Wide Web** sites; millions of individuals "surf" the Web from their homes. You're as likely to come across a site for a large corporation advertising its wares as you are of finding a site where someone is showing off pictures of his kids or sharing an old family recipe.

This chapter provides some background on the Internet, the World Wide Web, and **intranets.** It describes how FrontPage fits into this scene, explains how easily it integrates with Microsoft Office, and shows how *you* might fit into the latest wave of this technology.

### The Net, the Web: What's the Difference?

The Internet is older than you might think—it's been around for almost 30 years. Considering that the first electrical computer was built just over half a century ago, the Internet is quite the veteran in the computing world. It started out in the late 1960s as a U.S. government communications network (called ARPA-net), and was used mainly by the government, universities, and other research institutions until the mid-1980s, when it expanded and took on the name "Internet."

**So how does it work?** When computers interoperate with others within a group, they constitute a network. The Internet is one huge network of computers consisting of thousands of smaller networks worldwide. You might think of a computer as a cell in your body—many similar cells make up your heart, your liver, and so on; each of these organs can be considered networks of cells. All of these networks together make up your entire body, which would be the Internet in computing terms.

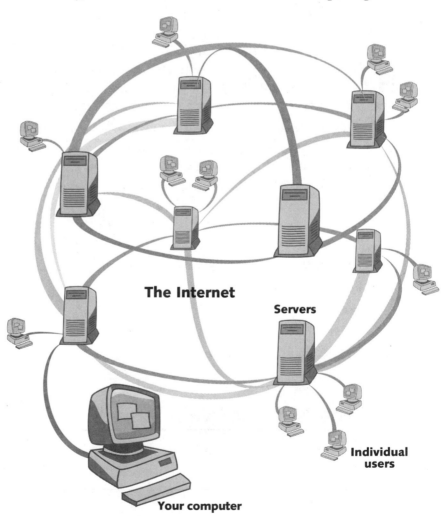

**The Internet**

**Servers**

**Individual users**

**Your computer**

And just as cells must communicate in order to live side by side, so must the computers of the Internet. They must use a common language, and that language is stated in **protocols**—a set of agreed-upon rules governing how they interact. The standard protocols used for exchanging data on the Internet are Transmission Control Protocol and Internet Protocol; the combination of the two is known as **TCP/IP**. TCP/IP organizes information into tidy little packages before shipping it across the network. Each package contains a portion of the information being sent, along with a description of what the information is, where it's coming from, and where it's heading. Sending data across the Internet is like disassembling a jigsaw puzzle in one room and reassembling it in another room. To put it together again quickly, you have to identify the pieces in relation to each other and put them back together in sequence.

**How about the Web?** In the late 1980s, when the Internet was growing gradually with the addition of a few major networks here and there, a scientist named Tim Berners-Lee began seeking a better way for his colleagues at the European Laboratory for Particle Physics (known by its French acronym, CERN) to communicate by computer. At the time, the only information that could be transmitted across the Internet appeared as simple text on computer screens. Berners-Lee and his associates created an interface for linking information from various sources. The eventual result was the defining of the **URL**, **HTTP**, and **HTML** specifications on which the World Wide Web is based. Today, Web technology allows creation of a formatted page of information that can be linked to other pages of information and accessed across a network.

In simple terms, the Web is a collection of information that is accessible via **Web browsers**. The first significant Web browser was Mosaic, developed by the National Center for Supercomputing Applications (NCSA) at the University of Illinois at Urbana-Champaign. The market now offers more than two dozen Web browsers, and the number is growing. Currently, Netscape Navigator and Microsoft Internet Explorer hold the lion's share of the Web-browser market. A Web browser consists of a window that displays Web pages. Typically, a Web browser has toolbars and menu commands that allow users to explore pages and sites and adjust the browser's settings. Because of the proliferation of Web browsers and the way that each can be configured to display information in different ways, a Web page viewed in one browser can, in theory, look very different in another browser. However, this problem has lessened as Netscape and Microsoft have come to dominate the browser market, since their browsers display pages similarly.

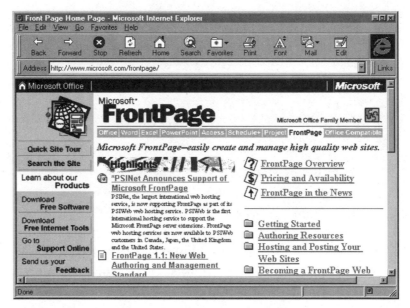

**A Web page from the FrontPage area of Microsoft's World Wide Web site, as viewed in Internet Explorer 3.0.**

Web pages can include graphics, sounds, animation, and other special effects in addition to text. Individual pages can be linked to other pages to provide access to additional information. All of this is transmitted using the physical medium and the protocols of the Internet. That's why many people think of the Web as being synonymous with the Internet.

The Web has grown at an incredible rate. Thousands of people have their own Web sites, and numerous businesses have put their names up in Web lights. (The term **home page** is often used to refer to a Web site; actually, a home page is the opening page of a Web site—its default page—and it usually has links to other pages.) The Internet and the Web have dramatically changed people's business habits in the last few years; have you noticed that it's now standard to include your e-mail and Web addresses on your business card?

Although more and more companies are attempting to do business on the Internet, the potential is virtually untapped. There are some basic factors underlying this somewhat slow development of commerce on the Web. Many sites are too slow, too unorganized, too difficult to read, and so on, and it's easy for a potential customer to move to another site with the click of a mouse. Part of the reason that access on the Web can be so slow is that technology is playing catch-up with demand. The Internet infrastructure was not built to handle the amount of information users would like it to carry.

Until the market dictates that costs come down and that more information travel for less money, we'll have to design Web sites for the existing infrastructure. These sites will need to be streamlined so that they download quickly, yet they'll still need to be professionally designed and frequently updated—all of which is easy to do with FrontPage. In the next chapter you'll get some pointers on how to create a successful Web site *now*.

**Where do intranets fit in?** Now that you know what the Internet and the World Wide Web are, you might be wondering what an intranet is. The key lies in the prefixes: *inter* (between or among) and *intra* (within). The Internet connects computers from a variety of different organizations; an intranet (sometimes called an *internal Web*) connects computers networked within a single organization. The term *intranet* also implies that the network supports Web technology. So basically an intranet is just like the Internet, except that an intranet's content is accessible only to the organization's users and not to users across the worldwide Internet. Intranets can also be linked to the Internet, but they don't have to be.

Large corporations are already realizing the potential of intranets, and smaller businesses are not far behind. Intranets are an effective and efficient way of communicating within an organization. In the coming years, intranets might do for businesses what e-mail has done in the past few years—make communication easier.

Typically, the networked computers on an intranet are at one location (such as one office), and they can span several departments within an organization. But an intranet can involve remote locations as well. Suppose Cascade Coffee Roasters has branches in Washington, Wyoming, and Wisconsin, and all the company's computers are networked. The company can set up an intranet so that its employees can communicate and share information via computer. This sounds just like a typical network, but what makes it an intranet is that it's a network that supports TCP/IP and has servers with content that can be accessed with a Web browser. The illustration below shows how one company's intranet might be set up.

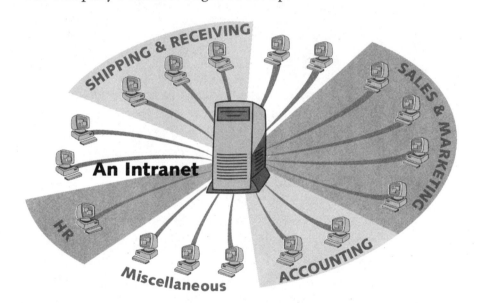

## FrontPage in the Spotlight

Web-site developers will find a "cast of thousands" when it comes to choosing a Web authoring tool, and competition between products is driving their improving quality. The choices include HTML editors that require HTML mastery; graphical Web authoring applications that require some HTML expertise; and the star performer, FrontPage, which requires very little or no HTML knowledge. FrontPage has entered the scene by offering a powerful product that makes it extraordinarily easy to develop professional-looking Web sites for the Internet or intranets. FrontPage is unique in that it exploits the current wave in computing—client-server computing—which makes it easy to integrate into many computing systems. Let's dig into that a little deeper.

**Client-server computing: It's hip, it's hot.** Client-server computing is the latest buzzword in business computing. In a client-server system, a **server** is a computer or application that supplies data or resources that can be accessed across a network. A **client** is a computer or application that takes advantage of the data or resources. In many cases, the server is a powerful computer and the client is a typical desktop system. For example, suppose the invoices received at Cascade Coffee Roasters are all stored in a database on the server. In a client-server invoice system, you input the information on a client computer and store the information centrally on the server when you complete the invoice. This way, an unlimited number of client computers can be hooked up to the server, and each can have access to the same data.

FrontPage works in a similar way; in fact, it contains both a client and a server. Its client software consists of the FrontPage Explorer, Editor, and To Do List. The Explorer allows you to view and administer your site in several different ways. You create new pages and edit existing pages in the Editor. The To Do List allows you to maintain an inventory of work that is yet to be completed in your site. As you build your site, you can add and check off items in the To Do List. Later chapters will describe these features in more detail, along with other client-side features such as **templates** and **wizards**.

For the server side of FrontPage, you can use the FrontPage Personal Web Server or the new Microsoft Personal Web Server on Windows 95 or Windows NT Workstation. On Windows NT Server, which ships with Microsoft Internet Information Server (**IIS**), FrontPage automatically detects and uses the IIS Web server. You can install the Personal Web Servers on a computer on a local area network (**LAN**) or a wide area network (**WAN**) running TCP/IP and instantly make that network into an intranet. You can even house the Personal Web Servers on the same computer you're using for the client software. If you need to create or edit new pages in your site, you can do that on any client computer that's linked to the server—even if your client-server setup spans halfway around the world.

The Personal Web Servers are best used as low-volume servers, and are ideal for developing and testing your sites internally. They are not recommended for use as World Wide Web servers, however—if you're expecting high volume for an intranet or Internet server, you'll probably want a more powerful solution, such as any of the leading Web servers on the market today. The Microsoft Personal Web Server and IIS are both excellent production Web servers. Note that the license for Windows NT Workstation (which is commonly used with the Microsoft Personal Web Server) permits only ten simultaneous Web connections, so if you want to support heavier traffic, you can move up to Windows NT Server and IIS, or use a UNIX-based Web server and one of the many FrontPage-supported Web servers for **UNIX**. For more information on servers, see Chapter 11.

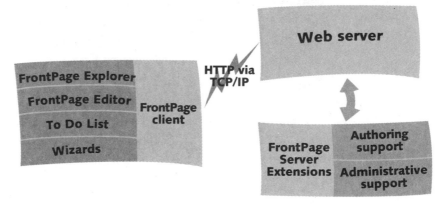

FrontPage also provides **FrontPage Server Extensions** to enable any of the leading Web servers to communicate with FrontPage. If your organization already uses a high-end Web server, the Server Extensions can be dropped in to provide seamless communication between FrontPage and the server. You'll find more details on the Server Extensions in Chapter 11.

# The Perfect Partnership: FrontPage 97 and Microsoft Office 97

The Microsoft Office 97 suite of applications includes Microsoft Word, Excel, PowerPoint, and Access. Office is the best-selling suite of office applications on the market. The content creation capabilities of Office combined with the Web-site management and Web-page creation features of FrontPage provide an ideal way to create Web sites. Here are some ways the two make a seamless partnership:

◆ In the FrontPage Explorer's Hyperlink view, Office documents are shown with the same icons you're used to seeing in the Windows Explorer.

◆ FrontPage's ability to verify and repair links extends to any Office documents within your site that contain links.

◆ You can casily copy material from Office files onto your FrontPage Web pages. For example, you can copy part or all of an Excel spreadsheet onto a page in the Editor, using either the Clipboard or drag-and-drop, and it will automatically be converted into an HTML table.

◆ You can drag Office documents from the Windows Explorer into the FrontPage Explorer, and those documents will be automatically imported into your site.

**As inexpensive as it gets** If you don't have Office running on your machine but still want to view an Office document that's in a FrontPage Web site, you can use an Office viewer. Office viewers are separate applications that users can download for free from Microsoft's Web site. As of this writing, viewers are available for Word, Excel, and PowerPoint. If you have a viewer installed, you can click on a link to a Word, Excel, or PowerPoint document in any Web site, and the document will appear as a read-only file in the viewer. You can configure a viewer in various ways, for example to show or hide various toolbars, bookmarks, and format marks. You can also print the file that appears in a viewer. More specific information on using the viewers is included in the README file, which you receive when you download and set up the viewer from Microsoft.

To download the viewers, connect to Microsoft's Web site at //www.microsoft.com. Select Products and find the appropriate application: Word, Excel, or PowerPoint. Click the link to the application's home page. On the application's home page, you will find instructions on how to locate and download the viewer.

**Ready for launch!** When you're building or updating your Web site, you can open Office files in their native application from within the FrontPage Explorer so you don't have to concern yourself with opening the Office application separately. When you double-click on a document created in Word, Excel, or PowerPoint from the Explorer, FrontPage automatically launches the appropriate application so you can edit the document in its native environment.

**Office look and feel** FrontPage sports the look and feel of Office. Toolbar buttons, menu commands, dialog boxes, and keyboard shortcuts are designed to be instantly recognizable by Office users.

**Office thesaurus** Just in case you're at a loss for words, the Editor includes the thesaurus used in Office.

**Office spell-checker** The Editor allows you to check the spelling of the current page, and the Explorer allows you to check the spelling of selected pages or the entire site. This is the same spell-checker used in Office.

None of us has ever won a national spelling contest. (If you have, you can leave the room.) But have you ever noticed the number of misspellings on Web pages? They can be thigh-slapping funny, but it's also very sad considering that the information on the Web is there for all the world to see. A misspelling in a site on an intranet can be even more embarrassing. Suppose you misspell your boss's name or title in a corporate bio. That could get you fired—or worse, your boss could force you to make the next two weeks' worth of bagel runs.

FrontPage might save you a bunch of bagel bucks by including the dictionary and suggestion routines available in Word, but no spell-checker can substitute for good spelling knowledge. Of course, you might as well use the best if you're going to rely on one!

## Coming Up

Now that you've got a better idea of how FrontPage fits into the Internet and intranet scenes, and how it works with Office 97, it's time to plan your first Web site. You'll learn how to do this in Chapter 2, and you'll also learn how to make your sites ones that viewers won't want to leave.

# Chapter 2
# Web-Site Development

## Planning the Information Flow

Surf on the **World Wide Web** today, and you'll find some very good sites—ones that download quickly, are pleasing to the eye, organize the flow of information into well-defined areas, allow for discoverable and easy-to-use navigation, and are well written. These sites simply *invite* you to come in, take off your shoes, stay a while, have some fun, and learn something new.

If you stay a long time at a site without realizing it, you've probably found a well-thought-out site. Take a step back and try to see the big picture here. Can you see the structure, the organization? Does the information flow easily? Understanding how information flows through a site is the first step in creating a functional, easy-to-use site. If you can understand how that concept works, and implement it in your site, you'll already be miles ahead of most other Web-site developers.

Many site developers don't take the time to understand the *flow;* they're only concerned with putting words and pictures on a page. Even though many sites proudly boast that they receive many more hits (connections) than their competitors, the number of visitors really isn't a good indication of how good a site is. How long a viewer stays at a site is a much better indicator. If users stay at your site long enough to go through the various levels and areas within it, then you know you've done the job right. That means they can find what they need, get around, and get back, without having to think too much about it.

To create an effective Web site, you need to visualize the flow of information and the various paths a user can take through it. In other words, you have to see your site from the user's point of view. Planning a site can involve a substantial amount of work, but it certainly doesn't have to be *all* work—if you have fun in the planning stages, you'll probably end up with a better site.

With FrontPage, you don't have to be a Webmaster to create a site that visitors will return to time and time again. The kind of site you create, and the kinds of information you include in it, depend on your target audience. This chapter will discuss sites targeted toward an Internet audience as well as sites for an intranet within your business or organization.

## Guidelines for a Good Site

The best Web sites are ones that look appealing, get the message across succinctly, and don't make users wait too long for information to appear on their screens. The following are some guidelines for creating a successful site:

◆ **Have a clear purpose.** What are your goals? Just to get on the Web? If so, you're like many others, and you shouldn't be surprised if your site ends up like most others. Make your goals as specific as possible. Perhaps you want your site to show off your company's products. That's all fine and dandy, but consider *how* you want to show off those products. How do you want your products positioned in the Web market? Asking these deeper-level questions will result in a clearly defined goal. Without a well-defined goal, your site is doomed for a trip to the Internet graveyard.

- **Always keep your audience in mind.** Who is the primary (and secondary) audience for your site? How old are they? What do they do for a living? How much time do they have to look at your site? For every piece of information, every graphic, and every content decision you make, ask yourself, "How will the audience react to this?"

- **Use items that download quickly.** The number-one reason that people leave a site quickly—or don't visit a site at all—is that it takes too long for the information to appear on their screens. Large file-size graphics cause users to twiddle their thumbs, and it's all too easy for them to click a Stop button in their browser to stop downloading your site. Use graphics with small file sizes. If you have to include a graphic that has a large file size, one option is to include a small, low-resolution graphic and give the user the option of downloading the larger one. For more ideas on how to streamline graphic size, see Chapter 8.

- **Make your site visually appealing.** You've undoubtedly seen some plain, boring sites on the Web. What makes them plain? Lack of color and lack of variation in text and heading sizes, perhaps. You've probably seen some cluttered and chaotic sites as well, ones that use too many fonts in too many sizes or too many colors. When building your site, remember that a well-laid-out page brings you one step closer to a well-done site.

- **Don't try to put everything on one page.** Be careful not to clutter your pages with too much information. We know that writers like to write and graphic designers love to create cool images. As the developer of the site, it's up to you to create that delicate harmony between these two very different groups of people.

> **TIP**
>
> We often think our sites are right on target with our intended audiences, but it's easy to miss the mark. To avoid this, be humble and try to have your site plan and content reviewed by as many people as possible, especially potential members of your audience. This step is critical but often overlooked.

Try to strike that balance between text and art: Think about who'll be reading those pages. Think about how difficult it can be to read a lot of text on a computer screen, and write the content for your pages accordingly. Think about your graphics in terms of what value they add to the page. Are they serving a purpose, or do they just look good? But remember that good-looking graphics sometimes serve the purpose by themselves. What we're all striving for as Web-site developers are pages that look good, contain useful information, and allow the user to easily explore the site.

◆ **Organize your content in intelligent ways.** Maybe you've heard the saying that "content is king." It's true. How many times have you visited a site and thought, "There's nothing here"? Perhaps some good content is buried deep within the site, but the only viewers who will "dig it up" are those who randomly come across it. If you have some information you feel your viewers *must* see, don't bury it in hidden pages. Make important information as obvious and easy to find as possible.

Don't forget that your site will likely be more than one level deep. Organize secondary material into groups of related information. For example, suppose you're setting up an online catalog for a music store. Would you list your jazz CDs and rock CDs in the same section? Of course not. This is a glaringly simple example, but if you look at all your information in terms of appropriate categories, you'll have a much better organized site than most of the ones out there.

◆ **Include appropriate buttons for exploring the site.** Most site developers use linked buttons to represent the various areas within the site. These buttons are usually found on all pages within a site, and are usually grouped together in the same place on the page. Keeping them together and in the same place increases their discoverability and usefulness. The user can simply click on a navigation button to move to another section of the site.

Here are some things to keep in mind while creating your navigation buttons:

- Include a button that takes the user back to the **home page**. If your viewers are buried five levels deep into a site, they should be able to click a button to get back to the first page so they can start over if they need to. If they're stuck using the Back button in their browser, chances are they'll get frustrated and leave your site.

- Be prepared for people to come to your site with graphics turned off in their browsers. It's a good idea to have a linked text version to go along with the linked graphical buttons. That way, the user can use either version to explore your site. Most of the time you'll see a text version right next to the graphical buttons.

> **TIP**
>
> Including a site map or an overview can save your audience the frustration of searching your pages for specific information. A site map is typically a single Web page that provides a diagram or an outline of what's available in the site. A good site map will describe the sections of your site and provide links to those sections. If you use a site map, it's helpful to have a link to it that appears on every page. Doing so will make it easily accessible from anywhere in your site.

- Do you need forward and back buttons? If your site contains a lot of text and you want people to jump around from page to page within a story, you might want to add forward and back buttons. But be sure to make the buttons logical and easy to use. For example, you don't want users to use these buttons and be taken to a page they weren't expecting.

The bottom line is: Make it easy for viewers to move through your site. When designing your site, ask yourself whether you'd want to move between certain points. Ask that question, and you'll come up with good ways to make your viewers happy little surfers.

- **Consider charting the flow of information on paper** *before* **you build your site.** This is particularly helpful if you have a difficult time visualizing information. Start with your home page and work down. This visual representation can help you "see" your content, organize it more clearly, and avoid major reorganizations as you build your site. Once you begin to build your site, you can see a graphical representation of it on your computer screen in the FrontPage Explorer. This helps you see your site's structure more clearly, and might lead to new ideas for improving the structure and flow. For more information on the Explorer, see Chapter 3.

◆ **Test your site thoroughly.** The Web audience can use a number of different browsers, each of which can present your site quite differently. Test your site using as many different browsers as possible, on different platforms (such as Windows 95, Windows NT, UNIX, and Macintosh) and at different modem speeds. It's not unusual to find a navigation button properly appearing in a corner of a page in one browser but in the middle of a page in another browser. We're not kidding, either; this happens all the time. Wise owls test every page and every link in their sites using several different browsers. You can easily verify all of the links within your site using the Verify Hyperlinks command in the Explorer. For more information on the Verify Hyperlinks command, see Chapter 3.

> **TIP**
>
> Another good way to treat your audience kindly is to provide a searching mechanism so they can find information in your site quickly. With FrontPage's WebBot Search Component, you can add a complete search engine to your site in just a few seconds. To find out how, see Chapter 9.

Another great way to test your site is to use the Preview In Browser command in the Editor. It lets you preview your page using any browser installed on your machine, and at different window sizes. For example, if you normally run your screen resolution at 1024 x 768, you can find out how your Web page will look at a window size of 640 x 480. For more information, see Chapter 7.

# Planning an Intranet Site

If you're in charge of developing a site for an intranet at a business or other organization, you've got no small task ahead of you. You have many of the same things to think about as when you're developing a site for the World Wide Web, with a few interesting exceptions. Since you usually know the exact audience for the site, you have the luxury of being more focused and specific. You should have a good idea about such things as what types of computers are being used, how fast they are, which browser is most commonly used and how the site is being accessed (via modem or via direct connection). Knowing these details can greatly affect how you develop the site. As with a site for the World Wide Web, up-front planning is the key to developing a successful site.

Depending on the size of your company, the site can be large and can involve many people in charge of different sections. FrontPage makes managing intranets easy; see Chapter 5 for details.

Does your organization need an intranet? Traditionally you'll see companies generating internal information like corporate policies, training information, phone listings, and company news using the old-fashioned printed method. Once this information is printed, it has to be distributed, often across various geographical regions. Every time an update or a change is made, you need to reprint and redistribute the information. Not only is this costly, but it wastes resources.

With an intranet in place, you can easily and quickly update company information, and it can be made available to everyone or to those with the correct access rights. Different departments can be in charge of maintaining their area on the site and keeping the company abreast of changes as they occur. This process is seamless and painless.

## Questions to Ask

When creating a site for an intranet, you should pay attention to the same issues of design, organization, and navigation that you need to address when building a site intended for the World Wide Web. In addition, if you can address the following intranet-specific issues up front, you can save a great deal of trouble.

◆ **Audience** What members of the company or organization will have access to the site? What kinds of information will the site include? Will all of the information in the site be accessible to everyone?

◆ **Work in progress** Who will update the site? Who will be in charge of which sections and which tasks? Spell this out as clearly as possible before creating the site, because as you go along you'll probably discover more tasks that need to be performed regularly by *someone*. FrontPage makes assigning tasks easy with the To Do List, which is explained in detail in Chapter 5.

◆ **Keeping it under control** How will you keep the site from getting out of control? The key to controlling the size of a site is controlling who can add material to it. If everyone in your company can add pages, change information, add links, and so on, your site will seem like a runaway freight train bound for the bottom of Whiskey Gulch. You can control these privileges by setting author, end-user, and administrative permissions. You'll find more details on this in Chapter 5.

Perhaps your business or organization already has a network in place, and it's easy to route files and view others' documents and presentations. But the process really is cumbersome; you have to connect to a network location, move the files to your computer or open them on another computer, launch the appropriate application to help you view and manipulate the files, and so on. Plus, when you're looking at a network location, all you see is a list of files. There's little presentation involved. And unless you know where to look for a specific file, it can be difficult to find a file on a network, especially if you don't know the exact filename.

Intranets allow this sharing of information in a visual forum. Suppose you want to find out your company's sales information for the previous quarter, which is contained in a Microsoft Excel file. In a typical network setting, you have to find the appropriate file, open it, and then view the information in Excel on your own computer.

With a site on an intranet, company personnel can access information without having to memorize a network location. All they have to do is find the company sales information page on the intranet and then click on a link to open the file from the network. Or you could choose to have that information displayed directly on a page in the site. If they can't find the sales information page easily (which would be indicative of a bad design), they can search for it in a few seconds using a Web search engine.

## Servers

If you're setting up a site on an intranet, you'll need a Web server to run it on. Just as with traditional network servers, it's often necessary to dedicate a single computer for use as a Web server. The faster and more powerful the computer, the better your site will run. Fortunately, the Web-server market is wide open and getting more competitive all the time.

The Web server you use will depend on the amount of traffic you expect to see. If you have a relatively small company, you might be able to use the FrontPage Personal Web Server or the Microsoft Personal Web Server as your sole Web server. These servers weren't designed to handle a high amount of traffic, so you might need to choose a server that can handle higher volumes.

## Security

You can use your network security features to protect many of the files used on your intranet. After all, these files are stored on the actual network. For example, if you want only certain personnel to be able to change information in files used on an intranet, you can restrict access at the network level.

In addition to network security, FrontPage allows three levels of access to a Web site. The Web server you use for your intranet also might interact with these security features.

◆ End-user access (browsing).

◆ Author access (accessing, updating, and maintaining the site using FrontPage).

◆ Administrative access (updating security permissions). Administrators also have all author access rights.

With FrontPage, you have many options in configuring the security on your site. For more information, see Chapter 5.

# Content

A company or organization can harness the power of an intranet in many ways:

◆ **Make documents and other corporate information widely available.** Companies can use an intranet site to house policy manuals, training manuals, company schedules, product data, and the like. This can save tremendous amounts of time, effort, and money.

For example, suppose Linda works in the Bed & Bath department at a department store, and she needs specifics on what kind of perfume the store sells so she can propose a bundling of towels and perfume for a holiday promotion. Instead of calling the head of the Perfume department, who would pass the request to an assistant, who would then direct Linda to a file on the network containing pricing, availability, and sales information, Linda can simply go to the appropriate intranet site and access that information herself.

◆ **Update your employees on company news.** A site on an intranet is an ideal place to put news about your company. If you want to provide employees with information about the annual picnic, you can put it in one place for all to see. An intranet site is also an ideal place for gathering your company's press releases for employees to read.

◆ **Use the intranet site for in-house promotions.** Even though the primary purpose of an intranet site is to streamline information flow within a company or organization, that doesn't mean it can't be fun to use. Combining serious work information on an intranet site with something fun, such as an in-house contest, can lighten up the workplace and might make employees want to use the site more.

◆ **Connect your intranet site with the Internet.** Through the use of security measures such as **firewalls** and **proxy servers**, you can link your intranet site to the Internet and still keep the intranet secure. You can provide links to your competitors' Web sites to keep your employees up-to-date on their goings-on, or to other useful and timely information your employees might need to know. If information about your company appears on others' Web sites, you can link to those locations so your company's personnel can see what all the hoopla is about.

## Coming Up

Now that you have an idea of what you can do with a Web site, it's time to learn some specifics about how to use FrontPage to create your site. Chapter 3 starts you out on that journey with a detailed look at the FrontPage Explorer.

# Creating and Managing Your Site

# Chapter 3

# Inside the FrontPage Explorer

## Your Site, from See to Shining See

Okay, Web-site designers, it's time to 'fess up. How many of you
have posted sticky notes on the wall or laid note cards on the
floor in an attempt to map out a site? How many times have
people dropped by your office and said, "Look at that wall now,
Pete! You oughtta buy stock in 3M!" How many times have you
penciled out your site on paper, drawing squares, **links**, arrows,
and small letters that you can't even read with a magnifying
glass?

And as for you beginning Web-site developers, do you wonder whether you've gotten in over your heads with all this Web
stuff? When you put your ideas down on paper and chart out a
few pages, it seems pretty straightforward. But when you begin
drawing links between all your pages, it can seem as though
you're climbing Mt. Everest with a day pack, one bandage, and
a bag of BBQ chips.

Several good software flow-chart programs are available that
allow you to build a map of your site and manipulate it as you
wish. However, if you use one of those programs, you still need

to create your site with a Web authoring tool, which means you have to input the data in two separate programs. Wouldn't it be easier if you could input the data only once?

If you want to organize your site in a single program, you've come to the right place, because that's what the FrontPage Explorer does *for* you. The FrontPage Explorer gives you a Folder view and a Hyperlink view of your site, allowing you to view and manipulate it as a whole. And there's no need to worry about making separate, manual changes to these views—the FrontPage Explorer updates each view as you make changes to your site, so you can see the changes instantly in either view. This greatly simplifies site creation and maintenance, and it'll no doubt save you hours and hours of time for every site you work on. If you work with large sites, this could save your sanity.

You can think of your entire site as a single document, even though it is made up of individual pages and other associated files. You can maintain consistency, maintain links, and perform operations across the entire site. For example, just as you don't want to spell-check a word processing document one paragraph at a time, you don't want to spell-check a Web site one page at a time, so the FrontPage Explorer allows you to spell-check an entire site. FrontPage pioneered this notion of a Web site as a single document, and the FrontPage Explorer is the means by which you manipulate this new document type.

This chapter presents the FrontPage Explorer in detail. The FrontPage Explorer forms the framework of the FrontPage client software, giving you direct or indirect access to the FrontPage Editor, the To Do List, and the FrontPage **templates** and **wizards**. These tools will be explained in greater detail in later chapters; this chapter simply focuses on how to access them through the FrontPage Explorer itself.

The FrontPage Explorer should not be confused with the Windows 95 Explorer, although it was designed to have the same look and feel and similar operations. Nor should you confuse the FrontPage Explorer with Microsoft Internet Explorer, which is Microsoft's **Web browser**. The FrontPage Explorer gives you an overview of your Web site. In the rest of this chapter, and indeed in the entire book, the term "Explorer" refers to the FrontPage Explorer; the Windows 95 Explorer is referred to as the "Windows Explorer."

Also note that FrontPage uses the term *Web* to mean a Web site. To avoid confusion with the **World Wide Web** and other Web-related terminology, this book uses the term *Web site* or *site* throughout.

## Starting the Explorer

Whenever you launch the Explorer, you'll see the Getting Started With Microsoft FrontPage dialog box, which gives you numerous options for how to proceed. This cuts down on the hassle of having to learn how to open or create a new Web site using the Explorer's menu commands. The dialog box looks like this:

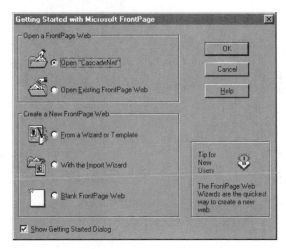

As you can see, from this dialog box you have several ways to proceed. Later in this chapter, in the sections titled "Creating a Site from Scratch" and "Opening an Existing Site," you'll learn how to create and open sites once you're in the Explorer, without having to access this opening dialog box. But for now, here's how to proceed:

**Open a FrontPage Web** In this section, you have two options: You can open the last FrontPage Web site you worked on in the Explorer, or you can open any other FrontPage site you have access to. Of course, the very first time you open the Explorer, you won't have the first option available to you. Select one of the two options, and then click OK.

If you opt to open the last FrontPage site you worked on, FrontPage opens the site in the Explorer. If you select Open Existing FrontPage Web, you'll see the Open FrontPage Web dialog box. This dialog box is described later in the section titled "Sites Authored in FrontPage."

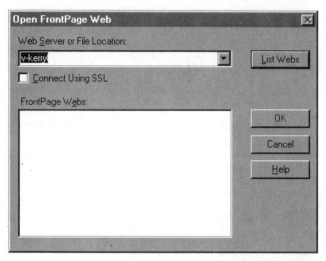

**Create a New FrontPage Web** You can also create a new FrontPage Web site from the Getting Started With Microsoft FrontPage dialog box. You have three options when creating a new site here. To create a new site, select one of these options, and then click OK.

◆ **From a Wizard or Template** Selecting this option brings up the New FrontPage Web dialog box, which presents a list of templates and wizards that create FrontPage Web sites. You can find descriptions of these templates and wizards in the next section, "Creating a Site from Scratch."

◆ **With the Import Wizard** If you have a non-FrontPage site that you want to import into FrontPage, you can do so by using the Import Wizard. Selecting this option and clicking OK opens the Import Web Wizard dialog box, where you specify the destination server or file location the site will be housed on, and the new site name. Clicking OK in the Import Web Wizard dialog box sends you to the Import Web Wizard, a series of screens that asks you to specify the folder (directory) where the site is currently located, and the files you want imported as part of the new site. You'll find a complete description of the Import Web Wizard in Chapter 4.

◆ **Blank FrontPage Web** Selecting Blank FrontPage Web allows you to start a new site from scratch. When you select this option and click OK, you'll see the Normal Web Template dialog box, where you specify the destination server or file location the site will be housed on, and the site name. When you click OK in this dialog box, FrontPage creates a site using the Normal Web Template, which basically is a site consisting of one blank page.

# Creating a Site from Scratch

When you first launch the Explorer, you'll see the Getting Started With Microsoft FrontPage dialog box, but after that you'll need to use FrontPage's menu commands to create or open your sites. If you're creating a site from scratch, it's wise to first construct the framework for it in the Explorer. The framework can consist of simply a name and a preconstructed page or two for you to work on later. FrontPage saves this framework on your Web server (or, if you want to create a site for only your own use, on your hard disk), and from that point you can work on it in the Explorer or the Editor, depending on what tasks you're completing.

But suppose you have some HTML pages from another Web site that you'd like to use. Can you use them in a FrontPage site? You sure can—you can open each of those pages in the Front-Page Editor, make any necessary changes, and then link them to other pages in your site. (See Chapter 6 for details on opening pages, and see Chapter 7 for details on linking.) Your previous work won't be wasted when you move over to FrontPage. Alternatively, you can recycle any HTML and graphics files by importing them into the Explorer. For more on this, see "Importing a File into a Site" later in this chapter.

So let's see how easy it is to create a Web site in FrontPage. Here's what you do:

1. In the Explorer, choose New from the File menu, and then choose FrontPage Web from the submenu; or click the New FrontPage Web toolbar button. The New Front-Page Web dialog box appears, presenting you with a list of several templates and wizards. The New FrontPage Web dialog box looks like this:

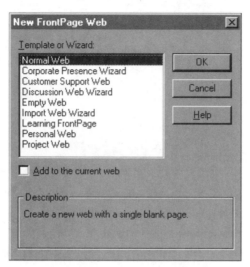

The easiest way to create a site is to use one of these templates or wizards, which can eliminate many pre-liminary design hassles. Templates and wizards are explained in detail in the next chapter, but for now, if you're creating your first site, here's a brief outline of what each can do for you.

**SHORTCUT**

You can also press Ctrl+N in the Explorer to create a new site.

**Normal Web**  This templates creates a new site with one blank page, so you can start with the absolute mini-mum. If you want to start without even a single blank page, you can use the Empty Web template.

**Corporate Presence Wizard**  This wizard is an excellent place to start if you're creating a business site. It asks you a series of questions and offers numerous kinds of pages to highlight your business.

**Customer Support Web**  This template sets up a customer support site for a business.

**Discussion Web Wizard** This wizard creates a discussion group with threads, a table of contents, and full-text searching.

**Empty Web** This template creates a new site with nothing in it. Generally, you'll want to begin with the Normal Web template.

**Import Web Wizard** This wizard allows you to import entire existing Web sites into the Explorer. You probably won't want to use this if you're starting a site from scratch.

**Learning FrontPage** You can use this template with the FrontPage tutorial in the *Getting Started with Microsoft FrontPage* manual.

**Personal Web** This template creates a personal Web site that you can fill in with information such as employee data, biographical information, your interests, and more.

**Project Web** This template creates a new site to help you manage a project. It includes a list of participants, project status, project schedule, and more.

2. Select one of these templates or wizards and click OK. Next you'll see a dialog box for the option you selected. For example, if you selected the Corporate Presence Wizard, you'll see the Corporate Presence Wizard dialog box.

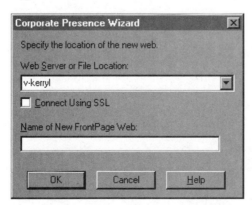

3. In the Web Server Or File Location text box, enter the name of the Web server where you want the site located, enter a pathname if you want the site placed on a hard

disk or a **LAN,** or select a location from the drop-down list. If you want to communicate with your site using **Secure Sockets Layer** (SSL) security, select the Connect Using SSL check box. For more information on SSL, see Chapter 5.

4. In the Name Of New FrontPage Web text box, enter a name for your site, and click OK. The name can include numbers and characters, but not spaces.

This name stays "behind the scenes"; you can give your site a different title if you like, which shows up in the title bar whenever your site is open in the Explorer. By default, the name and the title are the same; to change the title, see the section titled "Changing Site Settings" later in this chapter.

FrontPage then sets up your new site. This might take a few minutes, depending on the speed of your computer and your Web server, and the type of site you've chosen to create. Front-Page creates a folder for the site on the server you've designated. This folder has the same name that you just gave to your site. If you use a template to create your site, FrontPage adds files to this folder for each of the pages in the template. If you use a wizard, you'll see screens where you can customize your site before the pages are created.

When the process is complete, FrontPage displays the site in the Explorer.

# Opening an Existing Site

You can open any Web site in FrontPage, regardless of the Web authoring application it was created with.

## Sites Authored in FrontPage

If you've already created a site in FrontPage and want to open it in the Explorer, here's how to do it:

1. In the Explorer, choose Open FrontPage Web from the File menu. You'll see the Open FrontPage Web dialog box, which presents you with several options:

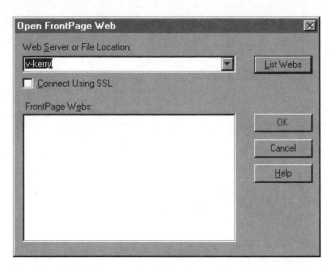

2. In the Web Server Or File Location text box, enter the name of the Web server where you want the site located, enter a pathname if you want the site placed on a hard disk or a LAN, or select a location from the drop-down list. If you want to communicate with your site using Secure Sockets Layer (SSL) security, select the Connect Using SSL check box.

3. Click the List Webs button. FrontPage will search the server or file location you specified and display a list of sites in the Front-Page Webs list box.

4. Double-click on a title or select a title from the FrontPage list box and click OK.

### SHORTCUT

To quickly open a site, you can click the Open FrontPage Web toolbar button, which is the standard Open button that you find in many Windows 95–based applications. Or you can choose a site from the list of recently opened sites on the File menu.

## Sites Authored in Other Applications

If you want to open a site authored in another application, the best-case scenario happens when the site is on a Web server that has the appropriate FrontPage Server Extensions installed. The Server Extensions gather the additional information needed by FrontPage and make the site's content available for editing. In this way, you might not need to change a site's format in order to work with the site in the Explorer.

To open such a site, follow the procedure outlined above. For more information on the FrontPage Server Extensions, see Chapter 11.

However, if you want to open a site from a server that does *not* have the FrontPage Server Extensions installed, it's still pretty easy. You use the Import Web Wizard, which is described in Chapter 4.

# Setting Explorer Options

Whenever you have a site open in the Explorer, you can set the following options so the Explorer displays the elements you want to work with.

 **Hyperlinks To Images** You can use the Hyperlinks To Images command to display or hide all links to image files in a Web site. If you have numerous image files in your site, it's a good idea to simplify the Explorer's view of your site by turning off Hyperlinks To Images. You can turn it back on whenever you need to see these links. You turn it on and off by choosing the Hyperlinks To Images command from the View menu or by clicking the Hyperlinks To Images toolbar button.

 **Repeated Hyperlinks** You can use the Repeated Hyperlinks command to display or hide multiple links between pages. By default, FrontPage displays only one link for a page with multiple links to another page. Turning on Repeated Hyperlinks is useful for getting an overall view of all the possible paths throughout your site, and for determining how many links a page has to another page. To turn it on and off, choose the Repeated Hyperlinks command from the View menu or click the Repeated Hyperlinks toolbar button.

 **Hyperlinks Inside Page** The Hyperlinks Inside Page command lets you view any links that a page has to itself—for instance, a link at the bottom of a page that returns the user to the top of the page. To turn this feature on and off, choose the Hyperlinks Inside Page command from the View menu or click the Hyperlinks Inside Page toolbar button.

**Toolbar**   At times, you might want to hide the toolbar at the top of the FrontPage window so that you can use the extra space to view more of your site. To hide and show the toolbar, choose the Toolbar command from the View menu. A check mark beside the command indicates that the toolbar in the Explorer is visible.

**Status bar**   The status bar at the bottom of the FrontPage window shows any activity between FrontPage and a server, as well as a brief definition of a selected command or button. To show or hide the status bar, choose the Status Bar command from the View menu. A check mark beside the command indicates that the status bar is visible.

# The Explorer Point of View

When you think of a Web site, do you see it spatially, as a bunch of interconnected pages, or do you think of it linearly, as a bunch of collected pages in a row? Either way is fine, of course, and it all depends on how each person thinks. Perhaps the most powerful feature of the Explorer is the way it presents your site in these different ways, which are called Hyperlink view and Folder view.

## Betcha Can't View Just One

Because people think differently, one Explorer view might be a more effective tool for you than another. The choice of Explorer views also provides an added bonus: It gives you a great excuse when you're staring blankly at the screen at the end of a long day, and your boss happens by. Just tell your boss you're lost in thought, trying to determine which view works best for you—no one has to know you're really envisioning yourself snorkeling off the sands of Kauai.

First we'll look at each of the views to see their unique ways of presenting a Web site. Then we'll explore the features that are common to both views.

# Folder View

**SHORTCUT**

To see a site in Folder view, first you must have a site open in the Explorer. Then, click the Folder View toolbar button, or choose Folder View from the View menu.

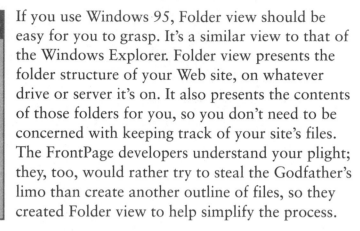

If you use Windows 95, Folder view should be easy for you to grasp. It's a similar view to that of the Windows Explorer. Folder view presents the folder structure of your Web site, on whatever drive or server it's on. It also presents the contents of those folders for you, so you don't need to be concerned with keeping track of your site's files. The FrontPage developers understand your plight; they, too, would rather try to steal the Godfather's limo than create another outline of files, so they created Folder view to help simplify the process.

Here's a look at Folder view for a customer support site called SupportWeb, which was created using the Customer Support Web template. For instructions on creating a site, see "Creating a Site from Scratch" earlier in this chapter.

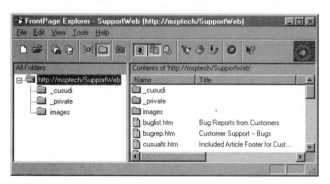

In the left pane is the folder structure of the site. The top-level folder contains files and subfolders. Every FrontPage site is created with specific folders according to the type of site it is. For example, a site created with the Customer Support Web template will have different subfolders than a site created with the Corporate Presence Wizard.

Notice in the graphic above that http://msptech/SupportWeb is highlighted. SupportWeb is the site name, and msptech is the server name. All the site's files are collected in the subfolders underneath this top-level location. The number of folders for a given site is not static, however; you can create your own folders to organize your files. To learn how, see the next section, "Creating Your Own Folders."

In the right pane is a list of the contents of whatever is highlighted in the left pane. You might recognize this as the same functionality used in the Windows Explorer. The folders and files listed in the right pane are accompanied by descriptive information, such as their name, title, size, type, the date they were last modified, who modified them, and any comments about the file.

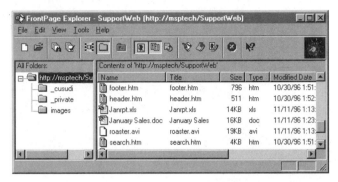

To sort the list based on a column in Folder view, click on the column heading. Files are sorted in ascending order, except for files in the Modified Date column, which are sorted in chronological order starting with the most recent date and time.

In your FrontPage journeys, you'll find numerous icons appearing in the right pane of Folder view, beside the file or folder name. First, there's the yellow folder icon itself. You'll also see an icon of a painting, which is used to denote image files such as JPG and GIF files. An icon that looks like a page with lines on it, indicating an HTML file, will appear often, and you might also see an icon that looks like a plain page, which indicates files other than an image file or HTML file.

**The image file icon, HTML file icon, and "other" file icon.**

Once you populate your sites with Microsoft Office documents, you'll also see icons representing those files in Folder view. In the graphic above, you'll notice a Microsoft Word document titled *January Sales* in Folder view. The standard Word icon appears beside it. Your site might also contain documents from other Office applications, such as Microsoft Excel.

**Creating your own folders** Say you're a Webmaster in charge of maintaining a site on your company's intranet, and the site includes numerous Office files from various contributors. One way of organizing those files is to collect them in a folder structure called Office. Then, the Office folder can have a Word folder where your Word files will be stored. Here's how to go about it:

1. In the Explorer, with a Web site open in Folder view, highlight the folder under which you want the new folder to go, by clicking on the folder in the left pane.

2. Choose New from the File menu, and then choose Folder from the submenu.

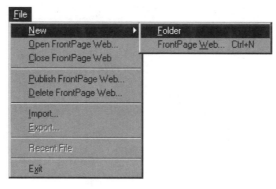

3. A new folder appears in each pane of Folder view.

4. Type in the name of the new folder, *Office*, and then press Enter.

5. Highlight the Office folder by clicking on it in the left pane.

6. Repeat steps 2 and 3, naming the new folder *Word*. Here's what the folder structure will look like:

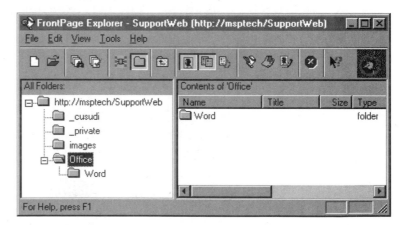

Now, when your co-workers send you their Word files for the site, you'll have a logical place to store them. Better yet, perhaps you can train them to import the files themselves! To learn how to import those files, see "Importing a File into a Site" later in this chapter.

**Uses for Folder view** Perhaps the most obvious use for the folders in Folder view is to collect your material in a logical, organized way. One way to do this is to create your own folders, as described above.

Folder view is especially useful for quickly locating summary information about files whose location in the site you're unsure of. For example, suppose you're in the Explorer and you need to find out the URL for a certain page in your site. Instead of searching for the page in Hyperlink view, you can go to Folder view, sort the list by title if necessary, locate your file alphabetically, and based on the folder it's in, you can determine the URL.

Here are some other good uses for Folder view:

◆ Finding all files of a specific file type in a folder, such as Office files. Group the list by type of file by clicking on the Type column, and then look for the specific file type.

◆ Finding images in a folder that might take a long time to download into a browser. Sort the files by size, and then look for larger image files at the bottom of the list.

◆ Finding all pages in a folder that you authored. Sort the Modified By column and then look for your name.

◆ Finding all the pages in a folder that haven't been updated in a long time. Sort the list by the Modified Date, and then look at the bottom of the column for older dates.

◆ Renaming a file. Rename a file in exactly the same manner as in the Windows Explorer. Just click on a file, wait a moment, and click again. You can then rename the file, and FrontPage will automatically update any links to that file.

◆ Modifying the folder structure. Rearrange the folder structure of your Web site by dragging files from one folder to another, just like in the Windows Explorer, and FrontPage will automatically reconfigure the links.

**Adjusting the column widths** Besides sorting the items in the right pane of Folder view, there's another way to change the view: You can change column widths. Place your mouse in the column heading area, near a border between the columns. When the cursor changes to a crosshair with left and right arrows, click and drag to adjust the width.

## Hyperlink View

The FrontPage developers figured out something that few others have even thought of. Many Web-site designers today are graphically minded folks who would rather look at a Monet than read about one. Since they think in terms of pictures, why not display a site in the same way?

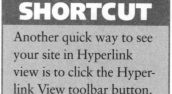

**SHORTCUT**

Another quick way to see your site in Hyperlink view is to click the Hyperlink View toolbar button.

Hyperlink view is the graphical representation of the links within a segment of your Web site. To see your site in Hyperlink view, choose Hyperlink View from the View menu.

Here's a basic look at a site in Hyperlink view. It's divided into two panes; the left pane presents an outline of your site, and the right pane shows the files of your site as large icons, linked together with a series of lines. Their names appear directly underneath the icon. Links are shown in a left-to-right fashion; links *to the page* come in from the left, and links *to other pages and elements* go to the right.

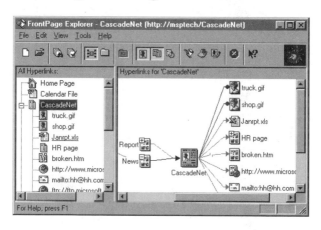

In the graphic on the previous page, the plus sign indicates that the view can be expanded; therefore, more links are either coming to or going from the page. Clicking the plus sign expands the view. Once the view is expanded, the plus sign changes to a minus sign, indicating that the view can be contracted.

If you let your mouse pointer hover over an icon, a ScreenTip pops up that indicates the filename and other information.

You'll notice many different icons in both panes of Hyperlink view. Envelope icons with a "mailto:" protocol indicate links that send e-mail. These are links on pages that allow users to send e-mail from the page, such as feedback to a Web administrator. Icons of paintings indicate image files, and globe icons indicate links to the World Wide Web. As in Folder view, you'll also see icons for Office files when they're a part of your site.

There are two more icons you should know about but that you won't want to see on your page: the icons for broken links and for errors on your pages.

**The broken-link icon and the error icon.**

The broken-link icon indicates that a link, whether internal to the current Web site or external, is configured incorrectly. You can fix a broken link by opening the page containing the link in the Editor and correctly configuring the link. (See Chapter 7 for more details.) If you see an error icon after opening the page in the Editor, that means a FrontPage WebBot component is not configured properly and needs to be corrected. (For more information on WebBot components, see Chapter 9.)

You might have noticed in the graphic on the previous page that some links end with an arrow, while others end with a bullet. An arrow indicates a link—in other words, that the item jumps to another item. A bullet indicates that the item to the right is included as a part of the item to the left—for example, a page containing a graphic. Bullets can also indicate that the page contains a WebBot Include Component.

In the left pane of Hyperlink view is an outline of the site. The home page of the site appears at the top, and is represented by a cute house. All of the material that appears in the site shows up below this icon in Hyperlink view at first.

Just as in Folder view, clicking on an item in the left pane causes the information in the right pane to change. In Hyperlink view, when you click on something in the left pane, that item appears centered in the right pane, along with any of its links to other files or addresses. Clicking the plus and minus signs expands and contracts the outline.

**Uses for Hyperlink view**  Hyperlink view is especially useful for determining just how many links you've got going and coming from each page, and also for seeing what other pages link to your page. Say you went live with a new page on your intranet a week ago, and you want to know how many others in your organization have linked to your page. You can simply look at your page in Hyperlink view to find out.

Hyperlink view is also useful for verifying that you've included all the links you think you have on a particular page. Suppose you promised several departments in your organization that you'd link to their home page from your "For More Information" page, and those links are embedded in the paragraphs on your page. Instead of looking at the page in an editor, finding the links, and then checking them against a master list, you can view all the links on your page in one place—Hyperlink view—and check *that* against your list.

Hyperlink view can also be used to find all pages that point *to* a particular page. Also, by expanding the links by clicking on the plus signs, you can find various paths through your site. This is useful, for example, to figure out how many mouse clicks it takes to get from one particular page to another.

**Modifying the view**  The size of the Hyperlink view window and the size of your monitor dictate how much of your site appears in Hyperlink view. You'll notice as you expand the site that links go off the screen. You can view the off-the-screen material in two ways: by using the scroll bar at the bottom of the window, or by clicking on any open area and dragging the material wherever you want it. When you drag in a blank area, the mouse pointer changes to a hand to indicate that you can move the material around.

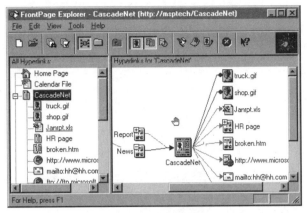

**When you click the mouse on a blank area, the cursor changes to a hand. You can then reposition the material on the page by dragging the mouse.**

There's also a way to center any item on your screen in Hyperlink view: Right-click on the item and choose Move To Center from the pop-up menu, as in the following graphic.

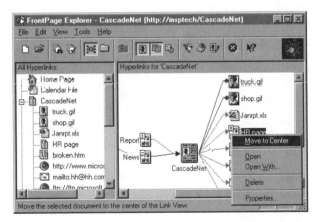

You'll also notice that because Hyperlink view is a representation of links, it can seem to go on forever. Again, think spatially, and you'll see that if page A is linked to page B, which is linked to page C, which is linked back to page A, you're already going around in circles. And that's only a tiny example. It's best to use Hyperlink view for viewing small portions of your site. You can get a good overall view of your site by collapsing everything; when you need to see specifics, it's time to expand those icons.

# What's Common to Both Views

Some features can be accessed from both Hyperlink view and Folder view in the Explorer. Here's the rundown:

**Opening files from a view** The two views are not just a compilation of pages and links; they are also avenues for opening their associated files in the Editor or whatever application you want to work in to manipulate those files. For example, to manipulate a Graphics Interchange Format (**GIF**) file that appears in any view, you can launch the application and edit the file with a few clicks of the mouse.

You can open files from the right pane in both views. To open a file, right-click on the title or the icon and choose Open from the pop-up menu. If the file is an HTML file, the page appears in the Editor, ready for you to edit. If you choose the Open With command, you can open the page with any other editor. After choosing Open With, you get a list of editors in the Open With Editor dialog box; you can select an editor and click OK.

**SHORTCUT**

You can also double-click on a file in Hyperlink view and Folder view to open it. The file opens with its associated editor.

But what if you want a different editor to open when you choose the Open command for a particular type of file, or what if your editor doesn't show up at all in the Open With Editor dialog box? You can change the editor type by choosing the Options command from the Tools menu and clicking on the Configure Editors tab. (See "Configuring Editors" later in this chapter.)

**SHORTCUT**

You can access the properties for an item by right-clicking the item and choosing Properties from the pop-up menu.

**Viewing file properties** To view properties for a file, select the file and then choose the Properties command from the Edit menu. On the Summary tab of the Properties dialog box, you'll find information such as when the file was created, who created it, when it was modified, and who modified it. There's also a text box to add comments to the file.

On the General tab, you'll find general information on the file, such as its name, title, type, size, and location. The location can be a file location or a **URL**. A URL indicates the address of a resource on a network and the method by which it can be accessed. URLs can use various **protocols**; the most common one on the World Wide Web today is **HTTP**. The terms *URL* and *HTTP address* refer to the same thing.

**Refreshing a view** To update the views in the Explorer, choose Refresh from the View menu. The command refreshes all views for the current site in the Explorer. If more than one person is working on a site at one time, refreshing the site allows you to see all of the changes.

**Changing the size of a view** A split bar separates the panes on each view. To move the bar and change the amount of the window devoted to each of the views, place your cursor directly over the bar until it changes to a double-line cursor with left and right arrows, and then click and drag the bar.

It's important to remember that the two views in the Explorer display your site according to its links, and not in a sequential order. Our increasing use of **hypertext** is causing us to think about documents differently than we used to. Before hypertext, we thought of documents in terms of their classic book form—one page stacked on another, perhaps indexed or referenced so you could manually find a cross-referenced term elsewhere in the book. Hypertext allows you to automatically jump to anywhere in a document. It's as if all the pages of a book are drifting in space, with links between any or all of them. If you think of your site in these spatial terms instead of in the standard book form, you'll fare much better in designing and manipulating your site.

# Other Functions of the Explorer

So far in this chapter, you've learned that the Explorer can be used to create and open sites, as well as to view them in several different ways. The Explorer also sports a host of other functions you can use in your everyday site management.

## Closing a Site

Because FrontPage can display only one site at a time, any time you open another site or create a new one, the current site is closed. To close the current site without opening another, choose Close FrontPage Web from the File menu.

# Publishing a Site

If you want to move your site to another server, FrontPage makes it easy. For example, suppose you've been testing your site locally on the Microsoft Personal Web Server or the FrontPage Personal Web Server, and you want to move the site to a higher-volume server that powers your intranet or is a Web server that is connected to the Internet. You can use the Publish FrontPage Web command on the File menu to copy a site that is currently open in the Explorer to a server. Assuming that the appropriate FrontPage Server Extensions are installed for the server you're copying to, and you've got administrative access, it's an easy task. Here's how to do it:

1. With the site you want to copy currently open in the Explorer, choose Publish FrontPage Web from the File menu. You'll see the Publish FrontPage Web dialog box.

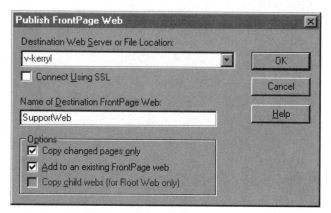

2. In the Destination Web Server Or File Location text box, enter the name of the Web server where you want the site located, enter a pathname if you want the site placed on a hard disk or LAN, or select a location from the drop-down list. If you want to communicate with your site using Secure Sockets Layer (SSL) security, select the Connect Using SSL check box.

3. In the Name Of Destination FrontPage Web text box, enter a name for the copy of the site. These names are subject to the naming conventions used by the destination server, so you might have to consider length as well as case-sensitivity conventions as you name the site.

4. In the Options section, you can select the Add To An Existing FrontPage Web check box if you're combining the copy with another site; otherwise, don't worry about this check box. If you're copying a **root Web site**, select the Copy Child Webs check box if you also want to copy all child Web sites (sites that have a link from the root Web site).

   If your site is already on the destination server, selecting the Copy Changed Pages Only check box will update the site only with the pages you've changed.

5. When you're ready to publish the site, click OK. Front-Page copies the site to the destination server and then notifies you that the copy is on the server.

Using the Publish FrontPage Web command, you can also publish to Web servers that do not have the FrontPage Server Extensions installed. In this case, FrontPage notices that the Server Extensions are not installed on the destination Web server, and automatically launches the Web Publishing Wizard (a separate component that you can install from the FrontPage Bonus Pack CD). The wizard will publish your site to the destination server using the FTP protocol. (It will ask you for information, such as the FTP server name, user name, password, and destination folder.) The wizard also knows how to save sites to online services such as America Online, CompuServe, and others.

## Deleting a Site

You must have administrative access to FrontPage to delete a site, and the site must be open in the Explorer before you can delete it. To delete the site that is currently open, choose Delete Front-Page Web from the File menu in the Explorer.

Consider this before you delete: Once you delete a site, even if you've removed it properly with the Delete FrontPage Web command, it cannot be recovered—not even

> **WARNING**
>
> Be sure to delete sites by using the Delete Front-Page Web command, not by manually removing their files from a server. If you remove the files manually, FrontPage might not recognize that they've been deleted.

from the Recycle Bin in the Windows Explorer. FrontPage posts this reminder every time you choose this command.

## Deleting Files

You must have at least author-level access to delete files in the Explorer. You can delete files by selecting them in any view and then choosing Delete from the Edit menu, or by right-clicking on the file and choosing Delete. FrontPage asks you to confirm the deletion before it carries out the action.

## Adding a New Page to a Site

You can add two kinds of pages to your Web sites: pages that you create from scratch, and preexisting pages. To add a new page to your site that you'll work on from scratch, you use the Editor. (See Chapter 6 for more details.) To add a completed page to your site, you use the Import command on the File menu in the Explorer. (For more information, see the next section.)

## Importing a File into a Site

An application's ability to incorporate documents created by earlier versions of the program or from competing programs is one way of determining its value: "utility" versus "futility." You shouldn't have to lose the work you've already done in another Web authoring application if you're moving over to FrontPage. If you've already created pages or files (for example, RTF or HTML files) that you'd like to include in your current site, FrontPage allows you to do it, and quite easily.

For those of you using FrontPage to construct a site for an intranet, here's where you'll be loading all those files into your site. You'll be able to import Word documents, Excel spread-sheets, and more into your sites—FrontPage allows you to import non-Microsoft files into your site as well. A site on an intranet can consist of dozens, hundreds, or even thousands of documents. If you're in charge of getting those documents into the site, you'll be relieved to know that you can import all those files at once if you want to.

You can import files into a site using two methods: by using a menu command or by dragging and dropping files into the Explorer from elsewhere on your computer. Here's how to use the menu command:

1. With the destination site open in the Explorer, choose Import from the File menu. The Import File To Front-Page Web dialog box appears:

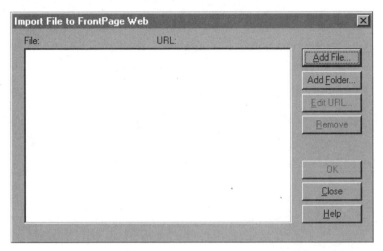

2. Click the Add File button. This brings up the Add File To Import List dialog box, where you specify the file or files you want to import. Locate the folder containing the file by using the folder controls at the top of the dialog box. Be sure to select the type of files to be listed by using the Files Of Type drop-down list. (If you're not sure of the type of file you're looking for, select All Files from the drop-down list.)

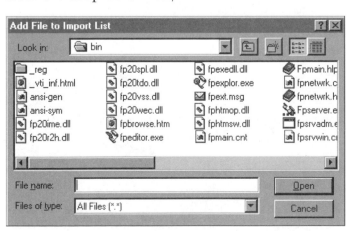

3. Select the file or files you want to import. You select files in the same way that you do in the Windows Explorer. To select a group of contiguous files, click on the first file in the group, press the Shift key, and then click on the last file in the group. To select multiple noncontiguous files, press the Ctrl key while clicking on the files you want to select. To remove a file from a selection, press the Ctrl key while clicking on the file.

4. Click the Open button. This closes the Add File To Import List dialog box and adds the files to a list in the Import File To FrontPage Web dialog box.

5. If you need to add more files to the list, repeat steps 2, 3, and 4. To remove files from the list before you add them to your site, select them and click the Remove button.

6. If you want to change the URL of any file, select the file in the Import File To FrontPage Web dialog box and click the Edit URL button. This is handy if you want to save the file separately from the other material in the site; you enter the new URL (pointing the file to the folder of your choice) in the Edit URL dialog box that appears, and then click OK.

7. Click the OK button to add the files to your site. When you click the OK button, it changes to a Stop button so you can halt the process at any time.

FrontPage closes the Import File To FrontPage Web dialog box after it finishes importing the files. The imported files are not linked to any pages in the site. If you try to close the Explorer while items are still in the Import list, the Explorer will warn you.

You can also add image files to your site by using the Import command. As described in Chapter 8, you can also do this in several different ways in the Editor, but if you know you're going to use certain files in your site, the Import command allows you to add them all at once.

**Dragging and dropping a file into a site** There will be times when you only want to import a file or two into your site, and the process of using the Import command is too lengthy for its own good. For those times, FrontPage supports dragging and dropping those files into the Explorer.

Let's suppose you're looking at a file called Recruiting Notes in the Windows Explorer that you want to add to a site that's open in the FrontPage Explorer. All you do is drag its icon into either view in the FrontPage Explorer. Here's an easy way to do it:

1. In the Windows Explorer (or wherever else the file might be), click on the file, and begin dragging it.

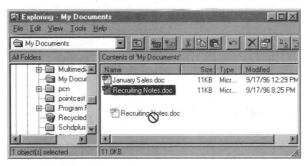

**The file is being dragged.**

2. Continue dragging the file and hover it over the Front-Page Explorer button on the Windows 95 taskbar. After a second or two, the FrontPage Explorer will become the active application on your screen, ready for you to drop the file into.

3. Drag the file into either view of the FrontPage Explorer and release the mouse button, "dropping" it into your site! The file is now imported into the site.

## Exporting a File from a Site

Suppose you want to copy an item, such as a page or an image, from your site to another location. You can save any file to your hard disk, a network location, or a floppy disk by choosing the Export command from the File menu in the Explorer. First, select the file in any view, and then choose Export. In the Export Selected As dialog box that appears, you can specify the location you want the file to be copied to. When you click the Save button, the file is copied to the specified location.

The Export command does not remove the file from your site. To remove a file from your site, you must delete it.

# Changing Site Settings

**TIP**

You can also change information on all of the pages in your site that do not use parameters and configuration variables, by using FrontPage's Find and Replace commands. For more information, see Chapter 7.

Nightmare on Web Street, scene one: You've just completed a site for your company, which includes the company's phone and fax numbers on nearly every one of its 169 pages. After you come up for air, you read in the morning paper that your area code is about to change. After you wonder where the heck you've been for the past nine months, you're faced with editing every one of those 169 pages. You could use a utility program to search for the old area code and replace it with the new one, and there are other ways to get the job done. But how about a one-stop-shop way?

FrontPage uses placeholders, also called *parameters* or *configuration variables,* so that it can track where this information is used in the current site. The templates and wizards in FrontPage add some parameters automatically. You can define your own and insert them using the WebBot Substitution Component discussed in Chapter 9. By using the Web Settings command on the Tools menu in the Explorer, you can update the information wherever it occurs in your site. Choose the command, and you'll see the FrontPage Web Settings dialog box, which has four tabs.

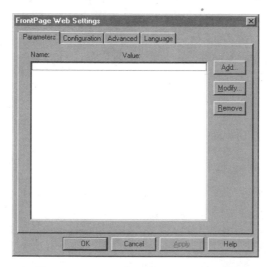

**Parameters tab**  If your site was constructed using a template or wizard that contained parameters for later authors to fill in, or if you've defined your own, those parameters will show up here.

◆ You can add parameters by clicking the Add button. The Add Name And Value dialog box appears, asking you for the name and value of the parameter (whatever information you wish to enter). Click OK to exit the dialog box and add the new parameter to your list. (Use the WebBot Substitution Component in the Editor to add the information to your pages.)

◆ To change the parameter information, such as in the scenario described above, select the parameter you want to change and click the Modify button. In the Modify Name And Value dialog box that appears, you can enter the new information. Click OK to save the information and exit the dialog box. This automatically updates the parameter in all pages of your site where the parameter appears.

◆ Clicking the Remove button removes the selected parameter from the list.

**Configuration tab** To change the name and title of your site, click on the Configuration tab of the FrontPage Web Settings dialog box, replace the information, and click OK. The name should not contain spaces, because the name will be used as part of the site's **URL**, and URLs normally do not contain spaces. The site title, however, can contain spaces.

It's important to give your site a name that you'll easily recognize among a list of sites. Each time you open a site to work on it in the Explorer, you'll select the site from a list; if you create numerous sites on your server, the list can get long and confusing. If you give your site an intuitive and distinctive name at the outset, you'll save yourself headaches later on.

**Advanced tab** The Advanced tab allows you to set or modify advanced settings, including the following:

◆ You can configure how FrontPage supports **image maps** in the Image Maps section. From the Style drop-down list, select the server type for the images, and then set an optional prefix if the Prefix text box is enabled. The default setting, FrontPage, allows image maps to be used no matter what Web server you use, as long as you have the FrontPage Server Extensions installed. Select the Generate Client-Side Image Maps check box if you want FrontPage to generate image maps from the client and not the server. It's a good idea to select this check box. FrontPage generates client-side image maps in such a way that if a browser does not support client-side image maps, it will simply ignore the client-side image map information in the HTML file. So, no harm can be done if you select this check box. (In fact, you can often gain more speed—see Chapter 8 for more details.)

◆ In the Validation Scripts section, you can specify the validation scripting language. The options available are VBScript, JavaScript, and <None>.

If you use the Form Field Validation feature of Front-Page, FrontPage will automatically generate JavaScript or VBScript right onto the page to perform the validation. This setting allows you to select which language to use. If you use JavaScript, it will work with both Internet Explorer and Netscape Navigator. If you choose VBScript, it will work only with Internet Explorer.

◆ In the Options section, select the Show Documents In Hidden Directories check box to display documents in **hidden folders**—folders preceded by an underscore (_). By default, you can't view pages and files in hidden folders when you are in the Explorer. This feature allows you to act as a moderator for a discussion group; individual messages in a discussion are kept in a hidden folder.

◆ In the Recalculate Status section, there are two check boxes that allow you to specify when FrontPage recalculates your Web site. These options are Included Page Dependencies Are Out Of Date and Text Index Is Out Of Date.

**Language tab**  The Language tab allows you to set the default language and HTML encoding for your site. The Default Web Language setting is used by the FrontPage Server Extensions so that when error messages need to be returned back to the browser, the specified language is used. The Default HTML Encoding setting specifies the default character set for new pages.

FrontPage 97 is available in English, French, German, Italian, Japanese, and Spanish editions. Even if the FrontPage user interface is not available for a particular language, you can still use FrontPage to *create* sites for essentially any language, using the extensive list of HTML encodings available from this dialog box.

## Changing a Password

Your officemate, Sissy LeJerk, looked over your shoulder and memorized your FrontPage administrator password as you were typing it in. What to do? Change your password when Sissy isn't looking over your shoulder. Here's how: First, tell her there's a mongo sale of her favorite perfume, Evening d'Armpit, in the mall next door. After she leaves the office, choose the Change Password com-

**TIP**

The Change Password command might appear grayed out. For several of Microsoft's Web servers, access control is handled by the system instead of by FrontPage. For more information, see Chapter 5.

mand from the Tools menu in the Explorer. You'll see a dialog box like the one shown below, asking you for your old password, which Sissy knows; your new password, which she'll never have a clue about because you'll be watching over your shoulder from now on; and a confirmation of that password. Enter the passwords, and then click OK to exit the dialog box and save your new password. Then put a small bag of used cat litter in Sissy's briefcase.

# Configuring Editors

Have you ever opened a file from the Windows Explorer? If you have, you know that the file opens in an application that it can be viewed and/or edited in. The FrontPage Explorer offers the same feature. When you double-click a file in your Web site, such as a **GIF** or **JPEG** file or any Office file, the FrontPage Explorer opens the file in the application specified in the Windows Explorer.

If you want to invoke a different editor than what is specified in the Windows Explorer, here's how: First, choose Options from the Tools menu. The Options dialog box appears. Click on the Configure Editors tab.

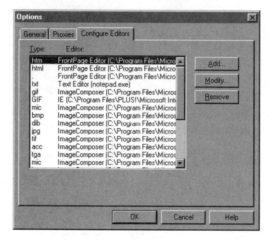

The list box on the tab has two columns, one for the extension of the file type to edit and the other for the application that's used to edit the file. As you can see, the dialog box includes default settings for some common file types and their editors.

To add a file type, click the Add button. In the Add Editor Association dialog box, add the extension that identifies the file type in the File Type text box and the name you want to use for the editor in the Editor Name text box. Then, enter the name and location of the executable file in the Command text box. If you don't know the exact location, click the Browse button to search your folders for the executable file. When you finish, click OK.

To modify settings for an existing entry, select the entry and click the Modify button. This takes you to the Modify Editor

Association dialog box, where you can change the editor name and the command to execute the editor.

You can also remove an entry in the list by selecting the entry and clicking Remove.

FrontPage allows you to designate only one editor application per file type. Each of the editors listed on the Configure Editors tab appears in the Open With Editor dialog box under the Edit menu. If you don't specify an editor for a particular file type in the Explorer, FrontPage uses the default Windows editor for that file type.

> **WARNING**
>
> FrontPage does not ask you to confirm the removal of an entry on the Configure Editors tab when you click Remove. If you remove an entry by mistake, you must reenter it by clicking Add.

## Verifying Internal and External Links

The testing of links is a vital component of any site-testing plan. You've got to be sure the links work. Broken links not only make your site look bad, they make *you* look bad. But even for small sites, this phase of testing can take a long time. FrontPage includes a tool to verify your links, which can save you oodles of time when you're in a crunch. You can use this tool to verify links in HTML files and Office 97 documents.

> **TIP**
>
> Verifying links in Front-Page ensures that the targets of your links exist, and that they will work in a browser. It does *not* confirm that your links jump where you want them to. You need to confirm this yourself.

To verify the links, do the following:

1. With the site open in the Explorer, choose Verify Hyperlinks from the Tools menu. The Verify Hyperlinks dialog box appears, listing all broken internal links along with all external links in your site (whether broken or not). If nothing appears in the dialog box, your site has no broken links and no external links.

   Each link is preceded by a yellow or red circle. The yellow circles will change color after you verify the links:

*Green*—indicates that the link is good.

*Yellow*—indicates that the link has not been verified or has changed since the last verification.

*Red*—indicates that the link is broken.

> **TIP**
>
> The Verify button changes to a Stop button while FrontPage verifies the links. Click the Stop button to stop the process at any time.

2. To start the process, click Verify. FrontPage checks all links, and then tells you their status in the Status column. To verify external links, such as links to the World Wide Web, FrontPage must be able to reach those links; in other words, to verify Web links, you must be connected live to the Web. Verifying external links can take a long time.

3. To fix a broken link right away, select that link and click the Edit Link button. In the Edit Link dialog box, change the URL in the With text box, and then click OK to return to the Verify Hyperlinks dialog box.

4. To move to a page that contains a link, select the link and then click the Edit Page button. The page opens in the Editor and scrolls to the link, allowing you to edit the link or remove it. (For information on editing a link in the Editor, see Chapter 7.) The Verify Hyperlinks dialog box remains open in the Explorer so that you can switch between the two programs.

5. If you don't have time to fix the link right away, or you need some time to find the correct address, you can add the task to the To Do List by selecting the link and clicking the Add Task button.

6. When you finish editing the links or adding them to the To Do List, click Close to exit the Verify Hyperlinks dialog box.

## Recalculating Links

Recalculating links updates or "refreshes" your site. If you've made significant changes to your site, such as removing entire pages, it's wise to go through the recalculating links operation.

This is especially true if you've added, deleted, or modified documents in your site without using FrontPage. All you need to do is choose Recalculate Hyperlinks from the Tools menu. FrontPage warns you that the process might take a long time, and asks you if you want to proceed.

When you use this command, FrontPage performs the following tasks:

◆ Updates the display for the current site for both Explorer views.

◆ Updates your list of links for the current site. If you delete material from your site and you want to check your links using the Verify Hyperlinks command, some of the deleted links might still be listed in the Verify Hyperlinks dialog box. Therefore, it is a good idea to use the Recalculate Links command after you have deleted material from your site.

◆ Updates the text index that's created by a WebBot Search Component. When you implement searching on a page using this WebBot component, FrontPage creates a text index for the component to use. When you add a page or save a modified page in your site, entries are added to the text index, but no entries are deleted. Thus, if you delete material from a page and then save the modified page, the text index still contains entries for the deleted material. Whenever you delete material, including entire pages, from your site, you need to use the Recalculate Links command to update the text index. (For more information on the WebBot Search Component, see Chapter 9.)

## Coming Up

As you can see, you can use the Explorer, the engine of FrontPage's client software, not only to view a Web site but to administer it. Two additional key parts of the FrontPage client, templates and wizards, are detailed in the next chapter.

# Chapter 4
# Templates and Wizards

## Life in the Fast Lane

Imagine what an announcer would say if FrontPage were ever featured in a late-night infomercial: "Tired of staying up night after night memorizing *thousands* of HTML commands? Tired of taking hours and hours to create that one final page that'll make your site shine?" In a fictitious world, you'd also be real excited about the prospect of losing five pounds and getting great abs while sitting there creating your Web sites, but we're here to tell you that FrontPage can actually save you so much time with its **templates** and **wizards** that you *might* even be able to take your family on that three-week cross-country trip to Wally World that you've been dreaming about for the past 15 years.

Everyone's looking for a shortcut, and you've got a huge one in FrontPage by not having to know a lick of HTML to create professional-looking Web sites. FrontPage also provides a couple of other pretty cool shortcuts in its templates and wizards. A template, as you might know, is a "shell" that you use as the basis for a new document. A wizard is a software module of one or more screens that asks you questions, offers you choices, and then generates a customized document as a result. Templates are not customizable up front, as wizards are. The result of both templates and wizards is a document that serves as a framework for your finished product—a framework that you can modify if you like, and add information to.

This chapter explores the FrontPage templates and wizards. It shows you how to work with them, and it gives you plenty of examples along the way. You'll find that using templates and wizards is a terrific way to get started on your Web site, and a sensational time-saver as well.

# Templates

Templates are examples of sites or pages that FrontPage provides to fill a particular need. Like wizards, they give you a framework, or a great place to start, for a site or a page. Wizards, however, offer you choices in creating a customized site or page; when you select a template, you get an exact copy of the template itself.

## Web Templates

Most of the Web templates in FrontPage are based on small sites; they have few items that need customizing. You can, however, enhance these pages by adding images, text, links, and so forth—in the FrontPage Editor. You can also add your own pages to sites created by Web templates.

The Web templates can be accessed in the FrontPage Explorer by choosing New from the File menu, and then choosing FrontPage Web from the submenu that appears. In the New FrontPage Web dialog box (shown on the facing page), you can select one of the following templates to use as the basis for your site or page:

**Empty Web**  When you want to create an entire site from scratch, you can use this "template." It creates an empty site with no pages, and you do all the rest by adding content in the Editor.

**Normal Web**  This template creates a new site with one blank page. Besides the Empty Web template, this is the least complicated template in FrontPage.

**New FrontPage Web**

Template or Wizard:

Normal Web
Corporate Presence Wizard
Customer Support Web
Discussion Web Wizard
Empty Web
Import Web Wizard
Learning FrontPage
Personal Web
Project Web

OK

Cancel

Help

☐ Add to the current web

Description

Create a new web with a single blank page.

**Customer Support Web** This template creates a place where your customers can go to report bugs, find solutions to previously reported problems, and suggest improvements for your products and services. This is an ideal site for software companies, but it is applicable to many kinds of businesses.

**Learning FrontPage** This is the template you use with the Learning FrontPage tutorial, which you'll find in the *Getting Started with Microsoft FrontPage* manual.

**Personal Web** This template creates a very simple site with a single personal home page. For a more in-depth and customized home page, you can do the following:

◆ Use the Editor to customize the Personal Web home page.

◆ Use the Personal Home Page Wizard instead of the Personal Web template. For details on using wizards, see the section titled "Wizards" later in this chapter.

**Project Web** Use this template to create a site that will serve as a central informational forum for a project. This template creates a home page, a page that lists members of the project team, a schedule page, a status page, a search page, various forms and discussion pages, and a page that links to all public discussions about the project.

# Page Templates

FrontPage offers you a wide variety of page templates, ranging from a bare-bones Normal page to a fairly complex "frequently asked questions" (FAQ) page. Adding pages to an existing site with a page template is a fast and easy way to customize a site.

**Using page templates** You create a page using a template in the Editor. The process is very simple:

1. In the Explorer, open the site that the new page will belong to. (You can skip this step if you want to; after you save the page, you can import it to any Web site.)

2. In the Editor, choose New from the File menu.

3. In the New Page dialog box that appears, select a template from the Template Or Wizard list, and then click OK. (Note that this list also includes page wizards; for more information on page wizards, see the section titled "Page Wizards" later in this chapter.)

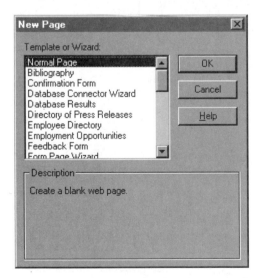

FrontPage creates the page using the template you selected, and presents it in the Editor for you to work on. Whenever you create a new page from a page template, it includes advice at the top about how to customize the page, as in the following example created with the What's New page template. The comment text will not appear in the browser.

FrontPage Editor - [Untitled What's New]

File  Edit  View  Insert  Format  Tools  Table  Window  Help

Normal | Times New Roman | A A' B I U

Comment: Once you create this page, keep it up to date by making an entry here every time you make a significant change to your web site. Clear out old entries every month so it appears fresh and up-to-date for frequent visitors.

## What's New?

For Help, press F1                           0:00 at 28.8

You can choose from 26 different page templates to create new pages in your site. The following are brief descriptions of the templates, starting with Normal Page, the most general template. The rest are listed alphabetically. You'll find that the templates have a wide variety of uses, and that some of them are designed to be used together in the same site.

**Normal Page**  This template simply creates a blank page. If you want to create a new page from scratch, this is the place to start.

**Bibliography**  If you need to compile a bibliography of sources, you can use this template to begin. It provides some examples for you to mimic, so you don't have to create each entry from scratch.

**Confirmation Form**  Use this template to display confirmation entries to users who have submitted information to your organization. The example provided in the template consists of a letter to confirm the submission of customer feedback.

**Database Results**  This template creates a blank database results or HTML template file. You typically use this template in combination with the Internet Database Connector Wizard, which is discussed later in this chapter and in Chapter 10.

**Directory of Press Releases**  You can use this template to produce a page on which your press releases are organized by date and title. The page includes sections for current releases and past releases. You can use the Press Release template, described later in this section, to create a release and then link to it from this directory page.

**Employee Directory** You can alphabetically organize your employee information using this template, which includes areas for you to enter an employee's title, project, office location, e-mail address, and more.

**Employment Opportunities** This is quite a complex template. It provides sections for job listings, job descriptions, and a place for users to submit general employment inquiries. Users can send you their employment history, goals, and contact information through this page.

**Feedback Form** This template creates a page for users to submit specific comments about your company, products, Web site, and so on.

**Frequently Asked Questions** You can use this template to create an FAQ page, where users can get answers to frequently asked questions.

**Glossary of Terms** This template produces a glossary page that is separated into alphabetized sections. Glossaries can be quite useful to viewers if your pages include technical terms that they might not understand.

**Guest Book** This template creates a page where your viewers can leave comments. Watch out when using this one; if your Web site contains controversial information, you could get negative comments on this page for the rest of the world to see. This page is best used in an intranet setting.

**Hot List** If you'd like your site to include a page that lists links to other sites, you can use this template to begin. You can use this page in any kind of site, whether it's a personal or business site and whether the site is on an intranet or on the World Wide Web.

**HyperDocument Page** This template creates a page that is intended to be one section of a linked manual or report. You can build a document by putting several of these pages together. Remember that you can include links to Office documents (such as Word, Excel, and PowerPoint documents).

**Lecture Abstract** This template creates a page describing an upcoming lecture. It includes space for a speaker name, organization, topics of discussion, and more. You can use this with the Seminar Schedule template, which is described on the next page.

**Meeting Agenda** When you want to make sure that everyone attending a meeting has an opportunity to look over the agenda, you can post the agenda on your intranet using this template. You can then build links to any documents that should be reviewed before the meeting.

**Office Directory** Use this template to produce a page that lists the locations of all your organization's offices. It includes placeholders for the 50 U.S. states, all of the Canadian provinces, and a collection of international listings.

**Press Release** This template creates a press release page, which when completed can be linked to a page created with the Directory of Press Releases template. You add these links in the Editor.

**Product Description** You can use this template to create a page containing descriptions of your products; the page is separated into product summary, key features, product benefits, and specifications sections.

**Product or Event Registration** This template produces a registration form page for users to fill out and submit. You can use it for product support, events, or other registration purposes.

**Search Page** Use this template to create a page where users can perform keyword searches of your entire Web site. The template inserts a WebBot Search Component for you, which includes all the code needed to perform a search. This template provides a ready-made search page; all you need to do is customize it in the Editor. For more information on WebBot components, see Chapter 9.

**Seminar Schedule** This template produces the main page for a collection of seminar information. The page is divided into several sections, each with placeholders where you can fill in specific information on sessions or tracks of the seminar. You can use this template in conjunction with the Lecture Abstract template, which was described above.

**Software Data Sheet** This template creates a page you can use to show off the benefits of your software. It contains places to list benefits, key features, system requirements, pricing and availability, and more.

**Survey Form** This template creates an extremely detailed survey form with several sections. Each section includes placeholders for different types of questions, with answers ranging in style from check boxes to drop-down lists.

**Table of Contents** This template uses a WebBot Table Of Contents Component to produce a Table of Contents page for your site, which will contain links to the other pages in the site. This WebBot component is described in Chapter 9.

**User Registration** This template creates a page where users can register for other protected Web sites on a server. It contains explicit directions for the user, and it must be loaded as part of the **root Web site** on your server in order to work correctly.

**What's New** You can use this template to create a simple What's New page that lists changes to your site by date.

# Custom Templates

Because everyone has a different style, and because you might have specific needs that the templates don't address, FrontPage allows you to create and save your own page templates in the Editor. (To find out how to create custom Web-site templates, see the next section, "Custom Web-Site Templates."

Perhaps you want to create several similar pages that don't look much like any of the existing FrontPage templates. You can create your own template to use when creating these pages and minimize the number of changes you need to make to each (rather than starting with a FrontPage template and having to modify it extensively to meet your needs).

Using a custom page template is a great way to streamline the gathering of employee information at a company. You can create a specific form with places for each kind of information you need from your employees, and then save that form as a template. That template can then be distributed within your organization for all to use.

Creating and saving a custom page template requires only a few steps:

1. Start with the Normal Page template in the Editor, and insert the content that you want to have appear in your new template (for example, custom logos, navigation buttons, and so forth).

2. Choose the Save As command from the File menu in the Editor.

3. In the Save As dialog box that appears, click the As Template button. You do not need to supply a template name or a **URL** before you click this button.

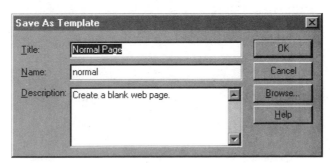

4. In the Save As Template dialog box, give your template a title and a name, and then enter a short description of the template in the Description text box. If you want to save the current template in place of another template, click the Browse button and find the template you want to replace.

5. Click OK in the Save As Template dialog box. Front-Page saves the page as a template and returns you to the page.

After you save the template, any time you create a new page in the Editor the template will appear in the New Page dialog box along with all the page templates and wizards included with FrontPage.

**Custom Web-site templates** You can use the FrontPage Developer's Kit to create custom Web-site templates as well as custom Web and page wizards, which are discussed later. For information on obtaining this free kit, see the FrontPage area of Microsoft's Web site at //www.microsoft.com/frontpage/.

# Wizards

How long do you suppose it would take to create a Web site for your business from scratch that includes all of the following?

◆ A home page with places for an introduction, mission statement, company profile, and/or contact information

◆ A What's New page that contains links for press re-leases, articles, reviews, and information about your site

◆ Numerous products and services pages, each with room for a description of the product or service, images, pric-ing information, and more

◆ A Table of Contents page that indexes your site and is updated automatically as your site structure changes

◆ A feedback form that asks users for specific informa-tion such as their name, title, address, phone number, fax number, and e-mail address

As you know by now, creating all of this from scratch and writ-ing it in HTML would take quite a long time. For many, it would be akin to putting an automobile together piece-by-piece—it's easy to see where the big pieces go, but incorporating the smaller pieces and getting it all to work smoothly is quite difficult. Would you be-lieve that with FrontPage, creating a site like the one just described can take less than five minutes? You can do it all with the Corporate Presence Wizard, which is one of several wizards included with FrontPage, and a couple dozen clicks of the mouse. And when you're done, you'll have a set of linked pages complete with elements that are ready for you to customize.

FrontPage offers two Web wizards that create the framework for entire Web sites, plus an additional Web wizard that allows you to import non-FrontPage Web sites. FrontPage also includes three page wizards that create Web pages, and a fourth and more complex page wizard, the Internet Database Connector Wizard, which assists you in querying databases from your site.

## Web Wizards

The two Web wizards that create brand-new FrontPage sites for you are the Corporate Presence Wizard and the Discussion Web Wizard. The Corporate Presence Wizard creates the framework for a site that includes the items described in the previous section, and the Discussion Web Wizard produces a site in which users can participate in discussions on various topics. First we'll walk through the Corporate Presence Wizard; after that, we'll provide a description of the Discussion Web Wizard.

Keep in mind that you can easily change the resulting site later on if you want to, using the Editor. You can customize text and graphics to give your site a unique look and feel, add to the pages, delete items or pages, and modify the pages in any other way you like.

**Corporate Presence Wizard** Using the Corporate Presence Wizard, you can create a site to highlight your business without having to do much up-front work. Let's step through the process of using this wizard, as someone might when designing a site for the fictitious Snake River Winery:

1. From the File menu in the Explorer, choose New, and then choose FrontPage Web from the submenu. In the New FrontPage Web dialog box that appears, select Corporate Presence Wizard.

If you already have a site up and running, you can select the Add To The Current Web check box to integrate your Corporate Presence site with it. For example, you can combine a Corporate Presence site with a Customer Support site. This is a great option to experiment with once you get to know the different kinds of sites Front-Page can create for you. If you're creating just this site, do not select the Add To The Current Web check box.

When you are ready to continue, click OK.

2. Next you'll be greeted by the Corporate Presence Wizard dialog box. In the Web Server Or File Location text box, type in the name of the server or file location where you want to save the site. You can also select a server or a file location, if available, from the drop-down list. Then, name your site in the Name Of New FrontPage Web text box.

The winery has a Web server of its own, called Silver-Dollar, so the person creating the site would type that name in the Web Server Or File Location text box. (For your own system, you would type in the name of your server.) Then the person would type the name of the site, Snake River Winery Cellar, in the Name Of New Front-Page Web text box. Because FrontPage doesn't allow spaces in the name of a site, underscore characters should be used to replace the spaces. Therefore, the name would be *Snake_River_Winery_Cellar.*

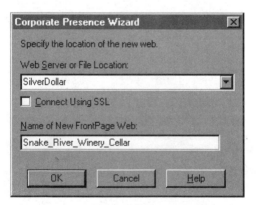

When you click OK, FrontPage creates the site on the server or at the specified file location.

3. Next you'll see the opening screen of the Corporate Presence Wizard. It contains a brief description of the wizard and informs you that you'll be asked a few questions about how you want your site to appear. Several buttons appear at the bottom of this screen and the following screens:

**Help**  At any time, you can click the Help button to open a Corporate Presence Web Wizard topic in online help.

**Cancel**  The Cancel button stops the wizard and takes you back to the Explorer. Because some of the material for the site will have already been created, you will be asked whether to delete the site.

**Back**  When the Back button is enabled, you can click it to return to the previous screen or screens and change any information you already entered.

**Next**  Clicking the Next button takes you to the next screen in the wizard.

**Finish**  The Finish button ends the wizard process at whatever point you click it. You can stop using the wizard anytime before the final wizard screen. When you click Finish, FrontPage immediately begins to populate the site with all the information you've supplied up to that point.

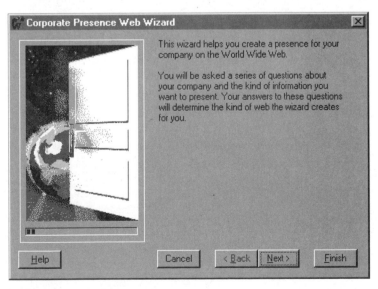

Click Next to proceed.

4. The next screen gives you several options for pages to include in your site. You'll notice that the Back button is now enabled.

The Snake River Winery is building a very sophisticated site and will include all of the available types of pages (listed below). The site starts with a required home page, the contents of which can be customized in the next step of the wizard.

**What's New page** This page is a must! For any users who return to the site multiple times, this page can provide information on recent updates to the site. Perhaps there's a new merlot being offered in the fall, or maybe there's a special group rate for tours of the winery in July. The What's New page can link to these items in your site.

**Products/Services page** Simply because the winery sells products, and especially because the products have mass appeal, the Products/Services page is a wise addition to the site. Here the winery can highlight all its wines and other products, and this might be a good place to tell people how to order.

**Table of Contents page** Those who want to see an overview of what the winery's site has to offer can go to this page, which links to all other pages in the site. It's wise to include some sort of overview page in your site. These pages can help prevent users from getting "lost" in your site.

**Feedback Form** The winery management wants to know what users think of the products offered in the site, and what they think of the site. Visitors to the site can use the feedback form to submit comments to the winery.

**Search Form** The winery considers a search form an attractive feature for its site. It allows users to search the site for any word that might appear on its pages. Enabling the search form is as easy as selecting the

Search Form check box in the wizard. FrontPage automatically compiles a word list that the search form uses when someone searches the site.

For each page you decide to include in your Web site, the wizard will present you with a subsequent screen to customize the page further. The wizard will not show screens for pages you did not select in this screen.

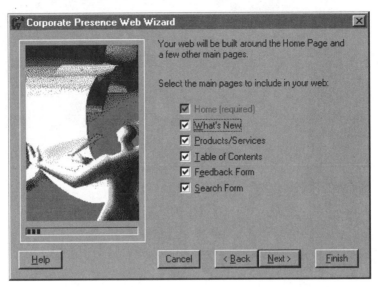

Click Next when you're ready to move on.

5. Next you'll see a screen with several options for the format of your home page. Your choices include creating spaces for an introduction, mission statement, company profile, and contact information for your company. You're not asked to supply the exact information, such as the text of your mission statement, at this time; you enter that later in the Editor. The wizard simply creates a space for you to fill with the actual content at your leisure.

The folks at the Snake River Winery want their site to look professional, so at the very least they'll include the introduction, company profile, and contact information. Including the contact information is vital; potential wholesalers or individual customers who view the site might want to find out more about purchasing products.

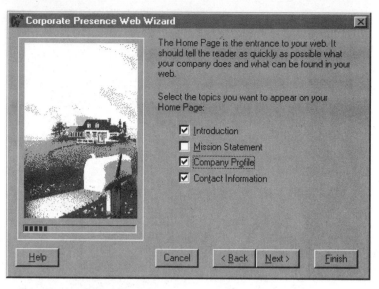

After you select the check boxes for the topics you want to include, click Next.

6. Options for the What's New page are presented in the next screen. Select any of the three check boxes if you want to include that type of information on the page. FrontPage creates subsections for any items that you want to include on the What's New page.

If a contact phone number changes at the Snake River Winery, the winery can alert its Web-site viewers to the new number on the What's New page in the Web Changes section. Any other breaking news about the company can easily be added to this page later on as well.

The What's New page is also a great place to put information about the industry, such as a list of upcoming trade shows, positive information about stock trends, or other business news. It's great to have a place in your site where visitors can expect new, timely content. Such information can lure your customers back to your pages, where they'll be exposed to your products again and again. You can use the Press Releases section and the Articles And Reviews section for this purpose.

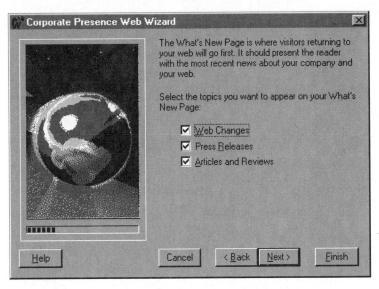

After you select the kind of information you want to include on your page to start with, click Next.

7. The next screen provides options for the Products/Services page. Enter the values for the number of products and/or services you want to highlight on this page; FrontPage allows you to enter between 0 and 5 for each. The wizard creates sections on the page for the number of products and services you enter in this screen.

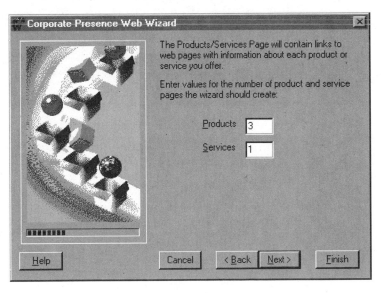

The Snake River Winery plans to highlight its three best wines in the Web site, so enter *3* in the Products text box. The winery also prides itself on providing top-flight customer service, so enter *1* in the Services text box to provide a section to highlight that aspect of the company.

Click Next to move to the next screen.

**TIP**

You can tab through the content options in the wizard screens instead of using your mouse. To select or deselect a check box, use the Spacebar.

8. Next you'll specify how you want to customize any product or service pages you have in your site. The wizard gives you choices to provide placeholders for product images, pricing information, and information request forms on the Products pages, and to provide capabilities lists, reference accounts, and information request forms on Services pages.

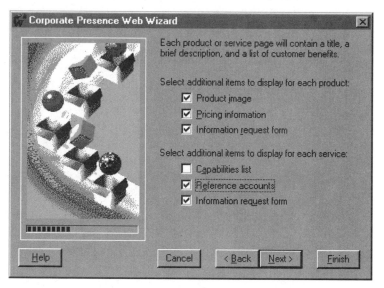

Select the options you want to include on those pages, and then click Next.

9. The next screen provides options for the feedback form, where you specify the information you want to receive from your audience. Think carefully about this, keeping in mind what kind of audience you expect to view your pages. If the audience doesn't have lots of time to fill out every item, seeing all of them at once might overwhelm them. Even though it takes only seconds to fill out a feedback form, Web surfers are keen on clicking out of a page if it looks like too much work.

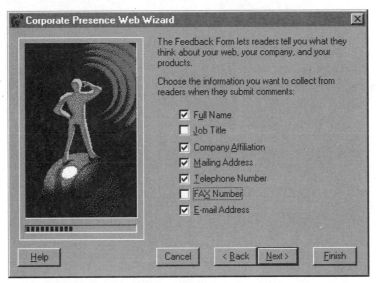

After you select the options you want for the feedback form, click Next.

10. The next screen features a neat option: It allows you to specify how the feedback you receive from your viewers is stored. If you plan to manipulate the information using a database or spreadsheet application (such as Microsoft Access or Microsoft Excel), select the first option and FrontPage will store the information in tab-delimited format. If you don't plan to use such an application, select the second option and FrontPage will store the information in Web-page format.

The Snake River Winery is not a large company, but management does expect its Web site to receive heavy traffic. It's easier to manipulate feedback information in Access and Excel—this reduces the workload significantly—so management wants to save the feedback information in tab-delimited format. That means the Yes, Use Tab-Delimited Format option should be selected.

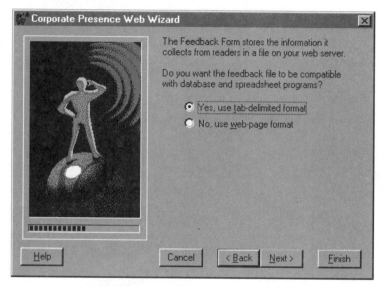

When you've made your choice, click Next to continue.

11. Next you'll see a screen with options to customize the Table of Contents (TOC) page. Here you can select options to update the TOC automatically each time a page is edited, to show pages not linked to the pages that appear in the TOC, and to use bullets for top-level pages.

If you anticipate that your site will be small or that it won't be updated often, it's a good idea to select the Keep Page List Up-To-Date Automatically check box. However, if you anticipate that your site will be large or that it will grow significantly, you should not select this check box. Updating the page list can be time-consuming in these cases. You can update the TOC manually later on, so don't be overly concerned about this option.

After you select the options to customize your TOC page, click Next.

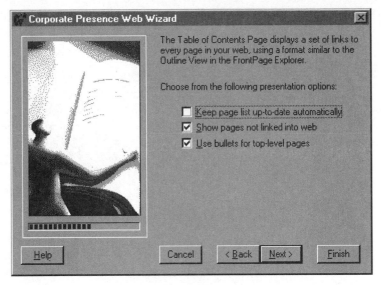

12. The next screen deals with the items you want at the top and bottom of every page in your site. You can include your company's logo, a page title, and links to your main Web pages at the top. You can also include links to your main Web pages at the bottom, along with your Webmaster's e-mail address, a copyright notice, and the date the page was last modified (which is supplied automatically by FrontPage).

Again, these options control whether FrontPage leaves room for the item, not the actual content for each item. Select the options you want even if you plan to use different items on different pages.

The winery Web site will sport a different logo for the pages in each section, so select the Your Company's Logo check box to include a space for the logo. Later, in the Editor, you can manually insert a different logo at the beginning of each page.

FrontPage doesn't check the contents of each space, so you can be flexible in how you use these options. For example, if the winery wants to include the e-mail address of someone other than the Webmaster on the pages, you should select the E-mail Address Of Your Webmaster check box to leave the space open. The e-mail address can be changed in the Editor later on.

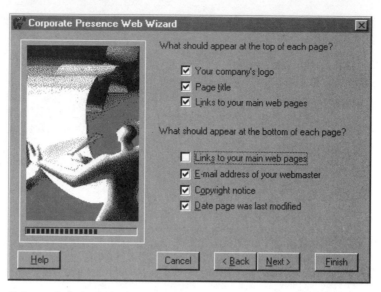

Select the options you want, and then click Next.

13. In the next screen, you can control the "look and feel" of your site. This screen gives you four options for the presentation style of your site—Plain, Conservative, Flashy, or Cool. Selecting one of these options displays the corresponding style on the left side of the screen.

As a young, energetic, up-and-coming business, the Snake River Winery does not want to present itself as conservative, so select the Cool option.

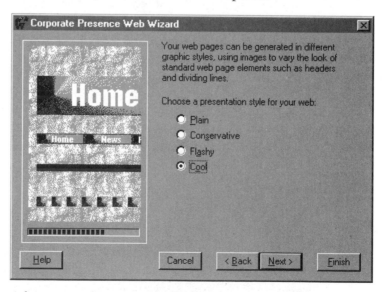

After you select a presentation style, click Next.

14. Next you'll see a screen that asks you to specify settings for the page background and text in your site.

You can set your colors as follows:

- In the Colors section, select the Custom option to set your own colors and background for the site, or select Default to use the FrontPage default settings. Clicking the Reset button refreshes the screen with the default settings. If you select Default, the options in the Background and Text sections become grayed out. If you select Custom, you can specify settings in the Background and Text sections.

- In the Background section, select any textured option from the Pattern drop-down list if you want a textured screen. The sample on the left changes to a preview of your selection. If you want a solid screen, select None from the drop-down list, and then click the button next to Solid. When you click this button, the Color dialog box appears, giving you 48 colors to choose from, as well as the option to define a custom color for your background. Select a color, and then click OK to return to the wizard screen.

- In the Text section, select a color for Normal text, links, **visited links**, and **active links**. Click the color button next to each item, and then select a color from the Color dialog box and click OK.

These settings are in no way permanent; you can always change them later by editing the properties of the Web Colors page that's created by this wizard as a part of the Corporate Presence site. You can locate this page easily in Folder View.

The winery wants to mimic as much as possible the look and feel of a wine cellar, so select the Brown Texture 1 background pattern. Retain the default black Normal text, which can be read easily against that background. Use the default colors for the links for the same reasons. (Default colors are blue for links, purple for visited links, and red for active links.)

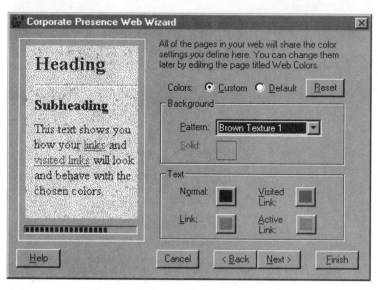

After you select all your color options, click Next.

15. The next screen gives you the option of showing an Under Construction icon on all unfinished pages of your site. It's always a good idea to label a page as "under construction" if it's not finished. This way, viewers won't think a page is final if it's not. For example, the winery wants to show its Products page, but the page is not yet complete. By using an Under Construction icon, the winery can at least expose the public to its products while the page is being completed.

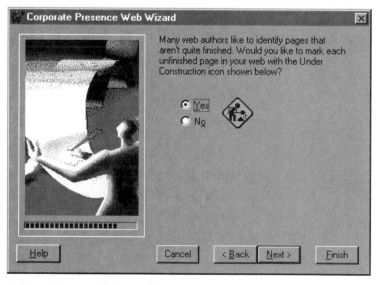

Select Yes, and then click Next.

16. The next two screens offer *huge* potential time-savers. They ask for your company information, such as the company's full name, one-word name, address, phone number, and fax number; the e-mail address of the Webmaster; and a general-information e-mail address. These screens are time-savers because you enter this information once, and FrontPage inserts the information into the placeholders already in your site. For example, on an earlier screen of the wizard (step 12), if you requested that FrontPage display your Webmaster's e-mail address at the bottom of every page, all you need to do is type the address here, and FrontPage will take care of the rest.

If you need to make changes to this information later on, you only need to change it in one place. (You can change these settings later on by using the Web Settings command on the Explorer's Tools menu.)

The Snake River Winery wants to start with all this information on its pages, even though it might decide later not to include some of it.

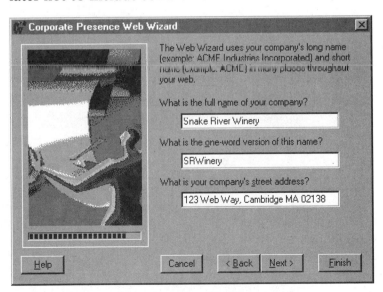

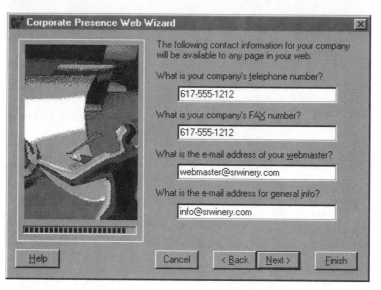

When you finish entering this information in both screens, click Next to move on.

17. The final screen tells you that FrontPage has gathered all the information it needs to create your Corporate Presence site. It includes a Show To Do List After Web Is Uploaded check box. The To Do List is a list of tasks that need to be completed in your site. FrontPage adds several tasks to the list after it creates this site; among them are customizing various pages with specific text and other files, and replacing images. The To Do List is explained in greater detail in Chapter 5.

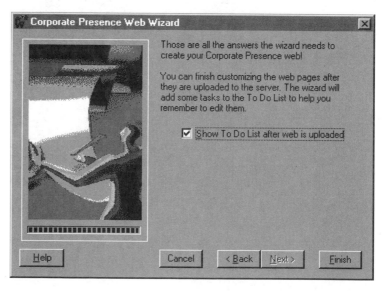

Click Finish, and FrontPage fills in the Corporate Presence site with the information you supplied and saves the site. Based on what you specified, the site will be saved to the server, or to a folder on your LAN or hard drive. Once saved, the site is displayed in the Explorer and FrontPage also displays the To Do List if you've directed it to. From this point you can fill in the fine details of your site and personalize it to give it your own "look and feel."

That's all there is to creating the structure for a Web site using the Corporate Presence Wizard—a bunch of tiny steps, all of which add up to a huge time savings.

**Discussion Web Wizard** The Discussion Web Wizard creates a threaded **discussion group** about a topic of your choice. Often this discussion group is added as part of a site. Each user can contribute thoughts and associate them with a particular ongoing conversation (thread). Each separate entry from a user is referred to as an **article**. The user also has the ability to search for existing articles. The wizard asks you to decide the following:

◆ What kinds of pages you want to include

◆ The title of the discussion

◆ Some input fields to separate topics of discussion

◆ Whether the discussion will take place in a protected site (meaning that only registered users can participate)

◆ How the table of contents should sort the posted articles

◆ Whether the Table of Contents page should be the site's home page

◆ The information you want reported about each article found in a search of past discussions

◆ The colors for the background and text

◆ Whether you want to create the site using **frames**

As always, you can change the look and feel and add or delete features to these pages later, using the Editor.

**Administering a discussion group** You can administer a discussion group in FrontPage quite easily by using the Explorer and the Editor. All you need is author or administrative access to the discussion site. If you're in charge of administering a discussion group, here are a few things you can do:

◆ Edit articles—Each page that a user completes and sends to the discussion group is called an article; it's saved as an HTML file in a hidden folder typically named _disc1. To see a list of articles, you need to tell FrontPage to show files in hidden folders. You can do this in the Explorer by choosing Web Settings from the Tools menu, clicking on the Advanced tab, and selecting the Show Documents In Hidden Directories check box. When you click OK, a dialog box is displayed asking you if you want to refresh the Web site now. If you click the Yes button, the hidden pages will display in the Explorer.

You edit an article by first finding it in the discussion folder and then double-clicking on it in the Explorer. The article appears in the Editor, where you can delete text—such as objectionable language. The modified article can then be saved and users will be able to view this edited article.

◆ Delete old articles—If you can see the files in hidden folders, you can sort the files and delete old messages that are no longer needed. In Folder view, sort the list of files in the discussion site by date, and then delete any files you don't need by selecting them and pressing the Del key.

◆ Limit administrative access—Any author can view and edit any message in the discussion group if he or she has access to the site. This amounts to little administrative control if a large number of authors are members of the discussion group. You can limit access to a discussion group so that users can browse the articles but not edit them. To do so, choose the Permissions command from the Explorer's Tools menu, apply the use of unique permissions settings for the Web site on the Settings tab, and then set Browse access for specific users on the Users tab (or specify that everyone only has Browse access). For more information on the Web Settings command, see Chapter 5.

An easier way to limit access to your site is by specifying that only registered users can access the site. To do this, use the Discussion Web Wizard to create your site. In the wizard you'll see a screen that gives you the option to have all discussions take place in a protected Web site, which means that only registered users of the discussion site can access the articles. If you opt to use the protected Web site, FrontPage will give you some simple directions for steps to complete on a registration page in the Editor after you complete the wizard and create the site.

**Import Web Wizard** If you have other Web sites that you'd like to turn into FrontPage Web sites, you can do so with the Import Web Wizard. This wizard imports a folder of files from your hard disk or LAN and creates a new FrontPage Web site from them. The folder doesn't necessarily have to be a complete Web site; any folder of files that you want to use to create a FrontPage Web site will do.

The Import Web Wizard is also handy for importing any older FrontPage site that might be stored in folders that your current Web server does not search when you're opening a site in the Explorer. For example, the Microsoft Personal Web Server does not search folders that early versions of FrontPage 1.1 stored its sites in. In these cases, you'll need to use the Import Web Wizard to import those older FrontPage sites.

Here are the sweet-and-simple directions for importing sites with the Import Web Wizard:

1. In the Explorer, choose New from the File menu, and then choose FrontPage Web from the submenu.

2. In the New FrontPage Web dialog box, select Import Web Wizard from the list of templates and wizards, and then click OK.

3. The Import Web Wizard dialog box appears. In the Web Server Or File Location text box, enter the server name or file location. You can also select the server or file location, if available, from the drop-down list. If you want to

> **SHORTCUT**
>
> You can also reach the New FrontPage Web dialog box by pressing Ctrl+N.

connect to the server using **Secure Sockets Layer** (SSL) security, select that check box.

Name your Web site by entering a name in the Name Of New FrontPage Web text box, and then click OK. FrontPage takes a few seconds to create a folder for your new site, and then proceeds to the wizard.

4. In the Import Web Wizard - Choose Directory screen, you'll need to locate the folder of files you want to import. Click Browse, select the folder in the Browse For Folder dialog box, and click OK. If the folder includes subfolders of files you want to import as well, select the Include Subdirectories check box in the Import Web Wizard - Choose Directory screen.

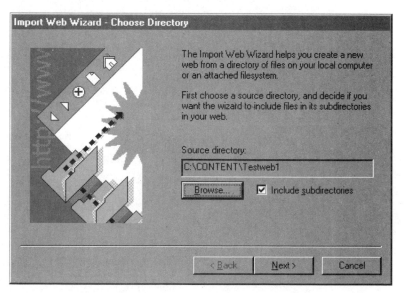

Click Next to continue.

5. Next you'll see the Import Web Wizard - Edit File List screen, which contains a list of all the files, including files in subfolders, within the folder you selected. You can specify which files to import at this stage. For example, if you plan to create a new site and are importing an older site as part of it, you might not want to include certain files if you do not plan to use them.

To omit a file from the list of files to be imported into your new site, select the file and click Exclude. If you remove some items from the list and want to start over with the original list, click Refresh, and the original list will appear again.

When you're satisfied that you want to include all the items in the list in your new FrontPage site, click Next.

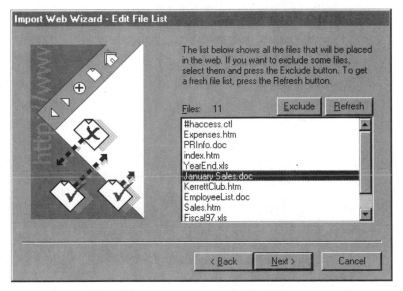

6. Now you've reached the Import Web Wizard - Finish screen, the last screen of the wizard. Click Finish to have FrontPage create the new Web site. If you want to change some information you've entered in the wizard, click Back until you reach the screen with the information you want to modify, change the information, and then click Next until you once again reach this final wizard screen.

That's all it takes for FrontPage to import a folder of files and create a new Web site from them. FrontPage will preserve the old folder structure that you've imported and add its own folders to the site, such as the _private and images folders for storing private and image files, respectively.

# Page Wizards

The FrontPage Editor includes three page wizards that make it easy to create customized pages. They are the Form Page Wizard, the Personal Home Page Wizard, and the Frames Wizard. A fourth page wizard, the Internet Database Connector Wizard, assists you in querying databases from your site.

The Form Page Wizard creates a form that you can use to gather input from users and save the results to a Web page or text file on the Web server. This form can be very useful in situations where you need to gather contact information, account information, product information, and so on, from your viewers. The Personal Home Page Wizard produces a page that includes placeholders for you to insert information on your work, current projects, favorite Web sites, biographical information, and more. The Frames Wizard allows you to divide one Web page into several sections, each of which displays an individual page on your screen.

You use these page wizards in the Editor. Each resulting page can be placed in your site and linked to other pages.

**Using the Form Page Wizard and the Personal Home Page Wizard** To add a page to your site using the Form Page Wizard or the Personal Home Page Wizard, do the following:

1. In the Explorer, open the site that the new page will belong to. (You can skip this step if you want to; after you save the page, you can import it to any Web site.)

2. In the Editor, choose New from the File menu. The New Page dialog box appears, as shown below.

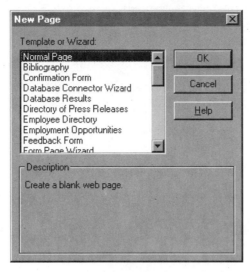

3. From the list of page templates and wizards, select either the Form Page Wizard or the Personal Home Page Wizard. Note that when you select a template or a wizard, a description of the item appears in the lower portion of the New Page dialog box. After you have selected a wizard, click the OK button.

4. Move through the screens of the wizard and answer the questions that FrontPage asks you. The process of using these wizards is the same as for using the Corporate Presence Wizard, described earlier in this chapter, but the questions are of course different. For example, you'll be asked to name the page instead of a site.

5. When you reach the final screen, click Finish and Front-Page will create the page and display it in the Editor. You can then edit the page, adding text and/or images, linking it to other pages, and so on. When you save the page, you can save it as a file, or if you have a site open in the Explorer, you can add it to the site.

**Frames** Frames allow you to divide a page into rectangular regions in a browser, each of which can display its own page. You can place one or more frames on a page (referred to as the **frame set** for that page). This means you can create a page on which different regions have different content. Changing the content of one region doesn't necessarily change the content of another, but if you want, links in one frame can cause the page that is displayed in another frame to change.

Here's the classic example of the use of frames: Imagine a Web page divided vertically into two regions, each of which is a frame. The left frame is occupied by a Table of Contents page, containing a complete list of links to all pages in the site. The contents of the frame on the right side of the screen change, depending on what link is clicked in the table of contents on the left side. If you click on a link to an Issues page in the table of contents, the Issues page appears on the right side; if you click on the Results link, the Results page appears, and so on. This scenario is depicted in the following graphic:

**A page divided into frames. Click on a link in the TOC on the left side, and that page appears on the right side.**

The graphic on the facing page shows a sample of frames being used in Microsoft Internet Explorer 3.0.

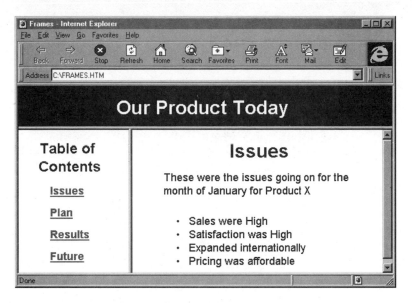

Frames are currently supported in several browsers, including Internet Explorer 3.0 and Netscape Navigator 3.0. Frames undoubtedly will be supported in even more browsers in the near future, and Microsoft is working to make frames in Front-Page compatible with the support provided by all the leading browsers.

You can include as many frames on a page as you want, and you can include frames on one page or on every page of your site. You can create pages containing frames in the Editor using the Frames Wizard; this process is described in the following section. You designate the content of your frames using various resources in the Editor. For details on this, see Chapter 6.

**Using the Frames Wizard** To create pages containing frames, follow this process:

1. Create all the pages that will be displayed within the frame(s) in your site. Also, it is a good idea to create an alternate page in your site that can be displayed if the user is using a browser that doesn't support frames. (If you select Make A Custom Grid in step 4, you will be able to specify the pages to display in each frame later in

this procedure. If you select Pick A Template in step 4, FrontPage creates a page for each frame; you can edit these pages later in the Editor.)

2. In the Explorer, open the site that the new page of frames will belong to.

3. In the Editor, choose New from the File menu. Select Frames Wizard in the New Page dialog box that appears, and then click OK.

4. From this step forward, you'll be in the Frames Wizard. In the first screen, you're asked to choose between creating a page by using one of six templates or by making a custom grid. Using a template, you can create a page with frames already arranged in formats appropriate for Table of Contents pages, pages for documents and footnotes, and other pages with hierarchical layouts. Select the Pick A Template option button or the Make A Custom Grid option button, and then click Next.

   If you decide to use a template, follow step 5a; if you decide to create your own grid, follow steps 5b–5c.

5a. Using a template: In the Frames Wizard - Pick Template Layout screen, select a layout from the Layout section. Selecting a layout yields a preview of the layout on the left side of the screen and a description of the layout at the bottom of the screen. After you select a layout, click Next. Then move on to step 6.

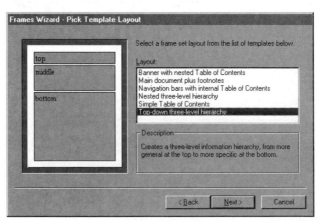

5b. Creating your own grid: In the Frames Wizard - Edit Frameset Grid screen, specify the number of rows and columns you want (thereby determining the number of frames). You can initially have up to five rows and five columns of frames on a page. The example on the left side of the screen changes to show the selected organization of frames. If you select a template and then change your mind and try to create a custom grid, the template's organization is used as the basis for the page. You can modify it, but be aware that some of the rows might have frames that have already been divided (as explained below).

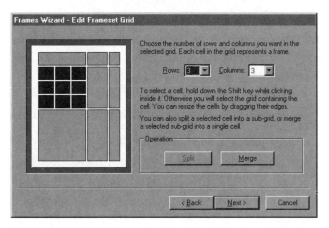

To resize a frame, move your mouse pointer over the border of the frame in the sample on the left, and when the pointer becomes a double-headed arrow, click and drag the border.

Each frame can further be divided into additional frames. To divide a frame, hold down the Shift key while clicking on the frame. Click the Split button in the Operation section of the wizard screen, and then use the controls at the top of the form to specify the number of rows and columns you want to subdivide the frame into. Be aware that using too many frames on a page can make the page download slowly in a browser. At today's bandwidth, try to use five or fewer frames per page. To merge a divided frame back to its former state, click on any frame within the split frame (which selects all of the original frame) and click the Merge button.

The small frames that are created when you divide a row can be used for many purposes, and we'll undoubtedly see some inventive ones on the Web in the near future. In general, rows are used to represent sections within the page (each with different topics), and the columns within a row are used for related (but independent) information. You might use small frames to display an image file or other element—an item that you want to appear on that row all the time. There are other ways of accomplishing this, of course, but designating content in frames is a handy and relatively easy way.

5c. After you create your grid, click the Next button. The Frames Wizard - Edit Frame Attributes screen appears, asking you to name all of your frames on the page. Click on each frame to highlight it, and then name it and specify the URL of the page or other file that you want displayed in it. Give your frames easy-to-remember names; you'll need to type these names in later when you create links to them.

You can specify links in one frame to load pages in another frame. To link the contents of one frame to another, select the frame that contains the page with the links, and then click the Edit button. This opens the page containing the links in the Editor. To have all of the linked pages appear in the same frame, right-click on the page, choose Page Properties, enter the name of the frame where the linked pages should appear in the Default Target Frame text box on the General tab, and click OK. To have a linked page appear in a specific frame, right-click on the link, choose Hyperlink Properties, enter the name of the frame where that page should appear in the Target Frame text box, and click OK.

In the Frames Wizard - Edit Frame Attributes screen, specify the margin width in pixels for the current frame, and specify whether the frame should be a scrolling frame. If you anticipate that your frame will be smaller than the pages or other content that will be displayed in them, you should specify the frame as a scrolling frame.

Here are some of the attributes you can give a frame and the values that you might use for placing a logo into an independent frame:

*Name*—Enter the name you'll use to refer to this frame (Logo Frame).

*Source URL*—Enter the location of the page that should be used for the contents of the frame (Logo.htm).

*Margin Width and Margin Height*—Enter the amount of space that should be left around the border of the frame, between the edge and the contents (2 pixels).

*Scrolling*—Specify whether scroll bars appear on the frame when the contents are too large to fit within the frame (no).

*Not Resizable*—Specify whether the frame can be resized within a browser. (Select the check box.)

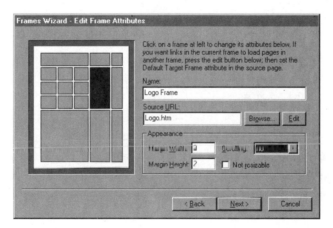

After you enter all the settings for your frames, continue on to step 6.

6. Now you'll see the Frames Wizard - Choose Alternate Content screen. Because some browsers don't support frames, it's wise to specify a page to appear in place of the one created with frames. Typically, this page contains a message to users that they are using a browser that doesn't support frames, and it can offer an alternative way to navigate the site without frames. Click the Browse button to search for the page you want to use.

Be aware that you must have a site open in the Explorer in order to select an alternate page. Once you have entered an alternate page or if you want to skip this option, click the Next button.

7. Now you'll see the final screen of the wizard, the Frames Wizard - Save Page screen. This one is a no-brainer; type in a title and a URL for the page, and then click the Finish button. Make the title intuitive and easy to remember, especially if you plan to have more than one page with frames in your site.

After you click the Finish button, FrontPage creates the page and saves it to the Web site, if one is currently open in the Explorer. To learn about editing frames and the content that appears in them, see Chapter 6.

**The Internet Database Connector Wizard** The Internet Database Connector Wizard creates an Internet Database Connector (IDC) file. The information in this file is used to communicate with any Open Database Connectivity (ODBC)–compliant database using the Internet Database Connector. The IDC file is a text file that typically contains a data source name, a Structured Query Language (SQL) statement, and the name of the HTML template file. The Internet Database Connector, or HTTPODBC-.DLL, is included with the Microsoft Personal Web Server and the Microsoft Internet Information Server. Using the Internet Database Connector Wizard along with the Internet Database Connector, you can make information in any ODBC-compliant database accessible from a Web page. One use of the Internet Database Connector Wizard is to display information from a database, even if you don't want to gather information from the Web site. For example, a store can provide a database of all its products online, and you can use a Web page to find out (from the database) the price of an item and whether it's currently in stock.

To use the Internet Database Connector Wizard, you need to have a Web site open in the Explorer. Then choose New from the File menu in the Editor, and select Database Connector Wizard from the list of templates and wizards. Then click OK. The wizard will ask you for detailed information regarding the ODBC data source, the query results template, the actual SQL query, and parameters. For more information on the Internet Database Connector Wizard, see Chapter 10.

## Custom Wizards

Anyone can create custom Web wizards and page wizards for FrontPage using Microsoft Visual Basic or Microsoft Visual C++. You can learn how by consulting the FrontPage Developer's Kit. Look in the FrontPage area of Microsoft's Web site at //www.microsoft.com/frontpage/ for information on obtaining this free kit.

FrontPage templates and wizards can free up some extra time for you to get more things done in your life. Maybe they'll free up enough time that you can put up one of your favorite signs on your office door: "Gone to the Monster Truck Races!!!"

## *Coming Up*

Speaking of freeing up time, FrontPage also helps you to administer a site once it's up and running. FrontPage makes it easier for you to implement security, manage tasks, update content, do testing, and go live with your site. Chapter 5 looks at these topics.

# Chapter 5
# Managing Your Web Site

## The Explorer Makes It Easy

You've worked hard to plan and design your Web site, and you've started putting it together. You've begun to turn all those ideas into actual pages, and now—whoa there, varmint! "How am I ever going to get all this done? Who's going to make sure it's kept up-to-date? How can I be sure it works perfectly before it goes online? And how can I be sure that my officemate, Georgio Trustnomore, who makes more than I do with half the talent, doesn't get into my site and mess it up?"

Dozens of questions like these can go through your mind at all stages of developing your site, especially if your company or organization has a large Web-site development team. But even one-person development teams have to consider numerous Web-site administration issues. Before those worries running through your head turn into a monster headache, read on and find out how FrontPage simplifies site administration.

Whenever you think of Web-site administration, think "Explorer." The FrontPage Explorer is the starting point for most of your administrative tasks—it's where you can see what work needs to be done in your site, assign those tasks as necessary, deal with **proxy servers** (also known as **firewalls**), set permissions, and much more. This chapter explains how FrontPage helps you deal with all these issues, beginning with security.

# Security

In the Old West, security came in the form of a weathered tough guy and his trusty six-shooter. Today, with information traveling over the air waves, and through phone lines at the speed of light, security is a little bit trickier. Especially when some 12-year-old hacker from Nebraska keeps finding ways to break through even the most complicated security measures. So, when it comes to protecting your Web site and restricting who sees it, you'll be glad to know that FrontPage makes available the toughest security components.

## Making Use of SSL

**Secure Sockets Layer** (SSL) is a protocol that allows for secure communication between a **server** and a **client**. SSL doesn't protect access to the communicated data, but it does encrypt the data. In order for SSL to work properly, both the server and the client must support SSL. Both FrontPage and Microsoft Internet Explorer 3.0 support SSL, as does Netscape Navigator. Front-Page also allows the creation of links that start with https:// instead of http://. Links that start with https:// indicate a secure link using SSL.

Before we go any further, you'll want to know whether the server you're communicating with supports SSL. There are a couple of ways to find this out:

◆ Check with the person administering the server. It's possible for the administrator to disable SSL support, so it's always a good idea to check first.

◆ If you're running Microsoft Internet Information Server or Netscape's Commerce, FastTrack, or Enterprise server, you're probably fine. But it can't hurt to check with the server's administrator in this case, too. (Note: The Microsoft Personal Web Server does not support SSL.)

◆ If you want to check for yourself, create a new Web site (using the Empty Web template, for example) in the

FrontPage Explorer as described in Chapter 3. Specify the server and the name of the site, and select the Connect Using SSL check box. If the Explorer opens the site and you don't encounter an error message, support for SSL is available on your server.

With an SSL-enabled Web server and with SSL enabled in FrontPage, all communications between the FrontPage client and the server, including any commands issued from the Explorer, the To Do List, or the Editor, are secure. This means the information is encrypted as it travels between FrontPage and the Web server, wherever they're located. This security comes in handy in several situations.

◆ If you're on the road and you need to make changes to a site that is on a server back home, you can open the site, make your changes, and save the changes back to the server.

◆ If your business or organization has more than one office but has only one Web server, someone at a remote office can make changes to the site.

◆ If your corporate Web site or personal Web site lies on an Internet service provider's "staging" server (a server that houses in-production Web sites), and you access that server to make changes to your site with Front-Page, the information is encrypted as it's being sent. This prevents a hacker from looking at the information before you go live with the site.

## Permissions

Permissions give you, the Web-site developer, the final say over who has access to your site. You can set permissions to control who can browse, author, or administer a site, no matter what kind of site you're developing—a site for an intranet or for the World Wide Web. If you've set permission to registered users only, someone on the Web who is not a registered user will not have access to your site, plain and simple. (You might want to limit access to a list of registered users while you are developing the site.) When your site is ready to go live, you can simply change the end-user permissions to allow access to everyone.

If you're using a World Wide Web server to author your sites in FrontPage, you'll use the Explorer to administer the setting of permissions on each Web site as well as to allow access to it for specified users. If you create your site and save it to a file location, such as a network drive, you can't use the Explorer to set permissions. You'll need to use the tools available on your file system to manage access to these sites.

Permissions can be manipulated by an administrator in the Explorer using the Permissions command on the Tools menu. By default, all Web sites on the server use the permissions that are set for the **root Web site**. You can, however, set permissions unique to a specific site. We'll discuss both options here.

**Setting and changing permissions for the root Web site** Here's how to set and change permissions for the root Web site:

Open an existing FrontPage site in the Explorer, by choosing Open FrontPage Web from the File menu. In the Open Front-Page Web dialog box, enter or select a Web server. Click the List Webs button, select <Root Web> from the list of sites, and then click OK. With the site open in the Explorer, choose the Permissions command from the Tools menu to open the Permissions dialog box, shown here.

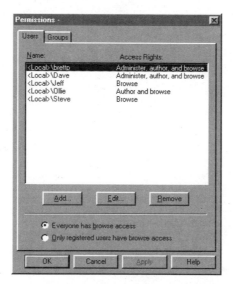

The first tab of the dialog box, Users, lists all users currently set for the root Web site, along with their current level of access.

It gives you the option to add, edit, or remove users, and provides two option buttons, Everyone Has Browse Access or Only Registered Users Have Browse Access.

◆ To add users, click the Add button and specify their access rights. You'll see the Add Users dialog box:

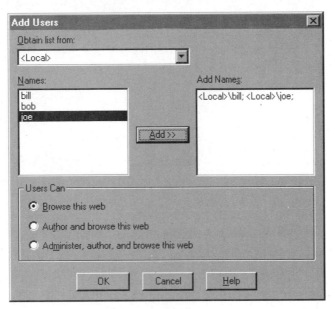

◆ To edit a user, select the user from the name list and click the Edit button to change the access rights for that user. You'll see the Edit Users dialog box, where you can change the level of permission for the user.

To remove a user, select the user from the name list and click the Remove button to remove that user from the list.

The second tab, Groups, lists all groups currently set for the root Web site, along with each group's current level of access. It also gives you the option to add, edit, or remove groups. These options work in exactly the same manner as those on the Users tab.

**Setting and changing permissions for a specific site** Here's how to set and change permissions for a specific site:

Open an existing FrontPage site in the Explorer, by choosing Open FrontPage Web from the File menu. Enter or select a Web server in the Open FrontPage Web dialog box. Click the List Webs button, select a site, and click OK. With the site open in the Explorer, choose the Permissions command from the Tools menu. You'll be greeted by the Permissions dialog box, which has three tabs, each dealing with a specific level of access. The following shows the Permissions dialog box for a site named OldWest.

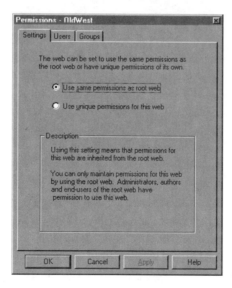

◆ The first tab, Settings, has two option buttons, one allowing you to use the same permissions in the current site that are used by the root Web site, and another allowing you to set unique permissions for the current site. Selecting either option yields a description of the option at the bottom of the dialog box. If you want to assign administrative, author, and/or end-user permissions to certain people for this site but not for the root site, select the second option. Otherwise, the first option should be selected, and you must make any changes to permissions to the root site, as described above.

**TIP**

If you make changes to settings on a tab, you must click Apply to keep those settings if you move to other tabs.

◆ The next two tabs deal with Users and Groups. Setting permissions for Users and Groups works the same way as described above for the settings for the root Web site. Be aware that when removing users and groups, Front-Page does not prompt you to confirm your action.

When you finish updating the permissions, click OK to return to the Explorer.

## Server Permissions

Web servers often have built-in permissions mechanisms that allow you to restrict access by using a password/user name scheme, an **IP address mask,** or a combination. (Note: Microsoft Internet Information Server, the Microsoft Personal Web Server, and the Windows NT Workstation Peer Web Services restrict access using standard Windows NT security, and do not support access restriction via IP address masks.)

An **IP address** contains four numbers separated by periods; each number is less than 256. An example is *150.200.45.65*. An IP address mask uses a combination of actual values and asterisks (also known as a *wildcards*) to create a model of an acceptable IP address. Masks are used to determine whether a computer has access to a location on the Internet—for example, a FrontPage site. An example of an IP address mask that would permit connections with the IP address above is *150.200.\*.\**. Computers with IP addresses beginning with *150.200* would be given access to a FrontPage site, and computers whose IP addresses did not begin with those numbers would be denied access. If an IP mask is in place, an administrator, author, or user must be working on a computer that has access to the location, and must also have the correct permissions to access the FrontPage site. By default, all computers are given permissions to access FrontPage sites.

For more information on server permissions, consult your server's documentation.

# Passwords

FrontPage requires passwords to author and administer your sites, but depending on the Web server you use, you might rarely see a dialog box asking for them. The Change Password command on the Explorer's Tools menu might even be grayed out.

If FrontPage asks you to enter a user name and a password, it will be for one of the following reasons:

◆ Some Web servers always require user name and password confirmation regardless of the user or situation.

◆ You're trying to access, author, or administer a site on a server and you don't have permission to do so.

When you install FrontPage, you're asked to supply a user name and a password for a single administrator to the sites you'll be creating. To add administrative access and to grant end-user and author access to others for your sites, you use the Explorer's Permissions command.

**Changing passwords** With several of Microsoft's Web servers, you're not allowed to change passwords in FrontPage. Microsoft Internet Information Server, the Microsoft Personal Web Server, and the Windows NT Workstation Peer Web Services use Windows NT user accounts, and FrontPage does not allow you to create, delete, or modify those accounts. Changing your password is the same as modifying your Windows NT account, and Windows NT considers that a breach of security.

So, if you're using one of these servers and you change access rights using the Permissions command in the Explorer, you'll notice that you are not allowed to change passwords for those users. Now you know why! That's also why the Change Passwords command on the Tools menu might be grayed out. When using these servers, FrontPage seeks the Windows NT user account information to verify user names and passwords. Therefore, in Windows NT, you must administer passwords at the system level. See the server-specific or network-specific documentation for information on changing passwords when using these Microsoft servers.

If you are using the Microsoft Personal Web Server with Windows 95, you administer users and passwords using the Personal Web Server administration tool, which can be accessed by double-clicking on the Personal Web Server icon in the Windows Control Panel. For more information, see Chapter 11.

With other Web servers, because the user list is completely independent of the system's user account list, you can freely add, delete, or modify passwords without fear of opening security holes. You do this through the Change Password dialog box, which you can reach by choosing the Change Password command from the Explorer's Tools menu. For more information, see Chapter 3.

## Proxy Servers

A **proxy server**, or **firewall**, protects a network from uninvited outside access. FrontPage makes communicating with proxy servers very easy, in either direction. For example, communication can be "inbound"—communicating from the outside through the proxy server and to your internal server, or it can be "outbound"—communicating from your server, through a proxy, and to another server on the outside. Communications related to the Web site are permitted only through the proxy, so uninvited guests are barred from your system.

If your local network uses a proxy server, you must specify that server in the Explorer in order for FrontPage to communicate with it. To specify a proxy server for your machine or to specify any server that can be used without going through the firewall, follow the procedure on the next page.

1. Choose the Options command from the Tools menu in the Explorer, and then click on the Proxies tab of the Options dialog box, which looks like this:

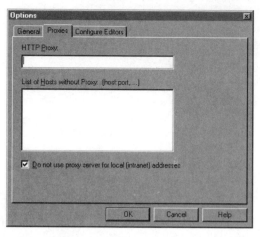

2. In the HTTP Proxy text box, enter the name of the proxy server and the port; for example, *itgproxy:1000*.

3. If your organization has servers that are inside the firewall, list them in the List Of Hosts Without Proxy text box. You can connect to these servers without using the proxy server. Port numbers are optional, and items in the list must be separated by commas. For example, *jeffserver:345,deborahserver:222*. To remove the proxy server or any servers in the list, select the information and press the Del key.

   If you want to use all available servers inside the firewall, select the check box labeled Do Not Use Proxy Server For Local (Intranet) Addresses.

4. When you finish updating the information in the Proxies dialog box, click OK.

   FrontPage saves the proxy server information and uses it for all future connections, so you don't have to enter the information again and again. Whenever you request a connection to a server (for example, when you are following a link), FrontPage checks whether Do Not Use Proxy Server For Local (Intranet) Addresses is selected and might check the List Of Hosts Without Proxy list. If the server is available internally, FrontPage makes the connection directly. If not, FrontPage first connects to the proxy server and has the proxy server connect to the server you want to use. This means that once you supply that information for the proxy server, all proxy communication is handled automatically by FrontPage, and you don't even have to be aware that a proxy server is in use.

# Managing Tasks: The To Do List

It's said that Albert Einstein chose not to memorize his phone number because he believed that memorizing such details took up too much space in his brain and too much energy. He preferred to reserve his brainpower and energy for his creative endeavors, and would simply write down any details that he could look up later.

Don't you wish you could do that with the small details about your site so you wouldn't have to remember them all? If you had to write down a long list of tasks, however, keeping track of them would be difficult. Luckily, FrontPage has a better solution, the To Do List. The Explorer creates a To Do List for every Web site that you create with FrontPage, and it shares this list with all authors across the site.

The To Do List is a list of tasks that need to be completed for a given site. It not only records all of those nagging details, but it allows you the luxury of not having to organize them. It lists each task, describes it, prioritizes it, indicates who's assigned to complete it, and more; this frees you up to take care of other details. Plus the To Do List is completely customizable, allowing you to change and rearrange the tasks to your heart's content. The following section describes the To Do List and explains what it can do for you.

## Showing the To Do List

To show the To Do List for your site, choose Show To Do List from the Tools menu in the Explorer. The number of tasks in the list is indicated in parentheses following the command on the menu. If the To Do List window is already active but is hidden underneath other windows on your screen, choosing the Show To Do List command brings it to the top. When the To Do List is open, it is also available from the task bar along with all other programs that are open. The following is the To Do List window, with a list of tasks to be completed after creating a new site with the Corporate Presence Wizard.

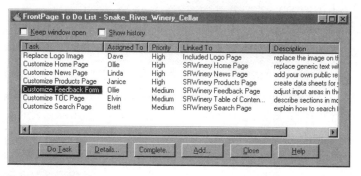

**TIP**

You can also show the To Do List by clicking its button on the toolbar in either the Explorer or the Editor.

The tasks are listed in the leftmost column, the Tasks column. You can see who is responsible for completing each task in the adjacent Assigned To column. A priority of high, medium, or low is assigned to each task and noted in the Priority column. The page or file that needs to be edited in order for the task to be completed is indicated in the Linked To column. Finally, a description of each task is provided in the rightmost column, the Description column.

Before you can begin using the To Do List, you should first understand the To Do List window. The following describes some of the features of the To Do List window.

**Keeping the window open**  Normally, when you click the Do Task button to begin working on the selected task, the To Do List window is closed. If you want to keep the To Do List window open, select the Keep Window Open check box at the top of the To Do List.

**Showing history**  Select the Show History check box if you want to see a list of all tasks, including those that have been marked as completed. When this check box is selected, a new column is added that lists the date the task was marked as completed. When this check box is not selected, the To Do List shows only tasks that still need to be completed.

**Sorting the columns** Sorting the columns can be useful for large lists, and it's easy—simply click on a column heading. Suppose you want to find out how many tasks are assigned to you. Just click on the Assigned To column heading, and then find your name in the column. All of your tasks will be grouped together. The To Do List sorts tasks in ascending alphabetic order; completed dates are sorted from most recent to oldest.

**Changing the view** It's often quite useful to maximize the To Do List window so it takes up the entire screen. Click the standard Maximize button in the upper right portion of the window—this will give you a much larger area to work in, allowing you to see many more details at once.

You can also adjust the column widths by moving your mouse pointer between the column headings until it changes to a crosshair with left and right arrows, and then clicking and dragging. This lets you expand a column to see detail descriptions that are too long to fit into a column.

## Using the To Do List

As you work on a site, you will need to update the information in the To Do List. For example, you can mark a task as completed, modify the details for a task, and add new tasks. These features of the To Do List are explained below.

**Completing a task on the spot** This is one of the most helpful features of the To Do List. If you see a task in the list that's assigned to you or someone else and you want to complete the task right then and there, you can do so. For instance, in the graphic on the previous page, suppose you want to complete the "Customize Feedback Form" task. All you need to do is select the task and click the Do Task button at the bottom of the To Do List window. The Editor opens to the page on which the task needs to be completed. Even better, the page opens to the very spot where the task needs to be completed, so you don't have to search for it. If a task is not associated with a particular page, the Do Task button is grayed out. When you save the page containing the unfinished task, FrontPage asks you whether you want to mark the task as completed in the To Do List.

**Changing the details for a task**  You can reassign a task, change the priority of a task, and change the description of a task by selecting the task and then clicking the Details button. You'll see the Task Details dialog box:

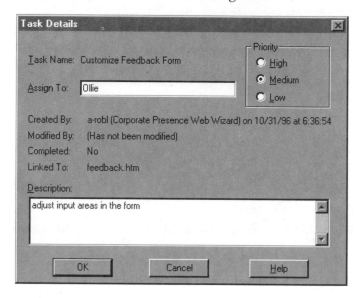

To assign the task to a different person, or to change the description of the task, simply replace the existing text. To change the priority, select the appropriate option button. You'll notice that not all details can be changed—only the three mentioned here. For tasks created by you or other users, you can also change the task name. Since these tasks were generated by the Corporate Presence Wizard, you can't change the task name. When you finish entering the new information, click OK to return to the To Do List.

**Deleting a task or marking a task as completed**  To delete a task from the list or to mark a task as completed, click the Complete button. You'll see the Complete Task dialog box, which gives you the two options. If someone worked on a task but wasn't certain whether the task was completed, he or she might not have marked the task as completed at that point. The Mark This Task As Completed option is useful at those times, for confirming that a task has indeed been completed. The Delete This Task option is useful when you no longer want a task to appear in the To Do List history.

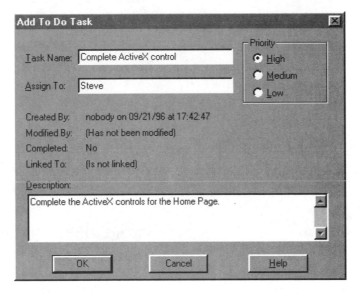

**Adding a task** If a task does not need to be linked to a particular page, click the Add button in the To Do List window to add the task. If you want to link a new task to a page in your site, start in the Explorer, select the page, and then choose Add To Do Task from the Edit menu. With either method, you'll see the Add To Do Task dialog box, which looks like this:

Enter the task name in the Task Name text box, and assign it to someone in the Assign To text box. Mark the priority as High, Medium, or Low in the upper right portion of the dialog box. Finally, add a description of the task in the text box at the bottom, and click OK. Be sure to use a short but specific description, because the column widths in the To Do List are often narrow. For information on changing column widths, see page 117.

## Managing with the To Do List

The To Do List can be a powerful management tool. It gives you the ability to assign or reassign tasks, observe what work has been completed in a site, and determine what work still needs to be done. You can perform the following team management tasks using the To Do List:

**Evening up the workload** If someone on your team has a great deal more work to perform on a site than others, you can even up the workload by reassigning some of that person's tasks to others.

**Seeing whether a task is completed** R. U. Awake, your team's resident procrastinator, often takes a long time to get things done. To check on her progress, you can look at the To Do List and sort the Task column to find a task. If the task doesn't appear in the list, R. U. gets a reprieve; if it's still there, it's time for R. U. to write on her whiteboard 50 times, "I will get my To Do List tasks done on time."

**Determining the state of your site** You can determine a site's condition in many ways using the To Do List. One way is to simply look at the number of tasks to be completed. Another way is to sort the tasks by priority—if you see many high- and medium-priority tasks remaining, you have more work to do than if most of the remaining tasks are at the low-priority level.

**Determining what pages or files need the most work** Sorting the Linked To column can give you an indication of which pages and/or files in your site need the most work. If you have many tasks associated with a few pages, you can assign more resources to those areas.

## Testing Your Site

Once your site is all nice and spiffy, and you think it'll run just fine, it's always a good idea to test it. Testing can prevent the following from happening: It's the morning that you are scheduled to present your finished, working site to the CEO for final approval. It's a small site, but you're mighty proud of it. Your officemate, Joan Clueless, who is jealous over your recent raise and subsequent purchase of a red sportscar, drops by the office around 11:30 the night before. She gets into your site and makes a teensy-weensy change to one of your links. So instead of linking to a profile of the CEO from the See Profile button as you've set it up, the button links to the "Little Johnny Visits the Morgue" Web site.

But you're craftier than Ms. Clueless, and you show up a little early the next morning to make sure your site runs fine. Here are three techniques you should use to check those links:

◆ You can check them individually in the Editor. It's a slow way to check links, but if you're ever in the Editor and want to make sure a link works, you can put your cursor on the link, press Ctrl, and click on the link. The Editor will take you to the page the link jumps to.

◆ You can wander through your site using a browser, such as Microsoft Internet Explorer, Netscape Navigator, or any other popular browser, and test each of the links. This way you'll be able to see first-hand that all the links work, including links to other sites on the Internet.

◆ You can have FrontPage verify all of your links in one step by using the Verify Links command on the Tools menu in the Explorer. This command is explained in Chapter 3. This command, however, only verifies that the targets of your links exist—it does not verify that what you linked to is what you *intended* to link to!

Finally, you can check that your image files are positioned on your pages where you want them. You should do this in the Editor and in the various browsers. When testing your images you'll want to look for things such as download time and visual quality. For more information on optimizing graphics for the Web, see Chapter 8.

The easiest way to test your site in a browser is to use the Preview In Browser command on the File menu in the Editor. This command allows you to select any installed browser to view your site, and at different window sizes. For more information on the Preview In Browser command, see Chapter 7.

You'll often get different results from testing a site locally than from testing the same site through a network or over the Internet because of variables that can affect speed and information transfer. If you can, test your site in as many ways as possible:

◆ Locally, on your own computer

◆ Over a network

◆ Remotely, over the Internet

◆ Through modems and other communication devices at different speeds

◆ On different operating systems

◆ With different browsers at different screen settings (such as different resolutions)

# Going Live with Your Site

Maybe you've got several thousand Benjamin Franklins to spare for the kind of party where you break bottles of champagne against your Web server, but most organizations do not. Nonetheless, going live with an intranet site or World Wide Web site is still a milestone event, and when it comes time, you've got to know how to do it.

There are a few ways you can make your site accessible to your audience. One common way is to develop your site on the server it will be viewed on, and let people visit your site as it matures. The Under Construction icons are very useful for this purpose; they let viewers know that a page isn't in its final form just yet. FrontPage can insert these icons if you use a wizard to create your site.

When you're not comfortable with people seeing your site under construction, and when there's simply not enough content to make a visit worthwhile, you can do one of two things: develop your site locally or limit end-user permissions.

**Developing Your Site Locally** The Microsoft Personal Web Server, the FrontPage Personal Web Server, and the Microsoft Internet Information Server suit local development to a "T." They allow you to develop and test your intranet or World Wide

Web site on your own computer or over a **LAN**. When your site is complete and you're ready to go live with it, you can copy it to its destination Web server using the Publish FrontPage Web command on the File menu in the Explorer. With this command, you can copy the site to any of the most popular Web servers. For more information on the Publish FrontPage Web command, see Chapter 3.

# Updating Your Site

The World Wide Web is a perfect reflection of information technology in general today—it changes constantly. One day you can e-mail a friend about a great site you visited, and the next day your friend won't be able to see what you saw because it's already changed. Even corporate intranets reflect this changing nature. One reason some sites change so often is because it's easy to make small changes to them. Once they're up and running, it takes little effort to replace a graphic, change a link, or even add a new page.

Another reason that sites change often is because audiences demand it. You must keep your site updated with the latest information, or else your viewers will not return. Visiting a site is like turning up a playing card that's face-down; if your audience doesn't see a different card now and then, they'll move on to a different game.

Updating large sites can be time-consuming, however, and the process can require more time as site size and the frequency of updating increase. You should have a plan for updating your site before you even begin to create your site. If you're planning a site now, or if you need to implement an update plan, read ahead for a few ideas on how to go about it.

## Updating Content

You can use a similar process for updating content that you used for gathering the content originally, but watch for ways to streamline the process. For example, when getting approval for your content, you can try routing it to people in a different order if the process was slow the first time around. Or you can eliminate a step in the process if you determine that the step wasn't necessary; for example, the material might need only one editing stage, not two. Also, check employee schedules to make certain a folder with Web-site content doesn't sit on someone's desk while he or she is lying on a beach in Tahiti.

If your company requires you to route material through a legal department, perhaps *all* of it doesn't have to be routed there, or maybe some of the material you want to put on your site has already been approved for use elsewhere in the company. If you can save some of the material from being rerouted, you'll save time and energy that you can apply elsewhere.

Never forget to *plan ahead*. If you've put forth a major effort to implement a site that's to be updated monthly, and if you plan to create a test site for your new material before you go live with it every month, leave yourself plenty of time for that test. For example, if you first went live in May, and you have an update planned for June, allow enough time to develop and test the update before June 1 rolls around. That might mean that all content for the June release must be finalized by mid-May so you have enough time to test the site and fix any errors you find.

Consider the time it will take you and/or your team to write, edit, and approve content. You'll need resources from different departments around your company, and even if you or an assistant are the ultimate go-getter who loves to make personal office visits for every bit of information you need, make sure you allow plenty of time to gather that material.

## Updating Content Remotely

Updating site content from a remote location is one of Front-Page's strongest attributes—few other Web-site authoring tools offer this feature. It's easy to do; here's all you need:

◆ You need to be able to connect to the Web server that contains the site you want to update. (Preferably, the server has the FrontPage Server Extensions installed.)

◆ You must have FrontPage installed on the computer you're using remotely.

◆ The remote computer and user must have author or administrative permission to change the site.

If you utter a resounding "YES!" to all three of those requirements, it's time to lobby your boss to allow you to work on the site, sipping an espresso from your favorite café along the Champs-Élysées. *Oui, oui!*

## Simultaneous Authoring

FrontPage makes changing the content of your site a simple task that can be performed by multiple authors at one time. If you update content while you're on the go, piece by piece, you can be changing one page in your site while someone else works on another page. The danger, of course, arises when two or more authors attempt to make changes to the same page simultaneously.

To help avoid this problem, FrontPage issues a warning if someone is overwriting a page that someone else has edited since you started working on your copy. Here is a sample warning dialog box:

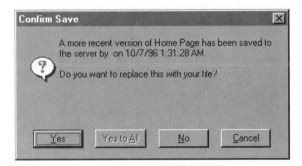

If you receive a warning like this, you'll need to decide which set of edits is retained. If you continue with your changes, the others might be lost. In the future, coordinate with the other person so that only one of you is working on a given page at one time.

Such complications can be avoided if your organization adheres strictly to the To Do List. In the To Do List, only one author is assigned a given task. If that author is not the one who should be performing that task, the task should be reassigned. Even if multiple authors are changing content in a site from separate locations, they still use the same To Do List for that site, and working on the same page simultaneously can easily be avoided if they are directed to work only on tasks assigned to them.

## Updating for Traffic

Are you or your company prepared to receive heavy traffic on your site? If your site becomes a popular one on the Web, you'll need a high-volume Web server to handle the hits. FrontPage makes it easy to move sites from one server to another, using the Publish FrontPage Web command on the File menu in the Explorer. So if a server in one location is taking a beating and you have a higher-volume server that can handle increased traffic, you can simply move your site to the new server. It's as easy as point-and-click. For more information on the Publish FrontPage Web command, see Chapter 3. For more information on Web servers and the FrontPage Server Extensions, see Chapter 11.

## *Coming Up*

This wraps up Part 2, where you've learned the basics of using the FrontPage Explorer to view, manipulate, and manage your Web site. In Part 3 you'll get familiar with the Editor and find out how to fine-tune your site so that no viewer will want to leave.

# Building Your Pages

# Chapter 6
# Creating Your Pages

## HTML Got You Down?

When our parents were young, they had to walk uphill to school both ways, in driving snow and subzero temperatures, right? So did early Web-page designers. Back in the Web's infancy, Web-page designers created their pages using simple text editors. They added the formatting to the page's content by inserting special codes around the text called Hypertext Markup Language, or **HTML**. Both the codes and the contents of the page were represented as simple text; only when they viewed the page with a Web browser could they see the results of the HTML.

Although we won't necessarily admit it to our kids, we didn't have to walk uphill to school both ways, and we also don't need to create Web pages from scratch anymore. FrontPage doesn't require you to know any HTML to produce professional-looking pages for your intranet or for the Web. If you're editing a page and want to italicize a word or change the color of a heading, you just select the text, click a button, and *voila*—FrontPage creates the HTML behind the scenes.

If you want to, however, you can edit the HTML on your Web pages in FrontPage, to add some features that FrontPage does not yet embrace. For example, you can add cascading style sheets, which are supported in Microsoft Internet Explorer 3.0 but not directly supported in FrontPage, to the HTML of any page to work with text and graphics in cool ways.

So far in this book you've seen how to create, view, and manage Web sites in the FrontPage Explorer. Now it's time to get your hands dirty and find out how to use the FrontPage Editor to craft all the elements on your site's pages to get just the look and feel you want. To illustrate the many components you can add to your pages, we'll work with the pages from an intranet site of a fictitious company called Cascade Coffee Roasters. You'll see several examples of the integration between FrontPage and Microsoft Office 97.

# The Editor in Brief: WYSIWYG

One reason the Editor is so easy to use is that it presents pages in WYSIWYG ("what you see is what you get") format. This means that whatever you see in the Editor is what you or your audience will see when viewing the pages using a Web browser. In the days when every detail on a page had to be formatted with HTML code, you would painstakingly make changes to the code and then *hope* that the changes looked right when you actually viewed the results. Now all you need to do is make sure it looks right in the Editor *once*. What you see is what you get!

Using the Editor is much like using a word-processing application such as Microsoft Word. The Editor includes many of the standard buttons and commands found in Word, such as buttons for bold, italic, and underline; numbered and bulleted lists; undo and redo; and so on. You type text in the Editor's screen just as you do in Word, and you can spell-check the files in your site as you would a file in Word. You can also insert tables and use **frames** very easily in the Editor—with just a few clicks of the mouse.

And like Word, the Editor allows you to have more than one file open at a time. The Editor deals with pages, so it's correct to say you can have more than one *page* open at a time. This is useful for toggling back and forth between pages to ensure consistency, accuracy of information, and so forth. The Editor also allows you to copy a page (including all of its HTML) from the

World Wide Web and edit it as you wish. This is useful if you own other sites and need to garner information from them quickly. Be careful, of course, about copying information from others' Web sites—there are copyright laws to heed, and plagiarism should be left to those who don't mind shelling out the bucks for a defense attorney.

## Launching the Editor

How do you get to the Editor? Let us count the ways:

◆ By double-clicking a page in Hyperlink view or Folder view in the Explorer. The Editor opens with that page in its main window.

◆ By right-clicking on a page anywhere in the Explorer, and then choosing Open from the menu that appears.

◆ By selecting a task associated with a page in the To Do List window and then clicking the Do Task button. Again, the Editor opens with that page in its main window.

◆ By launching the Editor on its own (either from Microsoft Windows, by clicking the Show FrontPage Editor button in the Explorer, or by choosing the Show FrontPage Editor command from the Explorer's Tools menu). In this case, the Editor opens with a blank screen. You can then open a page using the Open command on the File menu, and begin editing.

When the Editor launches, it appears in its own window, with toolbars and numerous menu commands at the top. An example of the Editor is shown on the next page. It might look a tad formidable at first, but don't worry—we'll describe what many of the toolbar buttons and commands do in this chapter. Before you begin to use the Editor, though, you should learn how to customize it so you can use it to your best advantage.

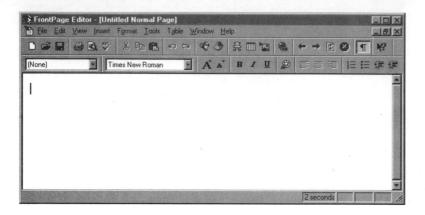

## Adjusting Settings

Surely you have a preferred way to work on your computer. (Even if you don't, we'll stop calling you Shirley.) For example, maybe you don't like working with toolbars—so what's the purpose of keeping them on the screen? Or maybe you like working in a smaller or larger window. Adjusting these elements in the Editor is easy; here are a few ways to tailor your environment.

**Changing the window size**  It's often useful to maximize the Editor to a full screen so you can get the largest view of the page you're editing. To do this, click the Maximize button, which is the middle button of the three-button set in the upper right corner of the Editor's title bar when the window is not maximized. To restore the Editor to its previous location and size, click the Restore button that appears in the same position for maximized windows. That three-button set is the same one that you see in all applications for Microsoft Windows NT 4.0 and Windows 95.

**Click the middle button of this three-button set to maximize the Editor to a full screen. If you don't see this button, the Editor is already maximized.**

You can also maximize and minimize individual pages in the Editor. To do so, click the Maximize button for the page. This button is the middle button of the set of buttons in the upper right corner of the *page's* title bar. You can *minimize* a page by clicking the leftmost button in the group of three. When you minimize a page, it's reduced to a button at the bottom of the Editor window, which makes it easy to see that you can have multiple pages open in the Editor at once.

**TIP**

If you have multiple pages open in the Editor, you can also move from page to page by clicking the Back and Forward toolbar buttons.

**Working with toolbars** The Editor includes the Standard, Format, Image, Forms, and Advanced toolbars. When they are all displayed, they take up a fairly large chunk of space in the Editor window. If you don't need some of them, you can hide them. To hide a toolbar, choose that toolbar's name from the View menu to remove the check mark beside it. To show a hidden toolbar, choose its name from the View menu (to add a check mark beside it), and the toolbar will appear in the same position it held before it was hidden.

The Editor's toolbars can be placed anywhere on your screen. If you prefer to work with the toolbars off to one side or at the bottom of your screen, you're in luck. To move a toolbar, click on a region of the toolbar outside the buttons and drag it to its new position. To have a toolbar "float," drag it from the toolbar region to a new position. To "dock" the toolbar again, drag it back to the toolbar region at the top of the Editor window.

**Showing and hiding the status bar and formatting marks** You can show or hide the status bar at the bottom of the Editor window by choosing the Status Bar command from the View menu. The Editor also uses formatting marks on the screen for some elements, such as paragraph marks, bookmark underlines, and form outlines. To show or hide these marks for the page you are currently working on, choose the Format Marks command from the View menu.

**SHORTCUT**

You can click the Show/ Hide Paragraph toolbar button, which looks like a paragraph symbol, to show or hide format marks.

Now that you've learned how to adjust some basic settings, it's time to dive into Cascade Coffee Roasters' RoasterNet site.

# Let the Construction Begin

This section describes most of the elements you can add to a page in the Editor. You can add all of the obvious page components, such as text, links, and headings, plus some that might surprise you—such as **tables, frames, marquees, background sound,** and video. These are discussed in this chapter and in Chapter 7. You can also add images, which are another major component of a Web page; the procedures are detailed in Chapter 8. You can also add forms and WebBot components in the Editor; these procedures are fully explained in Chapter 9.

When adding elements to your pages in the Editor, follow this simple guideline: Think as you would when using a word processing application such as Word. The Editor mimics many of the procedures and techniques you use in Word to add and manipulate page elements. The menus and toolbars also closely resemble those in Word. If you've used a word processing application, you'll have no trouble using the Editor, and you'll learn it very quickly.

## Moving Around in the Editor

**TIP**

The Editor implements the top 25 keyboard shortcuts of Microsoft Word, so Office users can feel right at home.

Once you have material on your page, you can use your keyboard to navigate in the standard ways. For example, you can use the PgUp and PgDn keys to move one screen up or down. Ctrl+Home takes you to the top of a page, and Ctrl+End takes you to the end of a page. You can also use the cursor keys to navigate on your pages, and you can use a scroll bar, if one is present, to move horizontally or vertically.

## Text

Adding text to a page is as simple as typing it in. Let's go through the motions of adding some text to a new Human Resources page in the RoasterNet site:

1. Create a new page in the Editor by choosing New from the File menu. In the New Page dialog box, select Normal Page, and then click OK. A blank page appears on your screen, with the cursor blinking in the upper left corner.

2. Type the words *Cascade Coffee Roasters.*

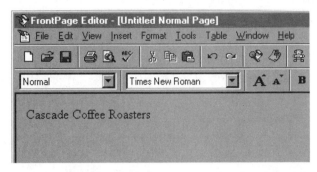

Notice that the text begins on the far left side of the current line. It doesn't have to stay there; you can indent the text, center it, or right-align it. You can also change the font and point size of the text, turn the text into a heading, and change its properties in many other ways. We'll discuss all those formatting techniques in the next chapter.

Whatever you type on the screen is what you see in the browser. And just as in Word, to start a new paragraph you simply press the Enter key.

**Cutting, copying, and pasting text** You can cut, copy, and paste text (and any other elements, for that matter) in the Editor just as you do in Office 97 applications. The Editor uses the Clipboard in the same way that Office 97 applications do; you can cut or copy material to other pages in the Editor, or to other documents in other applications. Simply cut or copy the material, move to the destination document (opening it first if necessary), and paste it in. Depending on the application you move the material to, you might lose some of the

**SHORTCUT**

The Editor uses common keyboard and toolbar shortcuts for cutting, copying, and pasting. Cut: Ctrl+X; Copy: Ctrl+C; Paste: Ctrl+V. You can also right-click to cut, copy, and paste.

formatting when you move the material. For example, if you're moving text of varying point sizes to a file in Notepad, all the text will appear in Notepad in the standard Notepad point size.

**Deleting text** Deleting text or other elements is also very simple, and you can do it in many ways. You can select the material you want to delete, and then press the Del key or choose Clear from the Edit menu.

### TIP

If you want to reinsert material you've just deleted, choose Undo from the Edit menu or click the Undo toolbar button. For more details, see "Undo/Redo" in the next chapter.

You can also delete words and characters in front of and behind the cursor. To delete a word to the right of the cursor, press Ctrl+Del, and to delete a word to the left of the cursor, press Ctrl+Backspace. Try these shortcuts to get comfortable with them; they're some of the least-used keyboard combinations in the FrontPage Editor and in Word, but they can make your editing work go much faster.

## Material from Office 97 files

A significant advance in FrontPage is its ability to seamlessly incorporate material from Office 97 files. This integration can be a big time-saver. For example, if you have material in a Word or Excel file that you want to use on a page in a FrontPage site, you don't have to recreate that material in FrontPage. This applies to entire documents as well; if you have documents in Word or Microsoft Excel that you want to turn into HTML files, you can do that in a matter of seconds in FrontPage.

**Copying and pasting from Office 97 files** Let's illustrate how easy it is to move material from Word into the FrontPage Editor. Michelle from the Human Resources department at Cascade Coffee Roasters has started to write the text for RoasterNet's home page in Word 97, but her officemate, Malina, advises that she should use FrontPage. Michelle had entered only a few lines in Word, but rather than lose those few lines, she cuts and pastes the text from Word...

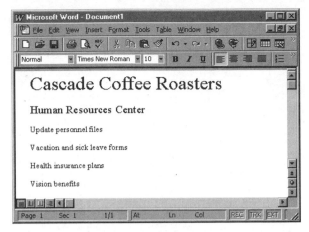

...into the FrontPage Editor:

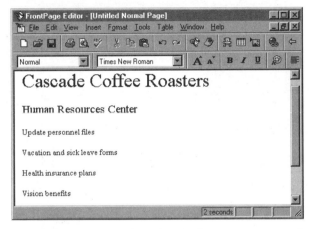

Michelle simply selects the text in Word, copies it, switches to the Editor, and pastes the text wherever she wants to on her open page. FrontPage automatically converts the material from Word into HTML for use on the page.

You can use the same simple technique with Excel files. For example, if you want to use some cells from an Excel spreadsheet on your HTML page in a FrontPage site, all you need to do is to select those cells, copy them, and paste them into a page in the Editor. The cells will appear slightly differently in FrontPage than they do in Excel; this is because HTML is not as "rich" an environment as the more advanced Office applications. Whenever you convert materials from Office files into HTML, you stand a chance of losing some or much of their original "flavor." The following graphic shows some cells copied from Excel 97 into FrontPage. These cells can also be dragged and dropped from Excel into FrontPage. For details, see the next section.

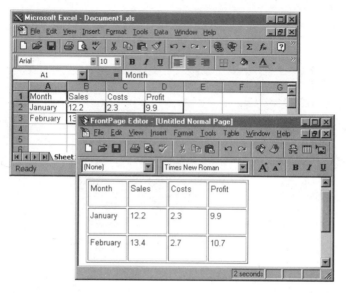

This is one reason that FrontPage allows you to link directly to Office documents from within HTML pages. When a user follows one of those links to an Office document, he or she will view the document in one of two formats. If the user has the native application for that document, such as Excel or Word, on a local computer, he or she can automatically launch that application and open the document. If the user does not have the application available, the document can be opened in an Office viewer, which is a tiny application that allows for viewing and printing Office documents. Office viewers are available for Word, Excel, and PowerPoint; see Microsoft's Web site at //www.microsoft.com for more details.

**Dragging and dropping Office files into the Editor** Now let's get on to some bigger things. In the example above, suppose Michelle has typed several *pages* of information into Word instead of just a few lines. Perhaps she was intending to type in the material and then use the Word Internet Assistant to turn it into an HTML file so she could use it in her company's intranet site. Nice thinking, Michelle—but your fellow HR Generalist, Andrea, knows that this step is unnecessary because Cascade Coffee Roasters uses FrontPage.

Andrea shows Michelle how to link to Office 97 files or insert entire files into the FrontPage Editor and automatically convert them into HTML files:

◆ If an Office 97 file has already been imported into the Explorer as a part of the site (in other words, with the intention of linking to it from within the site), you can drag that file from either view in the Explorer and drop it onto a page in the Editor. To do so, click on the icon representing the file in the Explorer (such as a Word or Excel icon), and while holding down the left mouse button, drag the file onto an open part of the page in the Editor. FrontPage creates a link to the file, using the name of the file.

◆ You can drag and drop an Office file from anywhere in Windows onto an open page in the Editor. For example, you can drop files from the Windows Explorer or even from the Windows desktop. FrontPage converts the entire file into HTML and presents it on the open page. If the file has links, they are converted to FrontPage links and still link to the same places.

> **TIP**
>
> You can also insert files onto a page in the Editor by using the File command on the Insert menu.

Remember when you're dragging and dropping that you don't need to have the Editor active on your screen when you begin. With the Editor open, you can drag the file over the Editor button on the Windows taskbar and wait for a moment (while still holding the mouse button down). The Editor will then become active on your screen, and you can then drop the file onto the open page.

> **TIP**
>
> The Editor allows you to drag and drop or insert files with any document format that Office recognizes. For example, you can drop WordPerfect documents or Lotus 1-2-3 spreadsheets into the Editor.

# Headings

One mark of an effective Web-page design is the wise use of headings. Too many large headings can make a page difficult to read, and too few headings can make a page look dull and perhaps make it difficult to understand.

To show you a simple use of headings, let's follow along as another Cascade employee, Cris, begins creating his Accounting home page. Cris wants the names of his department's personnel to appear on the page, which will later serve as links to their own pages. Here's the process he follows:

1. Create a new page in the Editor by choosing New from the File menu. In the New Page dialog box, select Normal Page, and then click OK. A blank page appears in the Editor, with the cursor blinking in the upper left corner.

2. From the Style drop-down list on the Formatting toolbar, select Heading 1. You'll notice there are six levels of headings in the list. The page heading should be a fairly prominent one, such as Heading 1. FrontPage adds space for the heading as a separate paragraph, placing it on its own line, ready for you to type the heading text.

3. Type in the main heading for the page, *Accounting*.

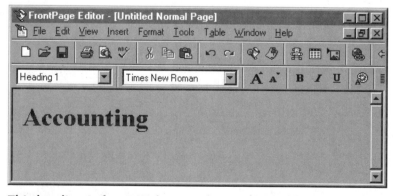

**This heading is formatted as Heading 1. Notice the Heading 1 option in the Style drop-down list.**

4. Now you want to add the names of your salespeople to the page. Press Enter to move the cursor to the next line, and then select Heading 3 from the drop-down list. A line formatted as Heading 3 appears below the title you just typed. Type *Judy*.

5. Repeat step 4 to enter the names of your other salespeople: Julie, Beth, John, and Bev. Your page should look like the figure below.

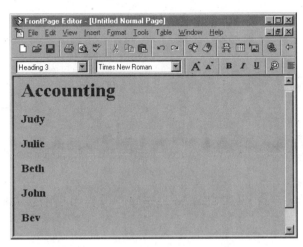

The following figure shows the relative sizes of the six heading formats:

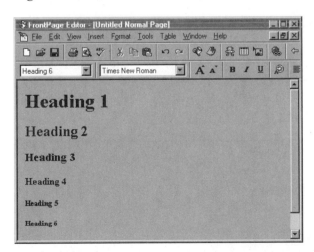

The Web browser you use will determine the exact formatting of the headings and might override FrontPage-specific formatting. No matter what, the formats are designed so that the more important headings (starting with Heading 1) stand out more than the less important ones (ending with Heading 6). Generally, the more important the heading, the larger the text, the more space above and below the heading, and so on. Some browsers even center some headings or italicize the less important ones.

## Lists

When you're designing your pages, consider using a list instead of cramming material into paragraph form; lists are much easier to read, so they tend to make your pages more user-friendly. If you use too many lists, though, your pages can become dry and tedious to read, and your audience will dash off to read *Particle Physics Illustrated* just to clear their minds.

The exact formatting of each kind of list is determined by the Web browser used to view the page. Here's a rundown of the kind of lists that are available from the Style drop-down list:

**TIP**

It is possible to modify the numbered list attributes. For example, the list can be ordered using uppercase and lowercase Roman numerals and uppercase and lowercase letters. You can also modify the starting value. For more information, see the section titled "List Properties" in Chapter 7.

◆ Numbered List—Presents items in an ordered sequence, typically using numerals and beginning with the number 1. Numbered lists are ideal for stating procedures.

◆ Bulleted List—Presents items with bullets. Bulleted lists are often used for related but nonsequential items.

◆ Directory List—Another bulleted list format. Some browsers recognize the coding for a directory list and format the list items differently than for a simple bulleted list. Generally, this format is used for very short items.

◆ Menu List—Another bulleted list format supported by most browsers.

**Creating a list** Back to RoasterNet. John, an HR Specialist, wants to create a numbered list to spell out the steps employees should take to declare their sick-leave days. (Of course, Cascade

Coffee Roasters employees, honest folks that they are, wouldn't even think of *not* declaring those days). Here are the steps that John followed:

1. On the page in the Editor, position your cursor where you want the list to begin. You can position the cursor at the beginning, middle, or end of a paragraph. If you position the cursor on a line that contains text, FrontPage will turn that text into the first item of the list. If you want to start a new list, position the cursor on a blank line.

**SHORTCUT**

You can convert existing text to a numbered or bulleted list by selecting it and then clicking the respective toolbar button. For more on formatting, see the next chapter.

2. Select Numbered List from the Style drop-down list. FrontPage formats the first line of the new list with a number; type the text for the first item in the list.

3. After you type the text for the first item, press Enter. The Editor inserts the next item in the list, and you can type that text in. Continue this process until you finish the list.

4. When you finish the list, press Ctrl+Enter. The Editor inserts a new line following the list and places the cursor at the start of that line. Here's a look at the short numbered list that John entered:

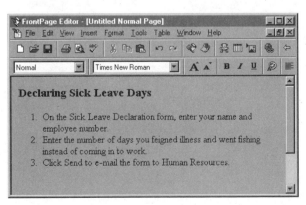

# Definitions

A **definition** is a type of formatting that is particularly useful for organizing a list of terms, called *defined terms*, and their definitions (although you can use definitions in any way you like). In many ways, a series of definitions is a special type of list. Rather than numbers or bullets, a word or a phrase is used to start each item. The remaining text for the item is formatted as the definition for that entry.

In many browsers, the word or phrase is positioned at the left margin and the definition text is indented next to it (similar to the way a bulleted list has the bullet at the left with the remaining text indented). In other browsers, the word or phrase appears on one line with the remaining text positioned below it.

Let's suppose that RoasterNet has a list of recommended drinks that the Cascade marketing team can access to use in its materials. The creator of the list can use a defined term for the name of each drink, and then insert the definition following that. You can see what a short definition list might look like in the following figure, and then you'll get to build your own by following the procedure below.

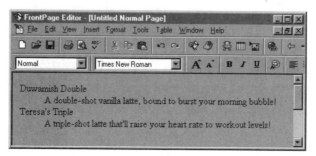

1. At the beginning of a blank line, select Defined Term from the Style drop-down list.

2. Enter the words *Duwamish Double,* and then press Enter. FrontPage expects you to enter the definition next, so it indents the new line in preparation for it.

3. Enter the following: *A double-shot vanilla latte, bound to burst your morning bubble!* Then press Enter. FrontPage formats the next line as a defined term, in expectation of your next term.

4. Enter the words *Teresa's Triple,* and then press Enter.

5. Type the following: *A triple-shot latte that'll raise your heart rate to workout levels!*

6. Press Ctrl+Enter to end the definition list.

## Tables

So many Web sites these days use tables to present information in a neat, orderly fashion. Tables allow you to compartmentalize the information on your pages. As a result, you can avoid having to format text and images manually so they appear in a structured way. Tables also allow for more consistency across Web sites, and especially across pages within a site. In addition, using tables increases the chance that information will appear the way you want it to regardless of the browser a viewer is using. Most browsers treat tables in similar enough fashion to ensure some consistency from browser to browser.

Tables in FrontPage have the same structure and are used in similar ways as tables in a Word document. Tables consist of columns and rows of cells that can contain text, images, background images, forms, WebBot components, or even another table. If you create a table and find later that you need to change the size of cells or add or delete rows or columns, don't fret—it's easy to customize an existing table in the Editor. When you create a table, you don't have to consider cell width and height if you don't want to; as you add material to the cells, the width and height automatically expand to accommodate the material.

> **TIP**
>
> If you open a Word document containing a table in the Editor, the table will be converted to an HTML table and can be modified in the Editor.

**Creating a table** The folks at Cascade Coffee Roasters have a need for many tables in their intranet site. Here's a process they can use to create a table and then customize it to fit their needs.

1. Position your cursor where you want the table to begin, and then choose Insert Table from the Table menu or click the Insert Table toolbar button. You'll see the Insert Table dialog box.

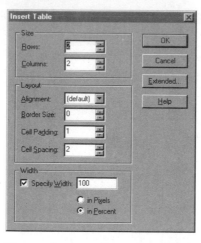

2. Enter the number of rows and columns you think you'll need in your table. You can add or delete rows and columns later.

3. Select an alignment option for the table: at the left side of the page, centered, or at the right side of the page.

**TIP**

If you create a borderless table and want to see what the table looks like without formatting marks, you can choose the Format Marks command from the View menu or click the Show/Hide Paragraph toolbar button. You'll see cell outlines in the Editor that will not appear in a browser.

¶

4. If you want a border around the table, enter the width in pixels for the border size. This setting is for the border that surrounds the entire table; each cell in the table also has a border representing the cell spacing (see step 6). If you do not want a border, enter 0. If you choose to surround your table with a border, you can specify border colors later on. The exact format of all table borders is determined by the browser being used rather than by settings within FrontPage.

5. Enter a number, in pixels, for the cell padding. Cell padding is the space between a cell's contents and each of its borders. This number pertains to all cells in the table; cell padding cannot be set for individual cells. The default is 1.

6. Enter a number, in pixels, for cell spacing. This controls the spacing between the cells in a table and is represented as a border around each cell (including those at the outer edge of the table). The default is 2.

7. Specify the width of the table. You can set the number in pixels or as a percentage of the page width. For example, if you set the table width to 50 percent, the table will span half the width of the page.

8. Click OK. The Editor creates the table and displays it on the page. FrontPage uses the number of columns and the width of the table to calculate the size of each of the individual columns.

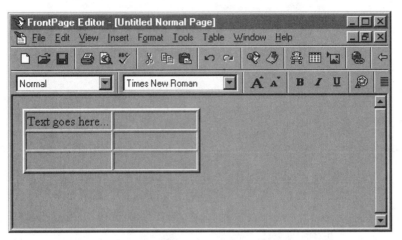

**The table above is three rows by two columns. It is left-justified on the page; has a 2-pixel border, 1-pixel cell padding, and 2-pixel cell spacing; and has a width setting of 50 percent.**

**Adding text** You can type in a table cell just as you would anywhere else on a page in the Editor. If you add more text than the cell is formatted to hold, the cell expands to accommodate it.

**Changing table properties** At any time, you can change settings for table alignment, border size, cell padding, cell spacing, and overall table width by using the Table Properties command. Simply right-click on the table and choose Table Properties from the pop-up menu. You can also access table properties by placing your cursor in the table and choosing Table Properties from the Table menu. The Table Properties dialog box opens.

**T I P**

You can quickly add a table to your page by clicking the Insert Table button on the toolbar and clicking the appropriate box on the grid that is displayed. The table properties are based on the last table property setting.

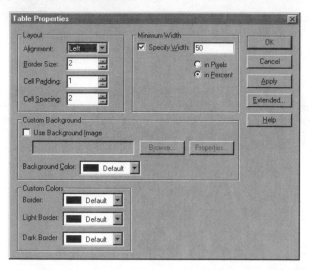

To get a "test view" of what your table might look like with different settings, you can change some settings in the Table Properties dialog box and then click the Apply button. You can change the settings and click Apply as many times as necessary.

In addition, you can insert a background image or add a background color by selecting the Use Background Image check box. When you make this selection, you'll see the Browse button become available. If you click the Browse button, the Select Background Image dialog box appears, which has three tabs for specifying the image you want to use.

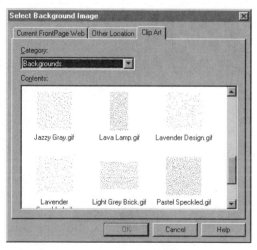

Do one of the following:

◆ If you want to use a background image that is currently in your Web site, click on the Current FrontPage Web tab, find the file in the folder presented, and click OK.

◆ If you want to use a background image from another location, such as a floppy disk, hard drive, or LAN, click on the Other Location tab, select the From File option button, click the Browse button, locate the background image in the Select Background Image dialog box, and click Open. You can also select a background image from the World Wide Web or an intranet by selecting the From Location option button on the Other Location tab, specifying the URL, and then clicking OK.

◆ You can also use FrontPage-provided clip art for your background image. To do so, click on the Clip Art tab, select the Backgrounds category from the Category drop-down list, click on a background image in the Contents window, and then click OK.

If your table has borders, you can specify their colors in the Custom Colors section of the Table Properties dialog box. To use a uniform color for all borders, select that color in the Border drop-down list. Selecting colors from the Light Border and Dark Border drop-down lists allows you to give the table a three-dimensional look. The light border color specifies the highlight color and the dark border color specifies the shadow color. Experiment with these colors to give your tables a customized look.

> **TIP**
>
> An easy way to expand the number of rows in a table is to position your cursor in the lower right cell and press the Tab key.

**Changing cell properties** You can also change some properties for cells, such as the alignment of text within them, their minimum width, the number of rows or columns they span, and their background images or colors. Here's how to view and change these properties:

1. Position your cursor in a cell whose properties you want to change. To change the properties for multiple cells at once, you need to select those cells first. To do so, position your cursor in one of the cells and then choose Select Cell from the Table menu. Then, hold down the Ctrl or Shift key to select additional cells with the cursor. Holding down the Ctrl key also lets you deselect selected cells. For information on methods for

easily selecting entire rows or columns, see "Selecting Rows and Columns" on page 154.

2. Choose Cell Properties from the Table menu or right-click over the selected cell(s) and choose Cell Properties from the pop-up menu. The Cell Properties dialog box appears.

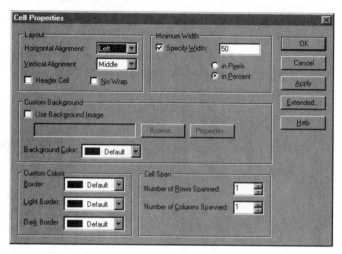

3. To change the alignment of text within the cell(s), alter the settings in the Layout section. For example, to align the text in the exact center of a cell, select Center for the Horizontal Alignment and Middle for the Vertical Alignment.

4. Enter a new number in the Specify Width text box to change the width of the cell(s). Normally it is a good idea to select the entire column the cell is in, and then change the width setting in the Cell Properties dialog box. If you increase a cell's width, the row width might also change accordingly.

5. In the Cell Span section, enter the number of rows or columns you want a cell to span. Changing this setting expands the cell to cross that number of rows or columns. This causes cells in the column to the right and/or the rows below to move accordingly to make room for the enlarged cell. One reason you might want to expand a cell in this fashion is to fill the area with an image.

   For example, suppose you have a two-row, two-column table, and you want an image to fill the area below the top two cells. You can expand the bottom left cell so it spans the two columns. The following figure shows the table before the column span, after the column span, and with an inserted image.

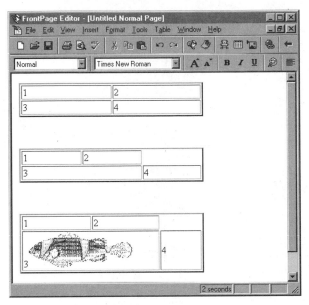

6. To insert a background image or add background color to the cell(s), select the appropriate options in the Custom Background section.

7. To add colored borders to the cell(s), select those colors in the Custom Colors section.

8. Click Apply to view your changed settings before closing the dialog box. When you have the settings the way you want, click OK to exit the Cell Properties dialog box.

**Creating header cells** Header cells are marked for special formatting; in FrontPage tables the text is made bold. Often a header cell is used at the top of a column or at the left end of a row, and will contain a title for that row or column, but a header cell can be any cell that you want to make prominent in your table. You can turn any regular cell into a header cell by doing the following:

1. Select the cell you want to turn into a header cell. To select multiple cells, select the first cell and then hold down the Ctrl or Shift key while clicking on additional cells.

2. Choose the Cell Properties command from the Edit menu or right-click over the selected cell(s) and choose Cell Properties from the pop-up menu. In the Cell Properties dialog box, select the Header Cell check box, and then click OK.

Any existing text in a cell that becomes a header cell is shown in bold, and any additional text you type in the cell will also be bold. Be aware that different browsers might treat header cell formatting in different ways.

**Selecting rows and columns**  To select a row or a column, position the mouse pointer near the top of a column or near the left border of a row until it turns into a solid arrow, and then click. You can also place your cursor in a cell, and then choose Select Cell, Select Row, Select Column, or Select Table from the Table menu.

**Moving around within a table**  You use the arrow keys to move from character to character (or element to element) within a cell, and the Tab key to move from cell to cell.

**Adding cells**  If you need to add a piece of information in your table but have nowhere to add it, you can always insert a blank cell. Inserting a cell into a table adds one more cell to the row it's inserted in, and can extend the row outside the original table boundary. In the following illustration, a cell was added to the right of the cell with *8* in it:

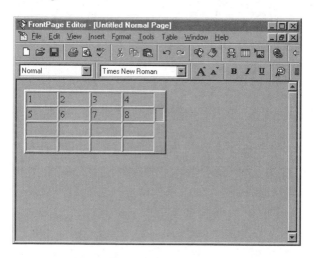

As you can see, inserting cells can make your tables asymmetrical, but that just might be your goal. To insert a cell, position your cursor in the cell directly to the left of where you want the new cell to appear, and choose Insert Cell from the Table menu.

**Adding rows**  To add a row or rows to your table, do the following:

1. Position your cursor in the row above or below where you want the new row(s) to appear.

2. Choose Insert Rows Or Columns from the Table menu. You'll see the Insert Rows Or Columns dialog box.

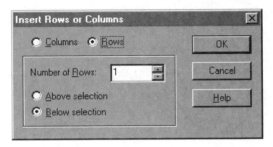

3. Select the Rows option, and enter the number of rows you want to insert. Then specify whether you want the row(s) to be inserted above or below the row you selected, and click OK.

**Adding columns**  To add a column or columns to a table, position your cursor in the column next to where you want the new column(s) to appear, and then choose Insert Rows Or Columns from the Table menu. Follow the same procedure outlined above in "Adding Rows," but select the Columns option and enter the number of columns you want to insert.

> **TIP**
>
> To add a blank paragraph after a table, position the cursor at the end of the lower right cell, and then press Ctrl+Enter.

**Deleting rows or columns**  To delete a row or a column, select the row or column you want to delete, and then press the Del key.

**Moving rows or columns**  Here's how to move a row or a column to another place in a table. In FrontPage, as well as in

Excel, when you paste a portion of a table, the pasted information replaces whatever was in the new location. Therefore, to move a row or a column without losing any other information, you must first insert a blank row or column into which you'll paste the row or column you want to move. For this example, we'll move a row, but the same procedure works for columns:

1. If there are no blank rows in the table, insert a row to serve as the destination row for the material you want to move.

2. Select the row you want to move, and then choose Cut from the Edit menu or press Ctrl+X.

3. Select the blank row you want to move the material to, and then choose Paste from the Edit menu or press Ctrl+V. The material is pasted in the new row.

This procedure also works for material you want to copy from one row or column to another. You can also cut and copy multiple rows and columns at once in the same way.

**Splitting cells**  To provide more detailed information in your table, or to clean up the formatting on a page, you might want to split a cell. When you split a cell, you divide a single cell into as many rows or columns as you need. Here's how:

1. Position your cursor in the cell you want to split.

2. Choose Split Cells from the Table menu. The Split Cells dialog box appears:

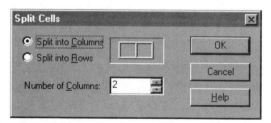

3. Specify whether you want to split the cell into columns or rows, and then enter the number of new columns or rows you want in that cell. Click OK.

Here's an example of a three-column table whose center column is split into three rows:

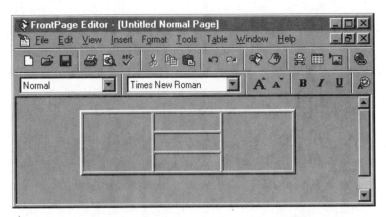

**Merging cells** There might be times when you want to combine material from several neighboring cells into one cell. This is called merging cells. Here's how to do it:

1. Select the cells you want to merge. To select multiple cells, select the first cell, and then click in the next cell while holding down the Ctrl or Shift key. When merging cells, you can select as many cells as you want, but ultimately you must have a rectangular area selected.

2. Choose Merge Cells from the Table menu. The Editor merges the cells. Any cell borders shared by the merged cells are removed, resulting in a larger cell. The content of each cell is retained and is formatted as a separate paragraph.

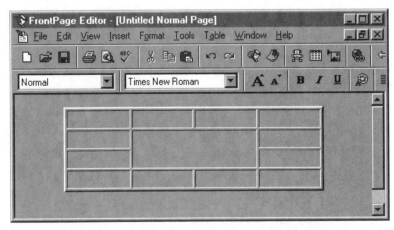

**In the table above, the centermost four cells have been merged.**

**Adding images to cells**  To add an image to a table cell, position your cursor in the cell, choose Image from the Insert menu, and then select an image from the resulting Image dialog box. You can also drag an image from the Windows Explorer or the FrontPage Explorer. For detailed information on inserting images, see Chapter 8.

**Inserting tables within tables**  The Editor allows you to insert a table within a table. You might want to use a table within a table to order your data in a special way. Or, you might want the look and feel of several bordered tables on a page. If you use tables for presenting thumbnail images for users to click on to obtain a larger version of the image, using a table within a table might help you to present the thumbnails in a more logical or graphically pleasing way than in an ordinary table.

Before you use the table-within-a-table strategy, consider if you can obtain the same results by splitting cells. Keeping your table design as simple as possible will probably save you time when you troubleshoot any problems on your pages.

To insert a table within a table, position the cursor in the cell where you want the new table to appear, and create the new table by using the Insert Table command on the Table menu or by clicking the Insert Table button on the toolbar. This process was described earlier in this chapter.

# Dividing a Page into Frames

**Frames** are rectangular regions on a Web page in which you can display other pages or images. In FrontPage, you create frames using the Frames Wizard; this process was described in Chapter 4.

## Uses for Frames

Frames can be used in a wide variety of ways, and their use is limited only by your imagination. You should use a frame whenever you want particular content on a page to remain static while other content on the page changes. A common use involves inserting a company logo in a frame at the top of a page, and dividing the rest of the page among frames for other content.

Another use of frames might involve presenting a list of your company's products in a frame on the left side of a page, and having a description of each product appear on a page in a frame on the right side. The page in the left frame is static; you want the list of products to appear all the time. The page that appears in the right frame changes according to what product the user clicks on in the left frame. You can associate each of the links on the page in the left frame with a target frame, which in this case is the right frame. Thus, when a user clicks on a link on a page in the left frame, the appropriate page appears in the target frame on the right side of the page.

In Cascade Coffee Roasters' RoasterNet site, one page might present a listing of each month of the year in the left frame, with each month linked to a sales report page for that particular month, which appears in the right frame. Or, a list of forms that employees need to submit periodically can be placed in a frame near the top of the page; the forms can appear in a larger window near the bottom of the page. The following figure shows an example of a Web page containing three frames viewed in Microsoft Internet Explorer.

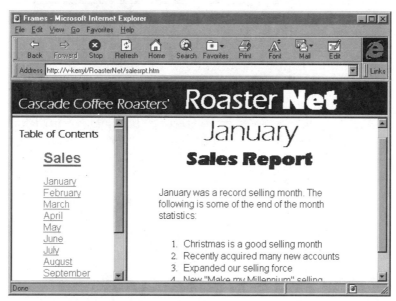

## Frame Sets

A collection of frames is known as a **frame set**. A frame set is saved as a single page by the Frames Wizard. The pages and/or image files that *fill up* the frames are regular page and image files from the same site. You create these pages in the Editor and import the images into your site.

There's a major difference between editing frame-set pages and editing standard pages in the Editor—you edit frame sets using the same wizard you used to create them. Keep this important fact in mind: You can never edit a frame or a frame set directly in the Editor. You edit frames and frame sets using the Frames Wizard. The *content that appears in the frames,* however, is edited either in the Editor (for HTML pages) or in an image editor such as Image Composer (for images).

## Creating a Frame Set

You create a frame set in the Editor using the Frames Wizard. Chapter 4 describes how to use the Frames Wizard to create pages containing frames.

## Editing a Frame Set

You use the Frames Wizard when you want to change anything about a frame set, including adding, removing, resizing, and renaming frames; changing frame attributes such as margins; and specifying different content to appear in a frame. You can reach the Frames Wizard in one of two ways. Suppose a designer updating RoasterNet wants to open Frameset1.htm, which contains the frame set she wants to edit. Here's what she can do:

◆ In the Editor, choose Open from the File menu. On the Current FrontPage Web tab of the Open File dialog box, select Frameset1.htm, and click OK. To reach the Frames Wizard this way, you must have the Web site that contains Frameset1.htm currently open in the Explorer.

◆ Or, in the Explorer, double-click the page labeled Frameset1.htm in either Hyperlink view or Folder view. Also, in either view, you can right-click on Frameset1.htm and choose Open from the pop-up menu.

The Frames Wizard appears, ready for you to edit the frame set. Here's a rundown of the edits you can make to the frame set:

◆ Changing the layout of a frame set—To change the layout of a frame set, such as splitting or merging frames or changing the number of rows and columns your frames are divided into, use the Frames Wizard - Edit Frameset Grid screen, which is the first screen of the Frames Wizard.

◆ Renaming frames and changing other frame attributes—To rename a frame, change a frame's content, change a frame's margin width or height, make a frame scrolling or nonscrolling, or change whether a frame is resizable, use the Frames Wizard - Edit Frame Attributes screen, which is the second screen of the wizard.

**T I P**

If you make changes to the frame set that you do not want to save, click Cancel anywhere in the wizard.

◆ Changing alternate content—To change the page that appears if the browser being used does not support frames, use the Frames Wizard - Choose Alternate Content screen, which is the third screen of the wizard.

◆ Renaming the frame set title or changing its URL— To rename a frame set and/or change its **URL**, use the Frames Wizard - Save Page screen, which is the fourth and final screen of the wizard.

When you have entered all the information you want to change, click Finish in the final screen. FrontPage displays a dialog box indicating that this page already exists and asks if you want to overwrite it.

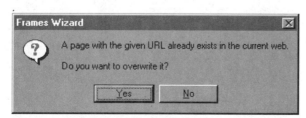

Click Yes and your change to the frame set will be saved. The content of your frames will not be modified—only the frame set itself. For more information on using the Frames Wizard, see Chapter 4.

# Displaying a Page in a Frame

To designate a page to appear in a frame, you can create a link
to the page and associate the link with the frame. This all happens in the Create Hyperlink or Edit Hyperlink dialog box. For
example, suppose RoasterNet has a Table of Contents page with
a word, *Sales,* that's linked to a page containing sales information. You want both pages to appear in different frames of a
frame set (on the same page). Here's how to set this up:

1. Open up your frame set in the Frames Wizard. Specify
   the URL in the Source URL text box in the Frames Wizard - Edit Frame Attributes screen to display the Table
   of Contents page in its frame.

2. Click the Edit button to open the Table of Contents
   page in the Editor.

3. On the Table of Contents page in the Editor, right-click
   on the *Sales* link and choose Hyperlink Properties from
   the pop-up menu to open the Edit Hyperlink dialog
   box.

4. On the Current FrontPage Web tab, verify the URL for
   the Sales page in the Page text box.

5. In the Target Frame text box, enter the name of the
   frame you want the Sales page to appear in.

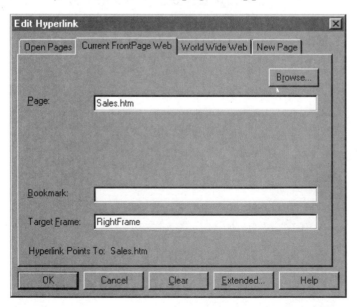

6. Click OK to close the Edit Hyperlink dialog box.

When the frame set that references the Table of Contents page is displayed in a browser, the user can click on the *Sales* link and the Sales page will appear in the frame named RightFrame.

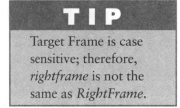

> **TIP**
>
> Target Frame is case sensitive; therefore, *rightframe* is not the same as *RightFrame*.

## Displaying Form Submission Results in a Frame

In the same way that you can direct a standard page to appear in a frame, you can direct the results of a form submission to appear in a frame. This is typically used with the Custom ISAPI, NSAPI, or CGI script, or with Internet Database Connector form handlers. Here's how to set this up:

1. In the Editor, right-click on any form field and choose Form Properties from the pop-up menu to open the Form Properties dialog box.

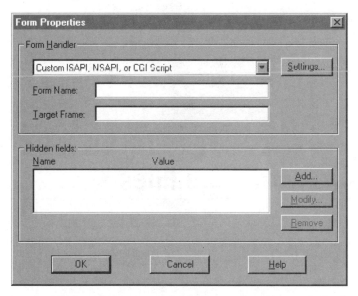

2. In the Target Frame text box, enter the name of the frame in which you want the output of the form to appear.

3. Click OK to close the Form Properties dialog box.

## Default Target Frames

If you have a page with many links and you don't want to assign a target frame to every one of them, you can associate them all with a default target frame. Default target frames specify a frame for any links on a page, including clickable images, that are not associated with a specific target frame. To assign a default target frame, do the following:

1. With the page open in the Editor, right-click anywhere on the page and choose Page Properties from the pop-up menu.

2. In the Page Properties dialog box, click on the General tab, enter the frame name in the Default Target Frame text box, and then click OK.

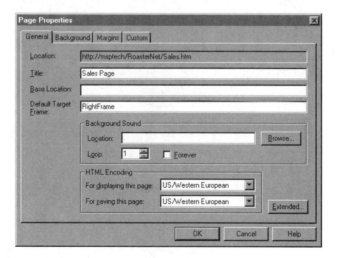

# Working with Page Files

Standard file management commands in the Editor are similar to their counterparts in the Explorer, except they work at the page level, not at the Web-site level. For example, the Close command in the Editor closes a page, while the Close command in the Explorer closes a site. Also, you can perform a few additional tasks with files in the Editor, such as printing. In this section you'll learn how to use the Editor's file management commands.

## Creating New Pages

Creating new pages in the Editor is easy, and FrontPage allows you to create numerous kinds of pages with its templates and wizards. Most often, you'll create new pages to add them to a Web site that is currently open, but you're not limited to that scenario. You can also create a new page, save it separately, and add it to any other Web site later on. (See "Saving Pages" later in this chapter for more information.)

### SHORTCUT

You can quickly create a new Normal page template by clicking the New button on the toolbar.

1. To create a new page, choose New from the File menu or press Ctrl+N on the keyboard. You'll see the New Page dialog box:

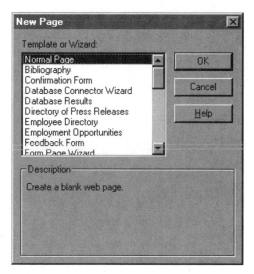

2. Select a page template or wizard from the list, and click OK. If you want to edit a blank page, select the Normal page template. You can find full descriptions of the templates and wizards in Chapter 4.

## Opening Pages

The Open command allows you to open pages in the Editor from the Web site currently open in the Explorer, existing pages that are stored as files in your system, and even pages from the World Wide Web. Not only can you open pages created with FrontPage, but you can open additional file types as well. This gives you many options for adding new material to your site. The file types you can open in the Editor include the following:

◆ HTML files (HTM, HTML)

◆ Preprocessed HTML (HTX, ASP)

◆ Rich Text Format files (RTF)

◆ Text files (TXT)

◆ Hypertext templates (HTT)

◆ Word Documents

  ■ Word 97 (DOC)

  ■ Word 6.0 and Word 95 for the Macintosh and Windows (DOC)

  ■ Asian versions of Word 6 and Word 95 (DOC)

  ■ Word 4.0–5.1 for the Macintosh (MCW)

  ■ Word 2.*x* for Windows (DOC)

  ■ Works 3.0 and 4.0 for Windows (WPS)

◆ WordPerfect 5.*x* and 6.*x* (DOC and WPD)

◆ Excel Worksheet (XLS, XLW)

If you have Microsoft Office 97 installed, and if during the Office setup you selected a configuration that installs additional document converters, those converters will also be accessible to FrontPage.

**Opening a page from the current site** If you need to edit a page that's part of the current Web site in the Explorer, there are two easy ways to do it: You can go to the Explorer, find the page, and open it from there (perhaps by double-clicking on it). Or (an even easier way), you can open it in the Editor by choosing the Open command from the File menu.

When you choose the Open command, you'll see the Open File dialog box:

Click on the Current FrontPage Web tab, which lists the files in the current Web site open in the Explorer. Select a file from the list, and click OK. The page opens in a new window in the Editor for you to edit to your heart's content.

**Opening a page from your file system** Say you're editing your Web site, and you need to add a page that is saved as a file but not saved as part of any site. For example, suppose someone in your organization is creating custom pages for several different Web sites and is saving them separately for others to add to their respective sites as needed. If you want to add a page like this to your site, here's how to do it:

1. Choose the Open command from the File menu. In the Open File dialog box, click on the Other Location tab.

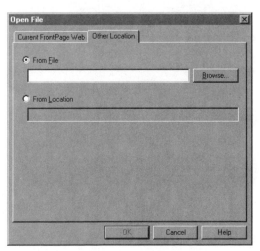

2. Select the From File option button, enter the path and filename of the file you want to open in the text box, and click OK. You can also click Browse to find the file in your folder structure. When you click Browse, a smaller Open File dialog box is displayed. In this Open File dialog box, select the type of file you're looking to open from the Files Of Type drop-down list. Then browse your file system for the file, select it, and click Open.

The Editor will try to open actual HTML files as they are, without conversions, and display all of their elements. However, if the file contains HTML that FrontPage does not recognize, the Editor will preserve it.

If you are opening a text file, you'll see the Convert Text dialog box, which gives you several nifty options:

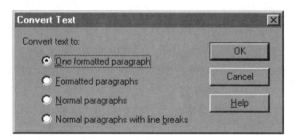

◆ One Formatted Paragraph—Converts all of the text in the file to one paragraph with the Formatted style applied.

◆ Formatted Paragraphs—Converts each paragraph to the Formatted style.

◆ Normal Paragraphs—Converts each paragraph to the Normal style, which is the default paragraph style in the Editor. This option loses multiple line breaks.

◆ Normal Paragraphs with Line Breaks—Converts each paragraph to Normal style and preserves line breaks.

When opening RTF files, the Editor uses the Office RTF-to-HTML converter, which preserves most list, table, image, footnote, and font-style formatting.

**Opening a page from any site**  You can open any page from any Web site you have access to—including those on intranets and the Web. All you have to know is the page's address. Here are the details:

To begin, choose Open from the File menu. On the Other Location tab of the Open File dialog box, select the From Location option button. Then type the address of the page you want to open in the text box, and then click OK.

The address must be in the form of an **absolute URL.** An absolute URL is the full address of a page, including the protocol, host name, folder name, and filename. With absolute URLs, you can open pages from any system that can create a connection to that site. For example, say Cascade Coffee Roasters is testing a Web site called RoasterTest1 on a local server named BeanThere, which includes a press release page (with the page URL PR3.htm) that you'd like to edit. If you have access and editing privileges to the Web site, you could open that page in the Editor by typing in *http://BeanThere/RoasterTest1/PR3.htm*—the absolute URL. It's that easy, even for bringing up World Wide Web pages in the Editor.

FrontPage might display a warning that the address you supplied is not a valid **IP address.** If you see this warning, check the address and try it again. Make sure you typed the correct characters; you'll need at least the server name at the beginning of the address. Be sure to use forward slashes instead of backslashes in the address.

> **TIP**
>
> If you still have problems opening pages from other sites, a corporate firewall might be blocking your way. In these cases, you can specify a proxy server in the Explorer. For more information on proxies, consult Chapter 5.

If you're attempting to open a page from the Web and you get an error message, you might not be connected to the Web. Make sure your connection is live by viewing the page with your browser, and then try again.

# Closing Pages

To close a page in the Editor, choose Close from the File menu. FrontPage will save and close the page in one of the following scenarios:

◆ If you opened the page from a Web site that is currently open, the Editor prompts you to save any changes to the page and then closes it.

◆ If you opened the page from a site that you've since closed in the Explorer, FrontPage will prompt you to open a site and then save the page again. To save the page to the site you opened it from, you must reopen the site in the Explorer.

◆ If you don't have any Web sites open in the Explorer, you'll be prompted to save any changes. In the Save As dialog box, the OK button will be grayed out, but you can save the page as a file or as a template. If you want to save the page to a site, you must cancel the save, open a site in the Explorer, and then close the page again.

◆ If you opened the page from a file that's not part of a site, the Editor will close that file after prompting you to save any changes.

# Saving Pages

Save your work in the same way that people in Seattle drink their coffee: early and often. Murphy's Law *will* strike you when it hurts the most; there will be times when the power goes down, or when your officemate, Tracy Tripsalot, rips the power cords from the wall sockets with her size-10 blue suede shoes. The Editor gives you three kinds of saving options:

◆ Save—Saves the active page in HTML format, to a Web site or to a file.

◆ Save As—Copies and saves the active page to a new page in the current Web site or to a file.

◆ Save All—Saves all pages that are open in the Editor.

**Saving for the first time** No matter which command you use, if you haven't saved the page before, you'll see the Save As dialog box, which gives you several options for how to save your file. You can also use the Save As command to save a page to a different location or with a different name.

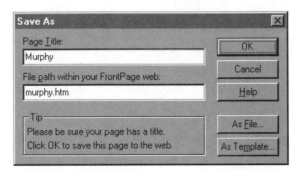

Here's how to use the Save As dialog box:

◆ Enter a page title and a page URL if you want to save the file as part of the site that's currently open in the Explorer. Give your page a unique and intelligent name so you can recognize it easily among other page names. After you enter that information, click OK.

◆ If you want to save the page as a file, such as to a floppy disk or hard disk, you don't need to fill in the title or URL. Click the As File button. This takes you to the Save As File dialog box, where you can type the filename and specify the location where you want the file saved. You can specify an extension as part of the filename, but if FrontPage does not recognize the extension, it will append an HTM extension to the filename when it saves the file.

**SHORTCUT**

You can quickly save a page by pressing Ctrl+S or by clicking the Save button on the toolbar.

◆ You can also save the page as a template from the Save As dialog box. For details on this, see Chapter 4.

## Saving Images

Images on a page are not saved within the same file that contains the HTML. Images are saved as separate files in their image formats (either **GIF** or **JPEG**). The HTML for the page just makes a reference to the locations of the images.

**Saving images to a Web site** When you're saving a page to a Web site, and the page you're saving includes images you've inserted, you'll see the Save Image To FrontPage Web dialog box for each image that was not inserted from the current Web site.

In the Save As URL text box, the name of the file you inserted will show up as a default name; you can type a different name if you wish. The buttons available at the bottom of the dialog box depend on whether the current Web site already includes an image with the same filename. Here are your options:

◆ The site does not have an image with the same filename— If this is the case and you want to save the image, you can click the Yes button to save it. If you'd like to save the page *without* saving the image to the current site, click the No button.

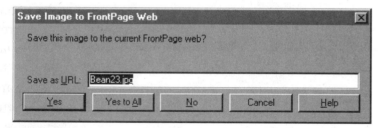

**WARNING**

When you replace an image in your Web site with another image, you overwrite *all instances* of that original image in your site.

◆ The site does have an image with the same filename—In this case, you have two options: You can click the Replace button to overwrite the image in the site with the current image, or you can click the Use Existing button to keep the existing image in the site and *not* save the current image in place of it. If you're unsure whether you want to overwrite an image in your site, you can give the image a different name to be safe.

Clicking the Yes To All button saves all images on the page to the current Web site, with their current filenames. If one of the remaining files has a filename that's currently in your site, you'll be asked to confirm to replace the image with the new image.

```
Save Image to FrontPage Web                              [X]

Save this image to the current FrontPage web?
(Saving will replace the existing image with the same name, and may affect other pages
in the current web that include the same image.)

Save as URL:  Bean23.jpg

 [ Replace ]  [ Yes to All ]  [ Use Existing ]  [ Cancel ]  [ Help ]
```

**Saving images to a file** If you're saving a page as a file, you'll be prompted to save any new images that you've inserted on the page from the current site since you last saved it. These images are saved as separate files in the location of your choice. For each image that you've inserted from the current site, you'll see the Save Image To File dialog box.

The options for saving the image are similar to those in the Save Image To FrontPage Web dialog box. The buttons available at the bottom of the dialog box depend on whether the selected location to save the image already includes an image with the same filename. Click the Replace button to overwrite the image with the current image. Click the Yes To All button to perform this task for all new images inserted from the current site since the last save. Or, click the Use Existing button to *not* overwrite the image with the current image. If you'd like to save the image with another filename or save it in a different location, click the Browse button. From there, specify a different filename and/or location for the current image, and then click Save.

## Printing Pages

Sometimes it's good to see a hard copy of a page you're working on, even if it's just to get a different "feel" for the page. Often you'll see things differently on hard copy versus on-screen. Many of us are used to working in the traditional "paper" office as opposed to the "paperless" office. It's hard to break old habits, isn't it?

> **TIP**
>
> Sometimes end-users will print your pages to save them for later reading. Thus, you might want to print your pages from various browsers, too, to see what they'll look like to your end-users.

If you're armed with a color printer, you've got an incredibly useful tool for seeing your Web site on paper, especially when it comes to determining effective color combinations on a page.

The Editor prints your pages as they appear on-screen, provided that your paper size is large enough to accommodate the page. The following sections describe how you can use the Page Setup, Print Preview, and Print commands to produce a paper version of the page you are working with.

**Page Setup** Choose Page Setup from the File menu to set up the header, footer, and margins of your printed page. These settings can be used to make your printed page easier to read and keep track of. You'll enter settings in the Print Page Setup dialog box, which looks like this:

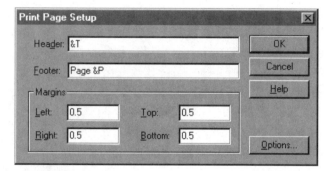

If you accept the default settings of the header and footer (shown as *&T* and *Page &P*), the Editor will print the page title as a centered header at the top of each printed page, and the current page number (with the word *Page*) as the footer. This emphasizes the difference between a Web page and the printed page. A single Web page might extend across several printed pages. Of course, your pages do not need to be numbered, but FrontPage numbers its printed pages in case you need to keep track of them.

Clicking the Options button in the Print Page Setup dialog box takes you to the Print Setup dialog box for your printer. The Print Setup dialog box is different from the Print Page Setup dialog box—it is controlled by Windows and allows you to change settings for your printer such as page orientation, paper size, and so on. When you're satisfied with your printer settings, click OK to return to the Print Page Setup dialog box. When you are finished in the Print Page Setup dialog box, click OK.

**Print Preview** You can choose the Print Preview command from the File menu at any time to see what your page will look like when printed. This is not necessarily what the page will look like in a Web browser, however, so be careful not to rely on Print Preview for that purpose. After previewing the page, you might want to return to the Print Page Setup dialog box to adjust the margins or the header and footer.

When the Editor shows your page in Print Preview, it presents a series of view-adjustment buttons at the top of the screen. You can zoom in or zoom out, and you can view the next page, the previous page, or a two-page, side-by-side view. You can also print directly from Print Preview by clicking the Print button. To exit Print Preview without printing, press the Esc key or click the Close button.

**SHORTCUT**

You can click the Preview In Browser button on the toolbar to preview your page in a Web browser. For details, see "Preview in Browser" in Chapter 7.

**Print** Choose Print from the File menu to print your page. The standard Print dialog box will appear on your screen; if you need to change printer settings, click the Properties button. You can change printer settings in the Properties dialog box that appears.

**SHORTCUT**

Press Ctrl+P or click the Print toolbar button to reach the Print dialog box quickly.

When you're satisfied with your printer settings, click OK in the Print dialog box to print your page. If your Web page runs longer than the length of paper you're using, the Editor will print it on multiple pages.

## Coming Up

With that, the grand discussion of creating your pages in the Editor comes to an end. In the next chapter, you'll learn how to format your pages in the Editor, and you'll also learn some of the Editor's utilities and useful commands.

# Chapter 7
# Fine-Tuning Your Pages

## I Wonder What *This* Would Look Like...

Once you've got the material you want on your pages, more than likely you'll want to fine-tune it. Your paragraphs don't have to stay left-aligned, your text doesn't all have to remain the same size and color, and the links and background of your pages don't have to stay the same, either. You can change all of this, and more, very easily in the FrontPage Editor.

You've probably noticed many Web pages that use plain, black text in a single size, which makes for plain, boring paragraphs. Even though the trend is moving in the other direction, there's still a long way to go before the majority of Web pages are pleasing to the eye. With FrontPage, you can format your pages so they really stand out. It's like a Ferrari next to a beat-up, rusted 1973 Pinto—your pages will catch more eyes and generate a positive reception if they're lively and clean.

With the integration of FrontPage with Microsoft Office 97, you have much more flexibility to format your pages than you had in earlier versions of FrontPage. Much of the formatting functionality is housed in the Format toolbar, which can be turned on and off by choosing Format Toolbar from the View menu.

# Fonts

The Editor gives you many options for formatting characters in different sizes, colors, and styles. You can change most of this formatting with the buttons on the Format toolbar, but all of the options are included in various menu commands. The following sections provide a primer on your character formatting options.

## Text Size

FrontPage follows the HTML standard and uses size levels rather than actual point size values for setting the size of regular text. The levels correspond to point size, and the smaller the number, the smaller the point size. For example, level 1 corresponds to 8-point text, level 2 corresponds to 10-point text, and so on. Even though this might seem confusing at first, you will quickly become accustomed to it.

**Changing text size** Here's the easiest way to change the size of your text. Select the text you want to change—it can be a single word, a line, a paragraph, or an entire page. (To select an entire page, press Ctrl+A.) Then, click the Increase Text Size or Decrease Text Size toolbar button. You can also use the Font command on the Format menu to change text size.

## Text Color

An occasional change of color in your text can attract attention, but we stress "occasional." Too many different colors of text can make a page look busy and cluttered. One good way to use a second text color is to make the first words of important paragraphs a different color. This can help to "index" the page; readers pay attention to anomalies, and a different text color is just that if it's used sparingly.

**Changing text color** You can make your text any of 48 standard colors supplied by FrontPage, or any other custom color. To change the color of your text, select the text you want to change, and then click the Text Color toolbar button.

In the Color dialog box that appears, click the color you want, and then click OK. If you want to use a custom color, click the Define Custom Colors button, define your color, and then click Add To Custom Colors to save it if you plan to use it again. When defining your custom color, remember that you can use the "elevator" arrow on the right side to adjust the color. This is a little-used tool in the Color dialog box.

## Font Type

With a wide range of fonts and several styling options to choose from, you can easily craft the look and feel that you want for your pages. As with most other design considerations for your Web pages, however, try to strive for consistency. Don't use too many different fonts or font styles on a page; if you get carried away, your viewers will run screaming from your pages quicker than a runaway semi down Teton Pass.

**Changing fonts** You've got oodles and oodles of fonts to choose from in FrontPage. If you've used the Font drop-down list in Microsoft Word, you'll have no problem getting used to that functionality in FrontPage. Here's the Change Font drop-down list:

> **TIP**
>
> Try to design your pages using standard fonts. If a user doesn't have the same fonts installed that you used to create your pages or if the user's browser doesn't support a font type being specified, typically a default font is substituted. If you need to use a rarely used font, for example for a logo, you can convert the font to a graphic.

Times New Roman ▼

To change fonts, select the text you want to change, and then select the font you want from the drop-down list.

## Font Style

A change in font style can add just the right emphasis to words, phrases, or even entire paragraphs on your pages. Be objective in your use of this technique and consider how all of your audience members will see your pages. For example, consider the visitors to your site with less-than-perfect vision. Those people will have trouble reading an entire paragraph of italic text; that's why the overuse of italics on computer screens is a big "no-no."

**Changing font style** You can easily change font style—to bold, italic, or underline—with a click of a toolbar button. FrontPage includes these buttons on the Format toolbar.

To change font style, select the text you want to change, and then click one of these buttons.

**Special styles** The Editor includes some additional styles called special styles. FrontPage supports these because the pages you open might contain special styles. Try to use regular styles, not special styles, when you create new text. The special styles might not display in a browser as they do in the Editor, because some browsers do not support many of them. If you want to apply a special style to selected text, choose Font from the Format menu. You'll see the Font dialog box. Click on the Special Styles tab, as shown here:

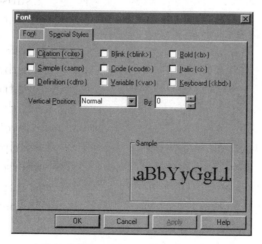

The following special styles are available. Selecting a check box displays an example of the style in the Sample section. To apply a special style, select the style and then click OK.

◆ Citation—An italic style that can be used for the name of a manual, section, or book.

◆ Sample—A typewriter-font style.

- Definition—A style that can be used for defining terms.

- Blink—A style that makes text blink in a browser. Many Web browsers do not support blinking text, however.

- Code—A typewriter-font style that can be used to represent code.

- Variable—An italic style that can be used to mark variable names.

- Bold—A simple bold style.

- Italic—A simple italic style.

- Keyboard—A typewriter-font style that can be used for text intended to be typed by the user.

You can also select multiple styles. For example, selecting both Italic and Keyboard will result in an italicized Keyboard style.

## Superscript and Subscript

FrontPage supports authoring of superscript and subscript styles. These styles are supported by some browsers, but not by all.

You set superscript or subscript styles on the Special Styles tab of the Font dialog box, shown above. To reach the Font dialog box (shown on the previous page), choose Font from the Format menu. Select Superscript or Subscript from the Vertical Position drop-down list, and then set its numeric level. The numbers correspond to varying heights that the superscript or subscript can appear at, and not to the size of the superscript or subscript. Selecting a superscript level of 1, for example, sets the superscript slightly above the sentence. A level 2 superscript sets up shop a little higher than a level 1, and so on.

## Symbols

Symbols are also called special characters; they contain characters beyond those found in the standard seven-bit **ASCII** character set. Say what? All you need to know is that the ASCII character set is the most widely used character-coding system in the world, but it does not include all of the characters from

European languages that use accent marks, many other foreign characters, and symbols such as a copyright mark or trademark. But you can use many of these special characters in FrontPage, and here's how:

1. Position your cursor where you want the symbol to appear on your page.

2. Choose Symbol from the Insert menu. This displays the Symbol dialog box:

3. Select a symbol, and then click Insert. FrontPage inserts the symbol on the page, but does not close the dialog box. You can insert more symbols directly following the symbol you just inserted by repeating this step.

4. Click Close when you're finished.

# Paragraph-Level Formatting

The other major type of formatting in FrontPage comes at the paragraph level. You can format lines and entire paragraphs, and you can implement such features as justification, different list styles, line breaks, and more. The following sections provide a hodgepodge of paragraph-level formatting options, many of which you'll probably want to get familiar with to give your pages a flash-and-dazzle touch.

## Creating a New Paragraph

Let's start at the simplest level. To create a new paragraph, press the Enter key. A blank line will appear, and the new paragraph will default to the Normal style.

To insert a new paragraph with a different style, do the following:

1. Position your cursor where you want the next paragraph to begin. If your cursor position is at the end of a line, press Enter once. If your cursor is in the middle of a paragraph, press Enter twice and the up-arrow key once.

2. Select a new style from the Change Style drop-down list. You can immediately begin typing in the new style.

If you insert a new paragraph in the middle of a paragraph, the Editor splits the original paragraph into two parts and adds the new paragraph between the two, keeping the original style for both parts. For example, inserting a Formatted paragraph in a Normal paragraph results in a paragraph containing the first portion of the Normal paragraph, followed by the new Formatted paragraph, and then the remaining portion of the original Normal paragraph.

## Changing Paragraph Styles

Suppose you want to change the style of a paragraph from Normal to Heading 3. There are several ways you can do this. First select the paragraph whose style you want to change (or simply place your cursor anywhere within the paragraph), and then do one of the following:

◆ From the Change Style drop-down list, select a new paragraph style.

◆ Choose Paragraph from the Format menu. Select the new style for your paragraph in the Paragraph Properties dialog box, and then click OK.

◆ Right-click on any text in the paragraph and choose Paragraph Properties from the pop-up menu. Change the style in the Paragraph Properties dialog box, and then click OK.

## Indenting a Paragraph

When you indent a paragraph in the Editor, the entire paragraph receives the indent. To indent a paragraph, position your cursor anywhere in the paragraph and click the Increase Indent toolbar button. To remove an indent, click the Decrease Indent toolbar button. (The Decrease Indent and Increase Indent buttons are shown at left.) You can indent as many times as your text will allow.

The following example shows the middle paragraph indented once.

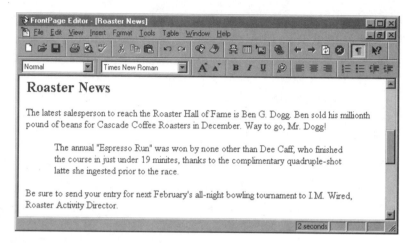

## Aligning a Paragraph

You can make a paragraph left-aligned, centered, or right-aligned with the click of a toolbar button. Just position your cursor anywhere in the paragraph, and then click the Align Left, Center, or Align Right toolbar button.

You can use these buttons to align paragraphs on a page or to align text in a table cell. Left-aligning a paragraph leaves a ragged right margin, right-aligning a paragraph leaves a ragged left margin, and centering a paragraph leaves both sides ragged and centers the paragraph within its margins.

**TIP**

If you're changing the style of a paragraph in the Paragraph Properties dialog box, you can also change the paragraph's alignment there at the same time.

# List Properties

FrontPage gives you a vast array of list style options, including several variations of bulleted lists and numbered lists. In Chapter 6 you learned how to create a list item-by-item; here you'll learn how to change the style of your lists once they're on the page.

**Turning regular text into a list** Suppose you have a number of lines on your page that you would like to turn into a list. You don't have to follow the process in Chapter 6 to recreate that list. You can simply select all the elements of text you want to turn into the list, and then choose Bullets And Numbering from the Format menu. You'll see the List Properties dialog box:

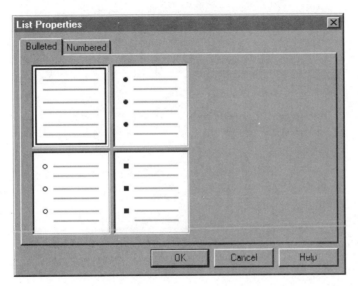

There are two versions of the List Properties dialog box; the first one, shown above, has two tabs, one showing the options for bulleted list styles and the other showing numbered list options. If you want to turn your text into a bulleted list, select one of the styles by clicking on it, and then clicking OK. The default style does not apply any formatting.

If you want to turn your text into a numbered list, first click on the Numbered tab. You can begin your list with a number other than 1 (or a letter other than "a" if you want a lettered list). All you need to do is select one of the styles on the Numbered tab, and then select or enter a number in the Start At text box. Then click OK.

**Changing the style of an entire list** To change a list from one style to another, right-click on the list, and then choose List Properties from the pop-up menu. You'll see a different version of the List Properties dialog box, this one having an extra tab called Other. You can select from bulleted and numbered styles on the Bulleted and Numbered tabs, or select a standard bulleted list, definition list, directory list, menu list, or numbered list on the Other tab, as shown below. When you select a style and click OK, FrontPage changes your list to that style.

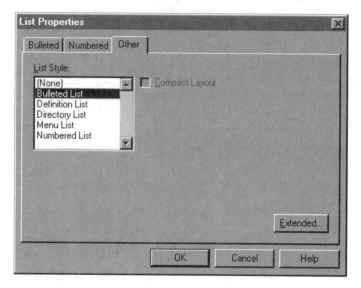

**Changing the style of individual list items** You also have the option of changing the style of individual items in a list—so all your list items don't have to be the same. It's a good idea to keep your list styles consistent, but if you ever want to change an individual entry to a different style, here's how: Right-click on a list item, and then choose List Item Properties from the pop-up menu. You'll see the List Item Properties dialog box with one tab pertaining to the type of list item that was selected. Select a different style, and then click OK to exit the List Item Properties dialog box.

## Line Breaks

A line break forms a new line on a page without creating a new paragraph. In other words, when you insert a line break, the next line starts below the previous line with the formatting used for the other lines within the paragraph. When you start a new paragraph, it too begins on the next line, but unlike the line break, the new paragraph can have different paragraph formatting than the previous paragraph.

**Inserting a line break** To insert a line break, position your cursor where you want the line break to appear, and choose Break from the Insert menu. This displays the Break Properties dialog box.

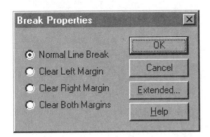

In the Break Properties dialog box, select among the following:

◆ Normal Line Break—Adds a line break and does not move based on any images in the left or right margins. In other words, even if there is an image in either the right or left margin, the new line starts immediately below the line break. (You can quickly insert a Normal line break by pressing Shift+Enter.)

◆ Clear Left Margin—Adds a line break, and if an image is in the left margin, moves the line following the line break down until the left margin is clear.

◆ Clear Right Margin—Adds a line break, and if an image is in the right margin, moves the line following the line break down until the right margin is clear.

◆ Clear Both Margins—Adds a line break, and if an image is in one or both margins, moves the line following the line break down until both margins are clear.

**Formatting a line break** To change the way a line break works with images, select it, right-click on it, and choose Line Break Properties from the pop-up menu. This displays the Break Properties dialog box, where you can change the type of line break.

**Deleting a line break** You can treat a line break as any other character. You can delete it with the Backspace or Del key.

## Horizontal Lines

**TIP**

FrontPage includes a selection of images that you can use as horizontal lines. They're included in the Lines category of FrontPage's clip art, which you can access by choosing the Image command from the Insert menu and clicking on the Clip Art tab. Since these lines are actually images and not standard HTML horizontal lines, their properties are specified differently. You change their properties in the Image Properties dialog box instead of the Horizontal Line Properties dialog box. For more information, see Chapter 8.

Using horizontal lines on a page is a neat way to separate sections, topics, or other elements. You can insert shaded or solid horizontal lines and format them in a few ways.

**Inserting a horizontal line** To insert a horizontal line, position your cursor where you want the line to appear, and then choose Horizontal Line from the Insert menu. A line appears, formatted the same way as the last horizontal line that was inserted in the Editor. If you're inserting a line for the first time, it will span the width of the page, have a shadow, and be two pixels high.

**Formatting a horizontal line** To change the appearance of a horizontal line, right-click on it and choose Horizontal Line Properties from the pop-up menu. The Horizontal Line Properties dialog box appears:

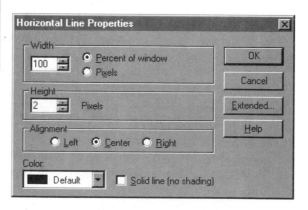

In the Width section, specify the length of your line as a percentage of the browser window width, or as a length in pixels. Then enter the line's thickness in pixels in the Height section. In the Alignment section, specify Left, Center, or Right alignment. From the Color drop-down list, select a color for the line. If the line color is set to the default color, you can also specify whether the line should be displayed with no shading by selecting the Solid Line check box. Solid lines set to the default color typically appear in gray, and shaded lines set to the default color appear shaded with the page's background color. Click OK to accept your settings and close the dialog box.

**Deleting a horizontal line** To delete a horizontal line, select it and then press the Del key or backspace over it.

# Further Enhancements

Now that we have covered some ways to format your pages, let's look into some other features that you can use to enhance your pages—for example, using bookmarks, links, marquees, sound, and video.

## Bookmarks

A **bookmark**, also known as an anchor, is a set of one or more characters on a page that is the target of a link. Using links to bookmarks allows a viewer of your Web site to jump to any point within a page (not just to the beginning of a page).

For example, suppose one of the pages in the RoasterNet site consists of a long, five-section document on the bright future of coffee bean sales in Seattle, and you link to that page from somewhere else within your site. When a user follows that link, the top of the page (i.e., the top of the document) appears in the browser. But if the document includes bookmarks at the beginning of each section, you can create your links directly to those bookmarks. That way, a user can jump directly to any of those sections instead of jumping to the top of the document and having to scroll down.

Bookmarks appear in the Editor as text with blue dashed underlines when Format Marks is selected on the View menu. See "Links" on the next page for information on linking to bookmarks.

**Creating a bookmark**   To create a bookmark, do the following:

1. Select one or more characters of text that will become the bookmark (the text you want to jump to).

2. Choose Bookmark from the Edit menu. The Bookmark dialog box appears.

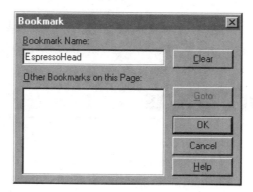

3. Enter a name for the bookmark in the Bookmark Name text box. Try to name your bookmarks intuitively, because later when you create a link to a bookmark you'll need to enter the bookmark name or select it from a list. It'll help to be able to easily discern one bookmark from another. If your page already includes other bookmarks, they will appear in the dialog box.

4. Click OK after you enter the bookmark name. In the Editor, the selected text will now have a blue dashed underline, indicating that it is a bookmark.

**Finding a bookmark**   Suppose you have a list of bookmarks on the current page in the Bookmark dialog box, and you want to find one of them. To find any bookmark in the list, select the bookmark, and then click Goto. The page scrolls to the bookmark location, and the bookmark is selected. This is a quick and handy alternative to scrolling up and down a page to locate your bookmarks.

**Clearing a bookmark** To remove a bookmark, select the bookmark and choose Bookmark from the Edit menu, or right-click on the bookmark and choose Bookmark Properties. In the Bookmark dialog box, click Clear. The dialog box closes, and the bookmark is removed. This procedure does not remove the text; it only removes the bookmark reference.

## Links

Links, also known as **hyperlinks,** are connections from one point to another. Viewers of a site can click on a link and jump to wherever it points to; this location is represented in HTML as a **URL.** You can link to and from text, images, other files (such as Microsoft Office files), or bookmarks. For information on creating links from images, see Chapter 8, and for information on changing the color of a link, see page 206.

If you have an intranet site populated with Office 97 documents, those documents can be interconnected with links. For example, a Word file can have a link that jumps to an Excel file. When you click on that link, the Excel file appears in Excel. You can link between Office 97 files and FrontPage HTML files very easily, creating a dynamic and powerful Office 97–style intranet site. This book describes creating links from FrontPage to Office 97 files. For information on creating links within Office 97 files only, see the documentation or online help for the individual Office 97 applications.

**Creating a link to pages or bookmarks** To create a link, select the text or image you want to link from, and then choose Hyperlink from the Edit menu. The Create Hyperlink dialog box appears, with four tabs that allow you to link to different places.

**SHORTCUT**

You can quickly create or edit a link by selecting the text or link and then clicking the Create Or Edit Hyperlink toolbar button.

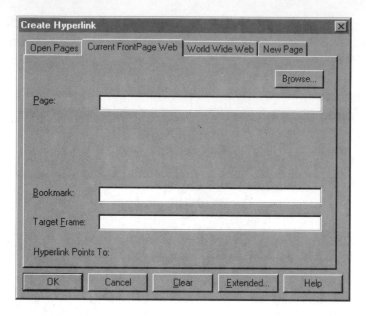

Here's how to use each of the tabs when creating links:

◆ Open Pages tab—Allows you to link to any page currently open in the Editor, select a bookmark on an open
page to link to, and specify a target **frame**. The Open
Pages list box lists all currently open pages; select a page
from the list. To link to a bookmark on a selected page,
select it from the Bookmark drop-down list, which is a
list of all the bookmarks for the selected page. To specify
a target frame for the destination of the link to appear in,
enter the frame name in the Target Frame text box. As
you work, FrontPage displays the **relative URL** of the current selection at the bottom of the dialog box. Once you
have completed your selections, click OK to create the
link and close the Create Hyperlink dialog box.

◆ Current FrontPage Web tab—Allows you to link to
any page or bookmark in the current Web site (the one
open in the Explorer) and specify a target frame. Click
Browse to select a page as the target page of your link.
If your target link is a bookmark, you can enter its
name in the Bookmark text box for the selected page.
To specify a target frame for the page to appear in, enter the frame name in the Target Frame text box. Clicking the Clear button clears your selection. FrontPage
displays the relative URL of the selection at the bottom

of the dialog box. Click OK to create the link and close the Create Hyperlink dialog box.

◆ World Wide Web tab—Allows you to link to a Web URL. Select a supported protocol from the Hyperlink Type drop-down list. A sample URL, using the selected protocol, is displayed in the URL text box. In the URL text box, enter the correct URL of the Web page you want to link to. Clicking the Clear button clears your selection. Click OK to create the link and close the Create Link dialog box.

**TIP**

If you want to create a link that allows users to send e-mail, select the mailto: protocol from the Hyperlink Type drop-down list on the World Wide Web tab. Then type the destination e-mail address following the protocol in the URL text box.

◆ New Page tab—Allows you to link to a page in the current Web site that has not yet been created. Enter a page title and a page URL in their respective text boxes. If the page will be a frames page, you can enter a target frame in the Target Frame text box. Use the option buttons to select between Edit New Page Immediately and Add New Page To To Do List.

After you make your selections, click OK, and the New Page dialog box is displayed, as shown in the figure below. Here you begin the process of creating a new page with a template or a wizard.

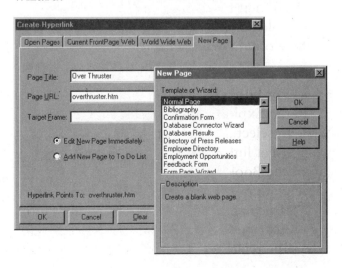

How this process is completed is based on your previous selections. If you selected the Edit New Page Immediately option, the new page will be opened in the Editor. If you selected the Add New Page To To Do List option, an entry is added to the To Do List reminding you to complete this page. When you return to the original page you were working on, you will see that a link was created to the newly created page.

**Selecting a link**   Once you have created a link and you want to modify it, you must first select it. All you need to do to select a link is to click anywhere within the link. You can also highlight text associated with a link to select it, but you do not need to. If the cursor is in a link, the toolbar buttons and menu items pertaining to links are enabled.

**Removing a link**   To remove a link, select it and then choose Unlink from the Edit menu. The link is removed, but the former link's text or image remains.

**Automatically created links**   Whenever you type in a supported protocol in the Editor followed by a destination, FrontPage detects that you want to make a link from the text and automatically creates one for you. In the figure below, the user simply typed the text *www.microsoft.com* in the first line. Because *www* only prefaces World Wide Web addresses, FrontPage assumed that the **HTTP** protocol would be used, and the user did not have to type it in.

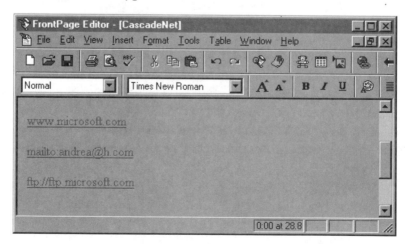

**Editing a link** To change a link's properties, select it, and then choose Hyperlink from the Edit menu. You can also right-click on the link and then choose Hyperlink Properties from the pop-up menu. You can change any of the link's properties in the Edit Hyperlink dialog box that appears. For more information, see "Creating a Link to Pages or Bookmarks" on page 191.

**Dragging a link from the Explorer** Here's another neat feature of FrontPage. If you have the Explorer and the Editor open simultaneously, you can create a text link to a page by dragging the page from the Explorer to a location on a page displayed in the Editor. Here's how to do it:

1.  Make sure the Editor and Explorer are open so that the target for the link appears in the Explorer window and the page on which you want the link to appear is open in the Editor. The Explorer can be in either Folder or Hyperlink view, and the target for the link can be any file you can create a link to, such as a page or an Office 97 document.

2.  Click the icon or file in the Explorer that will be the link's target, and drag it onto the page in the Editor. If you don't have enough room on your screen to drag the link directly into the Editor, drag the link to the Editor button on the Windows taskbar, and wait (while still holding down the left mouse button) until the Editor becomes active on your screen. Then finish the operation by dragging the file onto the page in the Editor. The cursor changes to the Windows shortcut cursor. Position the cursor at the exact spot where you want the link to appear on the page in the Editor, and release the mouse button. The name of the target is inserted and a link is created from that text to the target itself. This is just like any other link you might have added manually, and it can be edited in the same way.

**Creating links to the Web using a browser** In FrontPage, you don't have to recall and retype Web addresses if you want to link to a page on the Web. You can easily create such a link in two ways.

◆ With your cursor positioned on the page where you want the link created, click the Create Or Edit Hyperlink toolbar button, and click on the World Wide Web tab (as explained under "Creating a Link to Pages or Bookmarks" on page 191). Click the Browse button and follow the instructions that appear in your browser, which tell you to go to the page on the Web you want to link to, and then return to FrontPage. You can return to FrontPage by clicking the Editor button on the Windows 95 taskbar. FrontPage automatically grabs the URL from the browser. Click OK in the Create Link dialog box to finish creating the link.

◆ While you are browsing in Microsoft Internet Explorer or Netscape Navigator, simply click and hold on any link you see on a page, and drag that link onto a page in the Editor. Ta-da! FrontPage automatically creates a link to that page.

## Marquees

**Marquees** can turn people's heads and get them to pay more notice to your site. As Sheriff Buford T. Justice of the movie *Smokey and the Bandit* would say, they're "attention gettas." But as with any other catchy design element in your site, be careful not to overuse them—users might find them annoying or might ignore their messages. (Note: Marquees are supported in Internet Explorer 2.0 and 3.0, but not in Netscape Navigator 3.0.)

Marquees are HTML elements that allow text to move on a page. They turn an otherwise static page into one that's dynamic and lively. Let's use another example from RoasterNet to show what marquees can do for a page:

> **TIP**
>
> Another way to liven up your page is to use one of FrontPage's animated GIFs from its clip art library. For more information, see Chapter 8.

Gary, who's in charge of the National Sales department at Cascade Coffee Roasters, realizes the importance of evangelizing the sales message within the company, so he has instructed his department to create a Sales section for RoasterNet. He plans to have sections detailing general sales patterns, news from the competition and reactions to it, and up-to-the-minute news of the big "scores" his department earns. In the early stages, his pages are under construction, and he doesn't have much time to build them as he'd like. But one of his salespeople, Richard, has just made the company's largest-ever sale, and Gary wants the news to go up on a page on RoasterNet. If he just types the news on the page, it will look static and people might read past it, especially since his page is under construction and they might think that nothing has changed unless they look carefully. So Gary will use a marquee to get their attention. Here's the process he'll use to insert it:

1. Position your cursor where you want the marquee to be inserted. Choose Marquee from the Insert menu. You'll see the Marquee Properties dialog box:

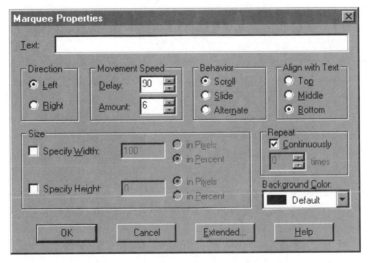

2. Type in the text of the marquee in the Text text box.

3. In the Direction section, specify whether you want the marquee to move toward the left or the right. (If you select Alternate in the Behavior section in step 5, you won't need to specify a direction here.)

4. In the Movement Speed section, specify numbers for Delay and Amount. Delay sets the length of time in milliseconds between each movement of the marquee. The higher the number, the longer the delay, and the slower the marquee moves. Amount refers to the distance in pixels between each movement of the marquee. You can make your marquee move faster, therefore, by

increasing this number. You can adjust the Delay and Amount values to make your marquees move at any speed, from very fast to very slow.

5. In the Behavior section, select one of the following options:

*Scroll*—This moves the text in the direction across the screen that you specified in the Direction section. Text appears and disappears from the sides of the marquee area.

*Slide*—This moves the text across the screen in the direction you specified in the Direction section. But instead of scrolling off the screen, the text stops when it reaches the end of the screen, and remains on screen.

*Alternate*—This moves the text back and forth across the screen. The text never leaves the screen when you select Alternate.

6. In the Align With Text section, you specify how you want the text to be aligned in the marquee area. (You set the marquee area in the Size section). You can align the text at the top of the marquee area, in the middle, or at the bottom.

7. The Size section is where you set the marquee area. To specify the width of the marquee area, select the Specify Width check box. If you want to specify the width of the marquee area in pixels, enter a number and then select In Pixels. If you want to set the width as a percentage of the screen, enter the number and then select In Percent.

## TIP

To give your marquee "space to breathe" from top to bottom so it can be easier to read, specify an ample height and select Middle in the Align With Text section. This centers the marquee from top to bottom in the area you've specified.

Select the Specify Height check box if you want to set the marquee area height. This number determines the amount of room, from top to bottom, that the text in the marquee area moves in. Enter a number and select either In Pixels to specify the height in pixels or In Percent to specify the height as a percentage of the page.

8. In the Repeat section, select the Continuously check box if you want the marquee to run all the time. If you want the marquee to move only a certain number of times when a reader comes to your page, deselect Continuously and enter that number in the text box below it.

9. Select a Background Color if you want the marquee to move against a colored background. Sometimes using a different background color than the rest of the page can have a pleasing effect, but beware of "overstunning" your audience with this option. The movement of the marquee might be enough to grab their attention.

10. When you're satisfied with all your settings, click OK to exit the Marquee Properties dialog box.

**Changing marquee settings** To change the settings of a marquee on your page, right-click on the marquee and choose Marquee Properties from the pop-up menu. This brings up the Marquee Properties dialog box. Change the settings, and then click OK.

## Sounds

**Background sound** can add another dimension to your site and give it more of a "multimedia" feel. Background sound plays whenever someone visits the page it's on, and it can play a specified number of times or loop continuously. Just as hearing a certain song can put us in a certain mood, background sound can set the tone for your viewers—and it can also annoy them if it's overused. Use background sound sparingly and wisely. (Note: Internet Explorer 2.0 and 3.0 support background sound, but Netscape Navigator 3.0 does not.)

FrontPage supports several types of sound files, ranging from Wave sounds (with WAV extensions) to Midi sequences (MID), AIFF sounds (AIF, AIFC, AIFF), and AU sounds (AU, SND).

Inserting a background sound and setting its properties require two different steps. Here's how to insert the sound:

1. With your cursor anywhere on the page you want the sound to be associated with, choose Background Sound

from the Insert menu. You'll see the Background Sound dialog box:

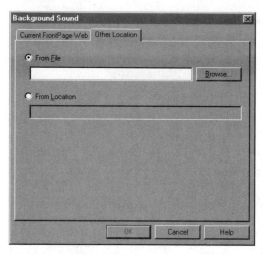

2. If the sound file you want to use already exists in your site, click on the Current FrontPage Web tab, select the file from the list, and click OK.

3. If the sound file is not already part of your site, click on the Other Location tab. To specify a sound file that you have on a floppy disk, hard drive, or LAN, select the From File option button, click Browse, find the file in the smaller Background Sound dialog box that appears, select the file, and then click Open. Both Background Sound dialog boxes will close.

You can also use sound files that you're using in other Web sites. Select the From Location option button, enter the URL for the sound file, and click OK to exit the Background Sound dialog box.

Here's how to adjust the sound's properties once you've inserted the sound:

1. Right-click on the page, and choose Page Properties from the pop-up menu (or choose Page Properties from the File menu). The Page Properties dialog box appears.

**Page Properties**

General | Background | Margins | Custom

Location:        http://msptech/RoasterNet/Sales.htm

Title:           Sales

Base Location:

Default Target
Frame:

Background Sound

Location:  file:///C:/Kalfiles/Sound2.wav        Browse...

Loop:  1      ☐ Forever

HTML Encoding

For displaying this page:  US/Western European  ▼

For saving this page:  US/Western European  ▼    Extended...

OK        Cancel        Help

2. On the General tab, specify in the Loop text box the number of times you want the sound to play. If you want the sound to loop endlessly, select the Forever check box.

3. You can also change the background sound that plays for this page by clicking Browse and selecting another sound in the Background Sound dialog box that appears.

4. Click OK to exit the Page Properties dialog box.

## Videos

Another great way to liven up your sites is to add video to them. As you might know, however, video files tend to be huge, and even though the bandwidth of the Internet is increasing gradually, it's not yet sufficient to transfer large video files in a speedy way. The situation can be different within a corporation if the intranet uses local connections where bandwidth is less of a concern. (Note: Internet Explorer 2.0 and 3.0 support embedded video in a page, but Netscape Navigator 3.0 does not.)

### TIP

In the Editor, the download time for a page at 28.8 kbps is displayed (in seconds) in the lower right part of the screen. As you change your page—adding or deleting videos, sounds, images, and other elements—the download time updates appropriately.

FrontPage supports the viewing of Windows-based AVI files in its Web sites. As with adding a background sound to a page, adding video requires two steps. First, you insert the video file on your page, and then you set its properties. Here's how to do it:

1. With your cursor on the page where you want to insert the video, choose Video from the Insert menu. You'll see the Video dialog box:

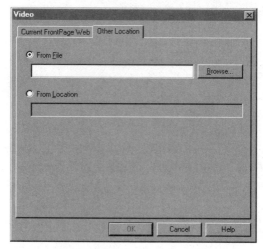

2. If the AVI file you want to use already exists in your site, click on the Current FrontPage Web tab, select the file from the list, and click OK.

3. If the file is not already part of your site, click on the Other Location tab. To specify an AVI file on a floppy disk, hard drive, or LAN, select the From File option button, click Browse, select the file in the smaller Video dialog box that appears, and then click Open. Both Video dialog boxes will close.

   You can also use AVI files that you're using in other Web sites. Select the From Location option button, enter the URL for the file, and click OK to exit the Video dialog box.

   The opening frame of the video file will appear on the page as a "placeholder."

   Once you've inserted the video file, you might need to adjust its properties. Here's how:

1. Right-click on the video-file placeholder on the page, and choose Image Properties from the pop-up menu. The Image Properties dialog box appears, with the Video tab selected:

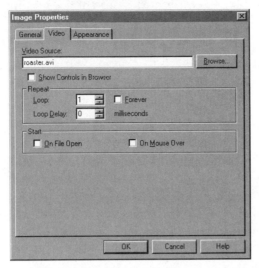

2. If you want to replace the video with another, click Browse, locate the replacement AVI file in the Video dialog box, and click OK.

3. Select the Show Controls In Browser check box if you want to show a set of controls—Play, Stop, and a slider—along with the video when it's displayed in the browser at runtime.

4. In the Repeat section, specify in the Loop box how many times you want the video file to play, and specify in the Loop Delay box the amount of time (in milliseconds) between playings of the video. If you want the video to play endlessly, select the Forever check box.

5. In the Start section, specify when you want the video to begin playing. Selecting On File Open starts the video whenever a person opens the page it's on, and selecting On Mouse Over starts the video whenever a user moves the mouse pointer over the video in the browser.

6. When you're satisfied with your settings, click OK to exit the Image Properties dialog box.

# Page Properties

You can set the properties for a page in the Editor by choosing the Page Properties command from the File menu or from the pop-up menu that appears when you right-click on the page. In the Page Properties dialog box, you can change general file information such as the page's title; set a page's background image, color, or sound; set default colors for text and links; and specify margins and custom settings. You must have a page open in the Editor in order to set these properties. (To open a page or create a new page, see Chapter 6.) Here's a primer on the properties, starting with the General tab:

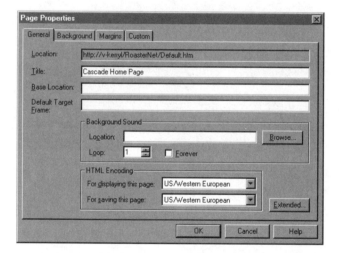

You can change the page's title by entering a new title in the Title text box, change the optional base URL by entering it in the Base Location text box, and assign a frame as the default target of all the links on the page by entering its name in the Default Target Frame text box.

In the Background Sound section, you can change the properties for a background sound. For details on this, see "Sounds" earlier in this chapter. The HTML Encoding section is used to specify settings to control the HTML character encoding for the page, which is used for Web pages of different languages.

The Background tab is where you can specify background colors and colors for various links:

```
Page Properties                                              [X]
  General | Background | Margins | Custom |

  (•) Specify Background and Colors:

    [ ] Background Image      [ ] Watermark
    [_____]  [ Browse... ] [ Properties... ]

    Background: [ [] White  |v]   Hyperlink:        [ [■] Default |v]

    Text:       [ [■] Default|v]   Visited Hyperlink: [ [■] Default |v]

                                   Active Hyperlink:  [ [■] Default |v]

  ( ) Get Background and Colors from Page:

    [_____]  [ Browse... ]

                          [ OK ]   [ Cancel ]   [ Help ]
```

In the Specify Background And Colors section, you can set the following properties:

**Background Image** By selecting the Background Image check box, you can specify an image to use as your page background; most browsers will tile this image automatically. You've probably seen this on the Web; a tiled background can be effective if it adds to the "viewability" of a page and does not impair viewing of text or other images on the page.

> **T I P**
>
> To adjust the properties of an existing background image, open the Page Properties dialog box and click the Properties button in the Specify Background And Colors section. This brings up the Image Properties dialog box. See Chapter 8 for information on this dialog box.

**Watermark** A watermark is a background image that does not scroll when you scroll the page. Select the Watermark check box if you want this feature. Click Browse to specify the image. (Note: Internet Explorer 2.0 and 3.0 support watermarks; Netscape Navigator 3.0 does not.)

**Background Color** You can specify a background color for your page if you don't want to use a tiled image. You might consider using a color with more flair. Just make sure your text and images are easy to read against whatever color you select. Use the Background drop-down list to select your color.

**Default text color** You can use the Text drop-down list to specify the default color of the text that appears on your page. Black is a safe standard, but don't hesitate to experiment with other colors that might look good against the background you selected. Any text that is formatted in a different color in the Editor will override the default color specified here.

**Hyperlink color** You can use the Hyperlink drop-down list to specify a color to use for all links on a page that have not been visited.

**Visited hyperlink color** Links change to this color after they have been followed. If a link appears on more than one page, following one instance of the link triggers the visited link color for all instances of that link in your site. You can specify the visited link color using the Visited Hyperlink drop-down list.

**Active hyperlink color** The active link color is the color of a link as it is being clicked. To specify such a color, use the Active Hyperlink drop-down list.

## TIP

The Get Background And Colors From Page option is a feature unique to FrontPage and is a great way to set up a "style page." For example, if you make changes to the background and colors on the style page, the changes will be reflected on all of the pages that this style page was applied to when you reopen them.

In the Get Background And Colors From Page section of the Background tab, you can specify use of the same background color, background image, text color, and link colors that are used on another page. Select the option button, and then click Browse to specify the page from the current site that you want to use for this purpose. If you've already set up those properties elsewhere, this saves you time by not having to set them up again for the current page.

**Margins** To specify top and left margins for your page, click on the Margins tab, select one or both check boxes, and enter the numbers, in pixels, in the appropriate boxes. If you are trying to move text or an image to the very edge of the browser window, set the margins to zero.

**Meta tags** The Custom tab displays a list of **Meta tags** that are used on your page. Meta tags live in the page's HTML and contain information about the page—for example, the content type, the character set, and the application that generated the HTML. They are never displayed, but they can supply information to a browser that recognizes them. You can add, modify, or remove Meta tags for system variables and user variables on this tab.

# Utilities and Useful Commands

You'll find numerous utilities and other commands in the Editor to make your work a little easier, and maybe even save your rear end if you make a mistake somewhere along the line.

## Preview in Browser

Believe it or not, many people use browsers other than Internet Explorer and Netscape Navigator. If your site is going to be accessible to the world, you should test it with as many browsers as possible. Therefore, you might want to install a variety of browsers on your computer and view your site using each one. You should also consider testing your site with different browser versions.

 At any time, you can see the progress of your work and how it'll appear to the throngs that will rush to see your pages online. You can choose the Preview In Browser command from the File menu, or click the toolbar button, to have FrontPage launch the current page in the Web browser of your choice.

When you choose the command from the File menu, you'll see the Preview In Browser dialog box:

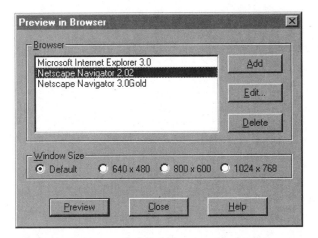

Select an available browser in the Browser section. You can add new browsers to the list by clicking the Add button. You'll then see the Add Browser dialog box, where you'll need to enter a name for the browser and the path and name of the executable file (EXE).

You can click the Browse button in the Add Browser dialog box to find the executable file for browsers you want to add.

In the Preview In Browser dialog box, you can also edit or delete browsers you have added to your list.

To edit a browser, select it from the list and click Edit. To delete a browser, select it from the list and click Delete. If FrontPage has automatically added a browser to the Preview In Browser dialog box, the Edit and Delete buttons are typically not available for it.

You can also set the browser window size by selecting one of the option buttons in the Window Size section. This is a great reason to use the Preview In Browser command—so you can test your site in different browser window sizes. Maybe you designed your Web pages using 1024 x 768 resolution but you want to see what the browser window size will look like to users with normal VGA (640 x 480) resolution. In order for the different window sizes to work properly, your display must have the same or higher screen resolution than the one you select. Clicking the Preview button causes the current page to be displayed in the selected browser and window size.

## Undo/Redo

The 3-2 hanging curve balls, interceptions in the end zone, and missed layups are on the record books to stay, but not the mistakes you make in the Editor. The Undo command can save you on the job. Use Undo to reverse the last action you made on a page, up to the last 30 actions. To undo an action, choose Undo from the Edit menu or click the Undo toolbar button.

> **TIP**
>
> For a quicker way to Undo, press Ctrl+Z, and for a quicker Redo, press Ctrl+Y.

To reverse the effect of an Undo command, you can choose Redo from the Edit menu or click the Redo toolbar button. You can redo up to the last 30 Undo commands.

## Following a Link

You can use the Editor as a mini-browser by using the Follow Hyperlink command. To see the actual page, file, or bookmark that a link goes to, select the link and choose the Follow Hyperlink command from the Tools menu.

**SHORTCUT**

To quickly follow any link on a page, you can press Ctrl and click on the link, or right-click on the link and choose Follow Hyperlink from the pop-up menu.

If the link leads to another page, the Editor opens that page if it is not already open. If the link is to a file, such as a Microsoft Excel document, the Editor opens the application configured for the file type and presents the file in its native environment.

## Show Explorer, Show To Do List, and Show Image Editor

If the Explorer is open, you can bring it to the front of the desktop by choosing the Show FrontPage Explorer command from the Tools menu or by clicking the Show FrontPage Explorer toolbar button. If the Explorer is not already open, these operations will launch it.

If the To Do List is open, you can bring it to the front of the desktop by choosing the Show To Do List command from the Tools menu or by clicking the Show To Do List toolbar button. You must have a Web site open in the Explorer to use the To Do List. If the To Do List isn't open, this command opens it. For more information on the To Do List, see Chapter 5.

If you have an image editor configured in the Explorer, you can launch it by choosing the Show Image Editor command from the Tools menu. You can install Microsoft Image Composer from the FrontPage 97 Bonus Pack CD, and it will become the default image editor.

## Add To Do Task

If you want to add a task to the To Do List, you can choose the Add To Do Task command from the Edit menu.

Add To Do Task

Task Name: Post new position openings

Assign To: John

Priority
○ High
○ Medium
○ Low

Created By:     (unknown) on 10/4/96 at 4:57:22 AM
Modified By:    (Has not been modified)
Completed:      No
Linked To:      Default.htm

Description:

OK          Cancel          Help

In the Add To Do Task dialog box that appears, you can add details to the task that appears in the To Do List, such as the task name, who the task is assigned to, the priority of the task, and a description. The task will be linked to the active page in the Editor. Chapter 5 discusses using the To Do List.

## Spell-Checker

**SHORTCUT**

You can quickly access the spell-checker in the Editor by clicking the Check Spelling toolbar button.

FrontPage is equipped with the Microsoft Office spell-checker, which provides outstanding consistency between Office documents and FrontPage Web sites. You can check the spelling of selected text, selected pages, or all the HTML pages in your Web site.

**To spell-check a page currently open in the Editor:**

1. To spell-check a selection of text, select it. To spell-check the entire page, you don't have to select anything.

2. Choose Spelling from the Tools menu, or press F7. The spell-checker begins checking at the top of the page if no text is selected. If it finds no unrecognized words, it presents a dialog box informing you that the spell-check is complete.

3. If the spell-checker finds words that it doesn't recognize, you'll see the Spelling dialog box.

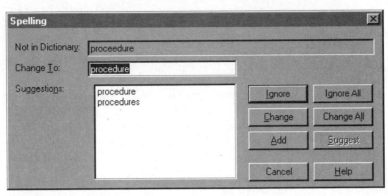

Use the dialog box as follows:

*Not In Dictionary*—This text box displays words that are not in the Office dictionary or the custom dictionary.

*Ignore*—Click this button to ignore the current word and search for the next unrecognized word.

*Ignore All*—Click this button to ignore all instances of the current word and continue.

*Change*—Click this button to replace the selection in the Not In Dictionary text box (the unrecognized word) with the selection in the Change To text box.

*Change All*—Click this button to change all instances of the current word on the page with the contents of the Change To text box.

*Add*—Click this button to add the selection in the Not In Dictionary text box to the custom dictionary and make no changes to the word. (Note: FrontPage shares the custom dictionary with Office, so any custom words you add while using Office applications are available in FrontPage, and vice-versa.)

*Suggest*—When this button is enabled, you can click it to list alternative words in the Suggestions list, based on the word in the Change To text box.

*Cancel*—Click this button to close the dialog box and quit the spell-check. Changes that have been made to the page and to the custom dictionary remain.

The spell-checker does not check the spelling in a file included on the page by a WebBot Include Component. You must open these files separately to check their spelling. For more information on WebBot Include Components, see Chapter 9.

**To spell-check multiple pages in a site:**

**SHORTCUT**

You can quickly access the spell-checker in the Explorer by clicking the Cross File Spelling toolbar button.

To spell-check all the HTML files in a site, you need to have that site open in the Explorer. Choose Spelling from the Tools menu in the Explorer, or press F7. In the Spelling dialog box, specify whether you want FrontPage to spell-check all HTML pages in the site, or just the ones you've selected in the Explorer. (To select multiple pages, press Ctrl while clicking on individual page icons in Folder view.) Then click Start.

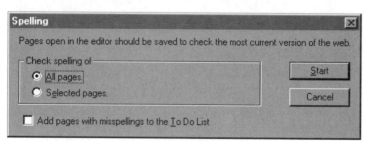

FrontPage presents the results of the spell-check in the Check Spelling dialog box. In this dialog box, you can see details such as the pages containing misspelled words, as well as the number of misspelled words per page. If you find yourself saying "Whoopsie," and you want to correct the error right away, click the Edit Page button. The page will be opened in the Editor, with the first misspelled word displayed in the Spelling dialog box, ready for you to change. If you don't feel like making the changes now, or would rather have Ralph down the hall do it because the game starts in half an hour and you've got to pick up the pizza on the way home, click Add Task to add the tasks to the To Do List. (From the To Do List, you can assign Ralph's name to the tasks.) When you're finished with the Check Spelling dialog box, click Close.

# Find/Replace

You can use Find and Replace in either the Editor (to search for and/or replace words on the current page) or in the Explorer (to search for and/or replace words across multiple HTML pages in your site). Take a second to imagine how useful this functionality can be. If your site contains dozens of instances of the word *board* that happen to be spelled *bored,* you've got a big problem on your hands. But luckily you've got a tool to search the pages across your site and fix any errors you know of in a straightforward fashion. We'll get to that Explorer tool in a moment; first, let's see how to use Find and Replace in the Editor:

**Find and replace words on a current page** Unlike in Word, when you use the Find command in the Editor you do not have the option to open the Replace dialog box when you find matching text. If you know you need to replace a selection of text with another, you must use the Replace command.

Use the Find command to find instances of text on an active page. To use the command, choose Find from the Edit menu, or press Ctrl+F. The Find dialog box appears:

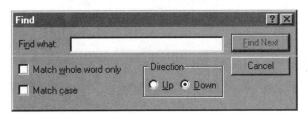

Type in the text you want to find. If you only want to find whole words, select the Match Whole Word Only check box. For example, if every word on your page is *the*, and you search for *t*, you won't find any instance of *t* if the Match Whole Word Only check box is selected. If the box is not selected, every instance of the letter *t* will be found.

Select the Match Case check box if you only want to find text that exactly matches the case of the selection you're searching for. You can specify the direction of the search, Up or Down, from the insertion point. When an instance of the selection is found, click the Find Next button to continue searching. Click Cancel to close the dialog box and stop the search.

To replace text with other specified text, use the Replace command on the Edit menu, or press Ctrl+H. The Replace dialog box appears:

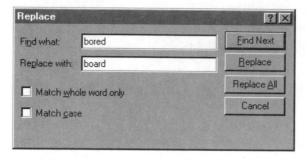

Type what you want to replace in the Find What text box, and enter your replacement text in the Replace With text box. To find text only if it matches a whole word or only if it matches the case of the text you're searching for, select the appropriate check box. To replace all instances of the text on the page, click the Replace All button. To locate the first matching instance, click the Find Next button to begin the search. When the Editor finds an instance of the text you're looking for, the text is selected on the page. To replace the text, click the Replace button. To move on without replacing the text, click the Find Next button.

**Find and replace words across an entire site** The Explorer can find and replace words across an entire site. To use this feature, you must have the site open in the Explorer. Let's suppose that most of the good typists at your company are on vacation, and the people filling in for them can't spell their way out of a bowl of alphabet soup. Someone has typed in *iz* for *is* all across the site, and you've got to fix it.

You can use the Find command to search for instances of *iz* in the HTML pages in your site. Choose Find from the Tools menu, or press Ctrl+F. You'll see the Find In FrontPage Web dialog box:

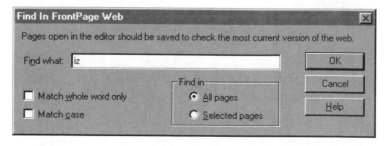

Type the word or words you want to find in the Find What text box. In the Find In section, you can specify all pages or selected pages. (To select multiple pages, press Ctrl while clicking on individual page icons in Folder view.) Make the appropriate selections in the Match Whole Word Only and Match Case check boxes. Click OK to begin the Find. When FrontPage finishes searching, you'll be presented with a Find Occurrences Of dialog box containing summary information about the search.

**SHORTCUT**

You can quickly access Find in the Explorer by clicking the Cross File Find toolbar button.

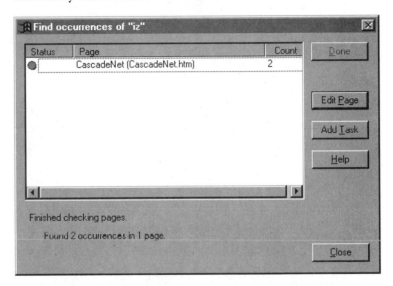

If FrontPage finds instances of the text you searched for, it will indicate the number of occurrences, and in how many pages, at the bottom of the dialog box. You can immediately open the pages in the Editor to fix the mistakes one by one by selecting the page from the list and clicking Edit Page. If you'd rather work on the task later, or if you have the power to assign the task to someone else and your tee time is rapidly approaching, click the Add Task button to add the tasks to the To Do List. When you're finished with this dialog box, click Close.

If you want to replace instances of text with different text in your site, choose Replace from the Tools menu or press Ctrl+H. You'll see the Replace In FrontPage Web dialog box.

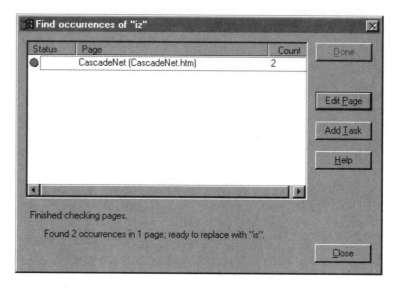

You use this dialog box the same way as described in "Find and Replace Words on a Current Page" on page 213. When you use this command, you'll see a summary dialog box such as this one:

Looks like the same dialog box as the one that appears when you use the Find command, doesn't it? It is, and you can use it in much the same way. But you'll see the difference when you click the Edit Page button: With Find, FrontPage opens the page in the Editor and selects the text you searched for, but to change the text, you must replace it manually. With Replace, FrontPage allows you to replace each instance or all instances of the text you searched for, with the text you entered as replacement text in the Replace In FrontPage Web dialog box. You can also specify other replacement text if you so choose.

# Thesaurus

You now also have the power of the Microsoft Office thesaurus in the Editor. The thesaurus comes in handy on those rainy days when you're sitting at your desk trying to find the right word that's on the tip of your tongue, and it doesn't help that your mind continually drifts back to the vacation you just spent in Cabo San Lucas.

To use the thesaurus for help on a specific word, select the word and choose Thesaurus from the Tools menu, or press Shift+F7. You'll see the Thesaurus dialog box, which you use in the same way that you use one in an Office 97 application.

◆ The Looked Up text box displays the word you're currently checking.

◆ The Meanings list displays meanings for the word you're looking up. If you select a meaning here, you'll see a list of synonyms in the Replace With Synonym list.

◆ Click on a word in the Replace With Synonym list if you want to use it in place of the selected word in the Editor, or if you want to use that word to search further. To use the word in the Editor right away, click Replace, and you'll be returned to the Editor with the new word in place. To keep on searching with the selected word as the new word you're looking up, click Look Up.

◆ If you don't want to use any new words from the thesaurus, click Cancel.

◆ If the Previous button is enabled, you can click it to return to the previous word you looked up.

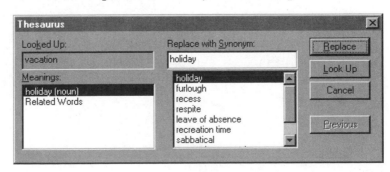

# Viewing and Editing HTML

The ability to edit HTML directly in the Editor was the most requested new feature for FrontPage 97. You can view (and edit!) the HTML for an active page by choosing the HTML command from the View menu. The View Or Edit HTML dialog box appears, showing the HTML for the current page. You can edit the code you see in the View Or Edit HTML dialog box using the same keyboard shortcuts you use on a page in the Editor, such as those for copying, cutting, and pasting. Below is an example of the View Or Edit HTML dialog box.

You have several options for how you can view the code, including the following:

◆ Select the Original option button at the bottom left of the dialog box to view the code of the page from the time it was last saved.

◆ Select the Current option button to view or edit the code in its current form. If changes have been made to the page since it was last saved, this is the most recent version of the code.

◆ Select the Show Color Coding check box to see the HTML tags, names, values, and other content in different colors. This really helps you see the code more clearly.

◆ After you make changes to the code, click OK to add those changes. FrontPage does not ask you to verify that you want your changes made, so if you make changes you do not want to keep, you must click the Cancel button before returning to the Editor.

## Moving Among Currently Open Pages

Use the Back and Forward toolbar buttons to move among pages that are currently open in the Editor. The pages are listed at the bottom of the Window menu in the order that they were opened, and you can move to a new page via that menu as well. You can also use the Back and Forward commands on the Tools menu.

## Refreshing a Page

To refresh an active page in the Editor with the last saved version of that page, click the Refresh toolbar button or choose the Refresh command from the View menu. If you have made changes since the last save, a dialog box will appear asking whether you want to save the changes. Click Yes or No, and the page will be refreshed. The Refresh command is handy when you've made changes to a page that you do not want to save, and you want to start over from the last version that was saved. It's also handy for viewing changes made to a page by another person.

## Stopping an Action

To stop an action in the Editor, click the Stop toolbar button (if it is enabled). This command is handy for ending actions that are taking a long time to finish or that might be "hung up," such as communications between the Editor and a Web server.

## *Coming Up*

With that, the grand discussion of formatting and using FrontPage's file commands and utilities comes to an end. In the next chapter, you'll learn how FrontPage works with images.

# Chapter 8
# Getting into Graphics

## Images: A Balancing Act

Ask a writer and he'll tell you that "content is king"; ask a graphic artist and he'll tell you, "content is one thing, but if you want anyone to read it, you'd better add some graphics." As a Web-site developer, you'll be walking this fine line and addressing the content vs. graphics issue for every page in your site.

The number-one issue when dealing with graphics in a Web site is file size, which translates directly to how long an image will take to display in the average browser. You can discuss graphic formats, resolution, image editing software, color palettes, browsers, and so forth until you're blue in the face, but the bottom line is that the best graphics are the ones that have reasonable image quality and small file sizes.

Since many people are still using 14.4-baud modems, many site developers set size limitations on their pages. Typically, a page in your site, including any images on that page, should not exceed 35–40 KB. That loud noise you just heard was a collective scream from the graphic designers of the world, saying, "Yeah, right!" That size doesn't sound like much to work with, and it's not, but with some helpful tips to optimize your images, you'll be surprised at what you can do.

This chapter will discuss three aspects of using images in your sites:

◆ The types of graphic formats used in Web-site development.

◆ How to optimize those formats, using color management, to achieve fast-loading images that still look good.

◆ Using FrontPage to handle your images, including placement, creating image maps, and creating transparent GIFs directly in the FrontPage Editor.

# Graphic Formats

As you might know, graphic formats are all referred to by an acronym or by the file extension associated with the format, and the names can get a little confusing. You've got BMP, GIF, EPS, TIF, JPEG, WMF, and many others. While working on your Web site in FrontPage, however, you'll be dealing primarily with two types of images, **JPEG** and **GIF**. Both are compressed graphic formats and are the most commonly used in Web-site development. But what if you have some graphics that are not JPEGs or GIFs, and you want to use them on a Web page? Well, you're in luck, because FrontPage can import many graphic formats, which are listed here:

CompuServe GIF (GIF)
JPEG (JPG)
Bitmap (BMP)
TIFF (TIF)
Windows Metafile (WMF)
Sun Raster (RAS)
Encapsulated PostScript (EPS)
Paintbrush (PCX)
Targa (TGA)

When you save a page that contains images you've inserted that haven't been saved yet, FrontPage will ask you whether you want to save each image to the current site. By default, Front-Page saves each image as a GIF. If you want the image saved as a JPEG, be sure to specify this in the Image Properties dialog box before you save the page.

The JPEG (Joint Photographic Experts Group) format is a scalable compressed format that can deliver high compression with very little image degradation. It's not uncommon for an image to lose some of its crispness in electronic form, especially when it's converted from one format to another. Because JPEG images handle compression and image degradation well, they're ideal for a Web-site environment in which they are often resized, converted, or otherwise altered. The JPEG format is most suitable for photographs or images with more than 256 colors. FrontPage looks at the number of bits used to represent each color in the image, also known as the file's bit depth. Images with eight bits of color information per pixel are capable of supporting 256 different colors. More bits mean more colors supported.

The GIF (Graphics Interchange Format) format is a compressed format for images that contain 256 or fewer colors. The GIF format is typically used with images that contain primarily solid colors, such as illustrations. The GIF format can also support transparency and interlacing.

| Bit Depth | Number of Colors |
|---|---|
| 8 bit | 256 Colors |
| 7 bit | 128 Colors |
| 6 bit | 64 Colors |
| 5 bit | 32 Colors |
| 4 bit | 16 Colors |
| 3 bit | 8 Colors |

**Various bit depths and their corresponding number of colors.**

FrontPage allows you to perform a little chicanery with GIF images in a Web site, using transparency. All images, including GIF images, are rectangular. But by using transparency, you can set any one color in a GIF image to not appear, thereby allowing the background to show through where the color was. For example, suppose your Web page has a white background, and on the page is a GIF image of a black rectangle with a red circle in it. If you set black to be transparent, the white background will show where the black was, and you'll see a red circle on the page. With transparency, you are not limited to using rectangular images on your pages, and you have more freedom to give your pages the look you want. We'll get into the "how" of transparent graphics a little later in this chapter.

# Color Management

The idea of color management might be new to a lot of graphic artists, but if you plan on being successful with your Web site, it will become your new best friend. The basic idea behind color management is this: How can I decrease the number of colors in my images and still have them look good? Decreasing the number of colors decreases the file size of the image, and smaller files download faster in a browser.

If you want users to see those impressive graphics you're about to create, you need to make sure they're built for speed. The last thing you want is for users to become frustrated as they watch their screens draw and redraw a bunch of large file-size graphics. Keep in mind the following tips for making your image file sizes smaller. (You can use Microsoft Image Composer, which comes with the FrontPage Bonus Pack, to manipulate your images.)

◆ Typically, the JPEG format works well for photographic images, and the GIF format works well for images containing solid colors, such as illustrations and line art.

◆ Size your images using your image editing software. Even though you can dimensionally size images in the Editor, this doesn't actually change the image file size. For example, if you insert a 2-inch square image that has a file size of 10 KB into the Editor and you size it to a 1-inch square, the image file size is still 10 KB.

◆ If you are creating an image that contains only black and white colors, save it as a black and white image.

This will make the image file size smaller. In Microsoft Image Composer, you can do this by setting the color format to Black and White when saving.

◆ If you are creating an image that will be saved as a GIF and it contains a gradient or straight lines, try to make these horizontal. Since the GIF format performs its compression by looking at each horizontal line, it can make the file size smaller if an entire line has the same color value.

◆ Experiment with the different JPEG compression levels. Try to use as much compression as possible and still retain acceptable image quality.

◆ View your images at different resolutions and bit depths, and view them in different browsers. A JPEG image of more than 8 bits will dither when displayed on a monitor that only supports 256 colors.

◆ If you're using Photoshop and you want to save an image as a GIF, change the RGB Color mode to Indexed Color mode, specify the bit depth (the smaller the better), and select the adaptive palette with no dither.

◆ If you are using Photoshop and you are saving images as GIFs and you know your image uses fewer than 256 colors, try using the Exact palette. Exact palettes contain exactly the number of colors in your image and thus decrease the image file size.

The key is to experiment. You might notice some flattening of colors, but you'll also notice a decrease in image file size. It's a judgment call, but it's one you'll have to make if you want graphics to display faster in a browser.

As crazy as this might sound, some people don't like to wait for graphics *at all,* so remember to take advantage of the alternative text feature (explained later in this chapter in the section titled "Alternative Representations"), and think about designing your pages so those "graphics haters" out there can still navigate through your Web site.

## Optimizing Your Backgrounds

If you want that cool background to appear quickly and still have acceptable quality, these tips can help you:

◆ Since a background image is just a tiled graphic, follow the guidelines described on the previous two pages to decrease the file size.

◆ Decrease the physical dimensions of the background image to decrease the file size.

◆ Don't put too much detail in a background. Remember that in most cases text will have to be read on top of it.

◆ Experiment with the backgrounds that are available in the Backgrounds category on the Clip Art tab of the Image dialog box. Many of these backgrounds are very small in size. See the next section for information on inserting them.

◆ Consider using a background color instead of a background image. This will decrease download time, sometimes significantly.

# Bringing in Those Images

Okay, now that you know a little bit about graphic formats and color management, it's time to find out how to get images on your pages. You do this in the Editor, by choosing the Image command from the Insert menu. Just follow these steps:

1. In the Editor, place the cursor where you want the image to appear.

2. Choose Image from the Insert menu. You'll see the Image dialog box.

3. You can select an image from one of three sources, listed below. When you select the image, FrontPage inserts it on your page with the cursor blinking after it.

**SHORTCUT**

You can insert an image by clicking the Insert Image toolbar button.

**Current FrontPage Web** This tab lists images that have been imported into the site. You can browse your folders to find the image you want. Sites created with FrontPage 1.1 store images in the folder titled Images, but FrontPage 97 sites can store images anywhere in the site.

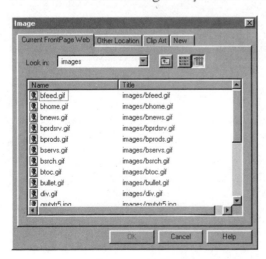

Each image is listed by its name for the currently selected folder. To insert an image from the current site,
select it from the list and then click OK.

**Other Location**  The Other Location tab offers two
choices. Select the From File option if the image you
want to insert resides on a floppy disk, a hard drive,
or a network. If you know the path and filename of the
image, you can type it in the text box, or you can use
the Browse button to locate the image. FrontPage gives
you the option to save the image with your Web site
when you save the page. Select the From Location
option if the image is in a different site on your Web
server or in a site on the World Wide Web. Type in the
**absolute URL** for the image, and then click OK.

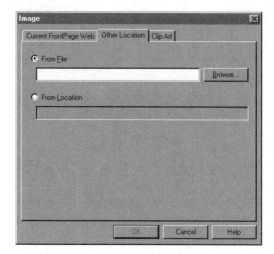

**Clip Art**  On the Clip Art tab, select the category you
want to view from the drop-down list. When you find
an image you want, click on the image in the contents
window and then click OK. The clip art included with
FrontPage is located in a folder that is shared with the
other Office applications you have installed.

FrontPage includes many categories of clip art. For example, the Animated category contains animated GIFs,
which are groups of images that display consecutively
in the same location, creating the appearance of mo-
tion. The Background category contains images you

can use as background tiles on your pages. Many people don't notice the Logos category because it is normally off-screen at the bottom of the Category list. Images in this category allow you to insert logos such as the "Site Created with Microsoft FrontPage" logo, the Microsoft Internet Explorer logo, and so on.

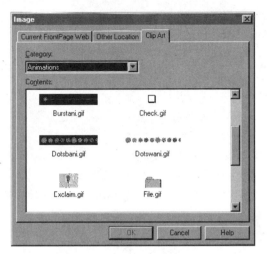

# The Images Are In—Now What?

After you insert an image, FrontPage gives you many ways to manipulate it using the Image Properties dialog box. Here you'll find useful information about your image, such as its type, dimensions, and much more.

## Changing Image Properties

If you want to alter an image and the way it appears on a page, you can manipulate that information to your heart's content. To change any of the image properties, here's what to do:

1. Select an image in the Editor by clicking on it.

2. Choose Image Properties from the Edit menu. You'll see the Image Properties dialog box, which has three tabs: General, Video, and Appearance.

3. Adjust the settings as necessary. When you finish adjusting the settings, click OK. Remember that the settings are not permanent; you can always return to the Image Properties dialog box to change them. The following is a detailed look at the settings in the dialog box, starting with the General tab.

**SHORTCUT**

You can right-click on an image and choose Image Properties from the pop-up menu to reach the Image Properties dialog box. With an image selected, you can reach the Image Properties dialog box quickly by pressing Alt+Enter.

Your options on the General tab are as follows:

**Image Source** This text box displays the image's **page URL** if the image is in the current Web site, its **absolute URL** if the image is from the World Wide Web, or its path and filename if the image is in a file. If you want to change the image, click the Browse button, which brings up the Image dialog box, as described above. If you want to open the image to work on it in your image editor, click the Edit button.

**Type** This section displays the graphic format of the selected image, either GIF or JPEG. The selected option is the image's current format. By selecting the other option, you can convert the image to that format.

When the GIF option is selected, you have two options for presenting the image: Transparent and Interlaced. You can use one or use both at the same time.

*Transparent*—Available only for GIF images, this check box is selected if a color in the image is currently specified as transparent. Deselect the check box to return the transparent portions of the image back to their normal color and make the image nontransparent. Later in this chapter, you'll find out how to make a color transparent (which automatically selects this option).

*Interlaced*—If the Interlaced check box is selected, the image will progressively render in the browser. A progressively rendered image slowly comes into focus as it downloads into a browser.

If the JPEG option is selected, the Quality text box becomes available.

*Quality*—You can adjust the image quality by entering a number between 1 and 100. A higher number means less compression, resulting in a better quality image, but it also means a larger image and slower performance. (Larger files take longer for the browser to download and display.) A lower number means more compression, resulting in a lower image quality but smaller file size. By default, the Quality setting is 75.

**Alternative Representations** Not all browsers support images, and most browsers can be set to disable images. Some browsers can display a low-resolution image in place of a high-resolution image while downloading the high-resolution image from the server. For all these cases, you can supply an alternative representation for the image.

*Low-Res*—Specifies a lower-resolution image to display in place of a higher-resolution image while the latter is downloading. Click the Browse button, and in the Insert Image dialog box that appears, select the image and then click OK. For you HTML buffs, this alternative image is the same as the LOWSRC attribute.

> **TIP**
>
> Neither FrontPage nor the browser checks that the low-res image is actually a low-res version of the real image, but an easy way to create a low-res image is to use Image Composer to create a grayscale version of the image, with very few colors.

*Text*—Specifies alternative text that will appear instead of the image if the user's browser cannot display images or is set to disable the displaying of images. This is useful if you anticipate that some users will view your site without its graphics. (Actually, it's a good idea to do this for all of your images.) In some browsers, this text will appear while the image is loading.

**Default Hyperlink** You can turn part or all of your image into a **hotspot** that links to other locations. (See the section titled "Creating Image Maps" later in this chapter to learn how.) If an image has multiple hotspots, you can set a default link for the parts of the image that are not covered by a hotspot.

*To set a default link:* Click the Browse button, and you'll see the Create Hyperlink dialog box. For your link, you can select from a list of currently open pages in the Editor; pages or files in the current Web site; pages or files from World Wide Web, Gopher, Newsgroup, or FTP sites; or a new page. Set your link, and then click OK to return to the Image Properties dialog box.

*To change a default link:* If the image already has a default link, when you click the Browse button you'll see the Edit Hyperlink dialog box. You can change the link in the same way that you set it—by selecting from among currently open pages in the Editor; pages or files in the current Web site; pages or files from World Wide Web, Gopher, Newsgroup, or FTP sites; or a new page. Edit the link, and then click OK to return to the Image Properties dialog box.

You can also specify a target frame for the default link in the Target Frame text box. For more information on links, see Chapter 7.

Use the Extended button to attach to the image any HTML **extended attributes** that are not directly supported in FrontPage.

The second tab of the Image Properties dialog box, Video, lets you insert an AVI (Audio Video) file onto your page. The image file you designated on the General tab is used as a placeholder that is displayed until the AVI is loaded and ready to run. Adding a video to your page using the Video command on the Insert menu is slightly different. For more information on using the Video command, see Chapter 7.

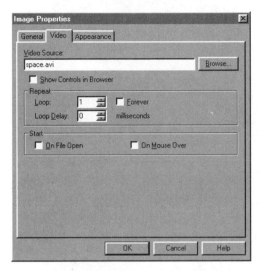

**Video Source** You can type in the path and filename to your video in the Video Source text box, or use the Browse button to locate the video file.

**Show Controls in Browser** Selecting this check box will show a set of controls: Play, Stop, and a slider, along with the video when it's displayed in the browser at run time.

**Repeat** This section lets you set how often and when the video will play.

*Loop*—Enter a number for the amount of times you want the video to play.

*Loop Delay*—Entering a number will delay the playing of the video between each playing. The delay is specified in milliseconds.

*Forever*—Select this check box if you want the video to loop indefinitely while the page is displayed.

**Start** This section lets you determine when the video will be played.

*On File Open*—Selecting this check box tells the video to play as soon as it's downloaded in the browser.

*On Mouse Over*—Select this check box if you want the video to play when the user positions the mouse pointer over the image.

The third tab of the Image Properties dialog box, Appearance, lets you manipulate the appearance of your image in a number of ways:

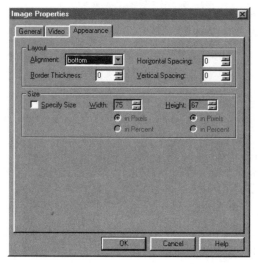

**Layout** In the Layout section, you control the position of the image on the page.

*Alignment*—Specifies a type of alignment between the image and the text around it. You can align the image in several ways.

*Bottom:* Aligns the text with the bottom of the image, so that the text begins at the bottom of the image.

*Middle:* Aligns the text with the middle of the image.

*Top:* Aligns the text with the top of the image.

*Absbottom:* Aligns the image with the bottom of the current line.

*Absmiddle:* Aligns the image with the middle of the current line.

*Texttop:* Aligns the top of the image with the top of the tallest text in the line.

*Baseline:* Aligns the image with the baseline of the current line.

*Left:* Places the image in the left margin and wraps the text preceding the image down the right side of the image.

*Right:* Places the image in the right margin and wraps the text preceding the image down the left side of the image.

These settings apply only to images that appear on the same line as text. If an image is the only element on a line, the setting will default to Bottom.

*Border Thickness*—Specifies a black border around the image; the width of the border is expressed in pixels. To change the width, select the number in the text box and type in the new number.

*Horizontal Spacing*—Sets a specified horizontal spacing in pixels from the image to the nearest image or text on the current line, on both sides of the image.

*Vertical Spacing*—Sets a specified vertical spacing in pixels from the image to the nearest image or text on the line above and/or below it.

**Size** This section displays the height and width of the image in pixels. Select the Specify Size check box to change the Width and Height of your image. Sizes are measured either in pixels or as a percentage.

**TIP**

You can also position the image on the left side, center, or right side of a page by using one of the alignment toolbar buttons in the Editor. The image alignment is **WYSIWYG** in the Editor, so you can see how the image will look from within a browser.

**SHORTCUT**

You can resize an image by selecting it and then dragging the sides or corners of the image. If you drag from the corners, the image is resized proportionally.

By specifying an image's width and height, you change only the image's HTML attributes, not the image itself. This allows you to have a single image in multiple sizes in your Web site—all referencing the same image file. By not having to replicate that image file in multiple sizes, you save disk space and decrease download time because multiple versions of the image don't have to be downloaded.

# Cool Stuff You Can Do to an Image

Once an image is on your page, you can do many cool things with it beyond setting or changing its properties. For example, with FrontPage you can create an **image map** from a **GIF** or **JPEG** image, allowing you to specify one or more portions of the image as a **hotspot** that links to other locations.

## Client-Side Image Maps

FrontPage makes use of client-side image maps. Traditionally, for an image map link to work, the **client** (e.g., a **browser**) would have to communicate with the server to figure out where the link goes to when the user clicks on a hotspot. However, with client-side image maps, the link destination information is stored at the client end, so the image map is no longer server dependent. This results in less communication between the client and the server, taking pressure off the server and reducing the time it takes to determine the link destination when a user clicks on a hotspot.

You set the image map style in your Web site via the Web Settings command on the Tools menu in the Explorer; this command is explained in Chapter 3. By default, FrontPage generates both client-side and server-side image maps, so that any browser can use the image maps on the page. The server-side image maps take advantage of the **FrontPage Server Extensions**. If you don't have the FrontPage Server Extensions installed, you can select a different server-side standard for image maps (NCSA, CERN, or Netscape standard) on the Advanced tab of the FrontPage Web Settings dialog box.

## Creating Image Maps

To create an image map, you use the Image toolbar.

**The Image toolbar contains six buttons. From left to right, they are the Select, Rectangle, Circle, Polygon, Highlight Hotspots, and Make Transparent buttons.**

If you don't see the image toolbar in the Editor, choose Image Toolbar from the View menu. Likewise, to hide the toolbar, choose the same command. The toolbar floats, which means you can move it anywhere you want on your screen, even outside the Editor. To move the toolbar, click inside the toolbar in an area not occupied by a button and drag the toolbar to its destination. You can dock the toolbar by dragging it and dropping it anywhere in the toolbar region of the Editor.

You can turn part or all of an image into a hotspot that links to other locations. For example, if you own a toy store and advertise your products on the Web, why not use an image of a teddy bear as a link to the section highlighting your stuffed animals? Or, in an intranet site, you can use an image of a dollar bill as a link to the Sales section.

You can create an image map in FrontPage in a matter of seconds. Here's how:

1. Select the image that you'll be creating the hotspot on. Notice that the Image toolbar becomes active and the Select button is depressed.

2. Decide which areas of the image you want "hot." For example, on an image of a house you might want the user to be able to click on the door and jump to an image of the foyer. If possible, make sure that the entire portion of the image you want to work with is visible on the screen.

3. Click the Rectangle, Circle, or Polygon toolbar button, depending on the area you want to define as a hotspot.

The Rectangle and Circle buttons create rectangular and circular hotspots, respectively, and the Polygon button allows you to create a hotspot of any shape. When one of these buttons is depressed, the cursor changes to a pencil when it's over an image, indicating that you're ready to draw the hotspot.

4. Carefully draw the hotspot around the portion of the image that you want to be clickable. Here's a rundown of how:

   *Rectangular and circular hotspots:* Position the cursor near where you want the hotspot to appear. Click and drag the cursor to draw and size the hotspot.

   *Polygonal hotspots:* Position the cursor where you want to begin drawing the hotspot. Click once to insert the first point of the polygon. Move the mouse and click again to draw the first side of the polygon. Continue drawing sides until your hotspot is complete; it's complete when you connect to the original point where you first clicked.

   Once the hotspot is drawn, you can always move and resize it if it's not quite what you wanted. See the next section for more information.

5. After you draw the hotspot, the Create Hyperlink dialog box appears. This is where you set the target link for your hotspot. You can link to currently open pages in the Editor; pages or files in the current Web site; pages or files from World Wide Web, Gopher, Newsgroup, or FTP sites; or a new page. If you add a link to a page that doesn't exist yet, you can select the option to add the task of creating the page to the To Do List. Set the link, and then click OK. For more information on creating links, see Chapter 7.

## Moving and Resizing Hotspots

Once you draw a hotspot on an image, you have complete control over its size and location. You can click and drag it to anywhere on the image, or use the arrow keys to move it and adjust

its location. To resize a hotspot, select it and then click and drag a size
handle (one of the small squares at
the corners of the hotspot). To return
a hotspot to its original position,
press the Esc key; this is similar to an
Undo command. You must use the
Esc key *before* you release the mouse
button.

**T I P**

If you resize an image
that already has hotspots
defined on it, the hot-
spots are not also sized.
You have to size the
hotspots individually.

## Editing a Hotspot Link

To change the target link of a hotspot, double-click the hotspot to
bring up the Edit Hyperlink dialog
box. You can also right-click on a
selected hotspot and choose Image
Hotspot Properties from the pop-up
menu to display the Edit Hyperlink
dialog box. Another way is to select

**T I P**

You can press the Tab
key to jump between
hotspots on an image;
you can press Shift+Tab
to select the previous
hotspot.

the hotspot and click the Create Or Edit Hyperlink toolbar button. Change the target link, and then click OK.

## Highlighting Hotspots

Sometimes it's difficult to see all the hotspots you've created,
especially on a complex image. Click the Highlight Hotspot
toolbar button to see all the hotspots on a selected image. The
image is removed and replaced with a white background, and
only the borders of the hotspots are shown. The toolbar button
toggles between the two views.

## Transparent Colors

Okay, so you've been on the edge of your seat, waiting patiently
to find out how transparency works. The truth is, it doesn't take
Houdini to make a color disappear in an image—it's very easy.
You use the Make Transparent button, which is the last button
on the Image toolbar. This enables you to make one color in a
selected GIF image transparent, allowing the background to

show through. Unfortunately, because of a limitation in the JPEG format itself, JPEG images cannot be made transparent.

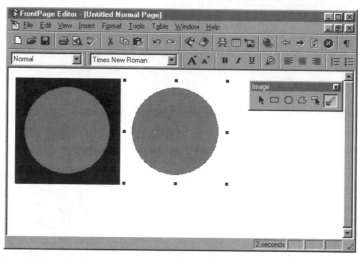

**An image before and after using the Make Transparent option. The dark area around the circle has been made transparent, letting the background show through.**

Here's how to make a color transparent:

1. Select an image to activate the Image toolbar.

2. Click the Make Transparent button. Once you click this button and move the mouse pointer over the image, the pointer changes to the Make Transparent pointer.

3. On the image, click on the color you want to make transparent.

4. *Voila*—every part of the GIF that contained that color is now transparent, and the background of the page shows through the image.

## WARNING

If the image you're making transparent is in JPEG format, FrontPage displays a warning dialog box telling you that the image must be converted and asking if you really want to convert it. If you click Yes, the image is automatically converted to a GIF.

Only one color at a time can be transparent in a GIF image. If you select a new transparent color on an image that already has one transparent color set, the first transparent color reverts to its original color.

GIFs are used for transparency because they contain fewer colors and more solid areas to make transparent. Because JPEG images can contain a wide tonal range, using transparency on a JPEG image would be similar to poking holes sporadically through a photograph with a pin. The image would be transparent only where the holes appear.

> **T I P**
>
> Many graphics packages try to use dithering in a GIF image to give it a more high-resolution appearance. The problem with dithering is that it actually uses many similar colors instead of a single color, which prevents transparency of a single color from working the way you would expect. When creating images that you want to make transparent, make sure that the background of the image is a single, solid color.

## Coming Up

The next chapter details FrontPage's powerful WebBot components and forms, which let you add numerous types of functionality to your Web sites.

# Chapter 9
# WebBot Components and Forms

## We All Need a Break

Traditional hunters and gatherers knew how to make the most of their time—they conserved their energy by optimizing their food gathering, tool making, and other tasks. They also knew how important it was to rest; many hunting and gathering cultures worked fewer hours than we do today, and they allocated more time for leisure activities.

FrontPage lets you live a life like that again. You'll save so much time by using FrontPage's **WebBot components** and **forms** to create your Web sites that you'll be able to live in a cave and gather roots for dinner if you want to. It might be a little rough, though—there won't be an outlet to plug your television and food processor into, so you won't be able to watch *Melrose Place* and *Seinfeld* while you're chopping up those roots. Think you can handle it?

## What Are WebBot Components?

FrontPage's WebBot components are drop-in programs that add functionality to a Web site. For instance, you can add a WebBot Search Component to a page with a few clicks of the mouse, and instantly your page has a full-text search engine for your users. Using the traditional way, a Web-site developer would have to do the following:

1. Create an **HTML** form that initiates the search.

2. Install a third-party full-text search engine on the Web server.

3. Write a **CGI** program on the Web server that connects the HTML form to the full-text search engine.

With WebBot components, you can forget all of this—there's no more need for complicated HTML and/or CGI programming to create sophisticated, interactive Web sites. Keep in mind that in order for WebBot components to work properly, the server hosting the site must have the FrontPage Server Extensions installed. These extensions are automatically installed with the Microsoft Personal Web Server and the FrontPage Personal Web Server, but must be manually installed with other Web servers. For more information on the Personal Web Servers and the FrontPage Server Extensions, consult Chapter 11.

You add WebBot components to a page by using the WebBot Component command on the Insert menu in the Editor. When you insert a WebBot component, you'll see one or more dialog boxes that let you configure it, and then the component is inserted on the page where your cursor was positioned. Some WebBot components are associated with **forms**, which are described later in this chapter.

The following sections provide a brief look at what you can do with WebBot components.

## Implementing Search Functionality

To give your users the ability to look for matching words or phrases in the text of a site's pages or in the text of all the messages in a discussion group, you can insert a WebBot Search Component on your page. The Search Component can be configured to check every word used within the site for a match. (This feature is called *full-text searching*.)

**Adding a WebBot Search Component** The WebBot Search Component creates a form that allows users to enter one or more words to locate in the site:

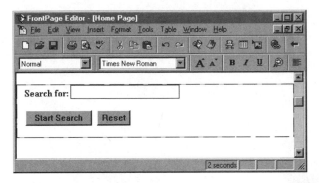

FrontPage doesn't actually have to examine each page of the site; instead, it searches a list of words that's maintained by the FrontPage Server Extensions. FrontPage returns a list of pages that contain the word or words the user is searching for. To add the ability to search for matching words or phrases in your site, do the following:

1. In the Editor, position your cursor at the place on your page where you want the upper left corner of the search form (the label, text box, and buttons created by the WebBot Search Component) to appear.

2. From the Insert menu, choose WebBot Component. Then select Search in the Insert WebBot Component dialog box, and click OK. You'll see the WebBot Search Component Properties dialog box, as shown on the next page.

**TIP**

If you want to exclude certain pages from a search, you can save them directly in the _private folder under the folder for your site on the Web server. (FrontPage typically does not search a folder with a name that starts with an underscore.) If you save the page to a different location and then move it to the _private folder with the Explorer, it is recommended that you use Explorer's Recalculate Hyperlinks command to update the search index.

**SHORTCUT**

You can insert a WebBot component by clicking the Insert WebBot Component toolbar button.

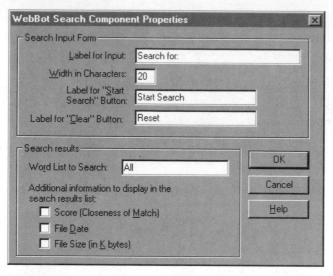

3. In the Label For Input text box, enter the text you want to use for the label of the text box. The default is *Search for:*.

4. In the Width In Characters text box, enter the width in characters of the input field.

5. In the Label For "Start Search" Button text box, type the text that will appear on the button that starts the search.

6. In the Label For "Clear" Button text box, type the text that will appear on the button that clears the search.

7. In the Word List To Search text box, enter *All* if the search is intended for an entire Web site. If you created a discussion group using the Discussion Web Wizard, you can enter the name of a discussion group folder. This restricts the search to only entries in the discussion group.

8. You can also select check boxes to display the following information in the search results list:

   *Score*—This indicates the quality of the match, or how closely the results match what you searched for.

   *File Date*—This indicates the date and time the document containing the match was most recently modified.

*File Size*—This indicates the size of the document containing the match, in kilobytes. This can be especially useful for users on slow dial-up connections, who can see how large a document is before they download it.

9. When you finish entering the information in the Web-Bot Search Component Properties dialog box, click OK. FrontPage inserts the search form on your page in the Editor.

The following graphic shows an example of a WebBot Search Component being used on a Web page, as well as an example of the search results.

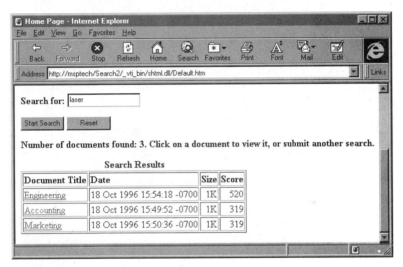

**Limitations of the WebBot Search Component** One limitation of the Search WebBot Component concerns the updating of the search index. Suppose a page called test.htm has the word *Fred* on it when you save it to your Web site. The index maintained by the Search Component will record the fact that test.htm has *Fred* on it. However, suppose that you delete the word *Fred* from test.htm. The search index does not get updated automatically, so it will still show that *Fred* is on test.htm. Thus, if someone were to use the Search Component to search for *Fred*, they would get a false hit for test.htm. The way to fix this problem, and to update your search index so it has the correct information, is to use the Recalculate Hyperlinks command on the Tools menu in the Explorer. For more information on this command, see Chapter 3.

# Creating a Timestamp

To insert a timestamp, which denotes the date and time the page was last edited or automatically updated, you use the WebBot Timestamp Component.

**Adding a WebBot Timestamp Component** To insert a time-stamp on your page, do the following:

1. In the Editor, position your cursor at the place on your page where you want the timestamp to appear. Often, the WebBot component is placed following a phrase such as *This page was last modified.*

2. From the Insert menu, choose WebBot Component, or click the Insert WebBot Component toolbar button. Then select Timestamp in the Insert WebBot Component dialog box, and click OK. You'll see the WebBot Timestamp Component Properties dialog box:

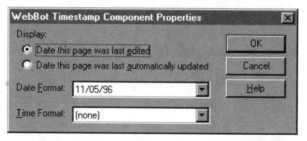

3. In the Display section, select the option for the date you want to display: the date the page was last edited or the date the page was last automatically updated. There's a slight difference in meaning between "edited" and "updated": A page is considered to be edited when it is changed and saved to the Web server. A page is considered to be updated when it is changed and saved to the Web server or when an included page is changed. You can include pages on other pages using the WebBot Include Component, which is discussed later in this chapter.

4. From the drop-down lists, select a format for the date and time that you want displayed by the timestamp.

The time format options containing the letters *TZ* indicate Time Zone. If you don't want to include either the date or the time, select None from the respective drop-down list.

5. When you finish entering your information in the WebBot Timestamp Component Properties dialog box, click OK. The timestamp is inserted on your page. You can then format the text used for the timestamp information using the standard tools within the Editor.

The following graphic shows an example of the WebBot Timestamp Component in the Editor.

## Including a Table of Contents

You can use the WebBot Table Of Contents Component to create an outline for your Web site, with links to each page. You can direct the component to update the outline each time pages are added, deleted, or edited.

**Adding a WebBot Table Of Contents Component** To insert a table of contents (TOC) on your page, you can do the following:

1. In the Editor, position your cursor at the place on your page where you want the TOC to appear.

2. From the Insert menu, choose WebBot Component. Then select Table Of Contents in the Insert WebBot Component dialog box, and click OK. You'll see the WebBot Table Of Contents Component Properties dialog box.

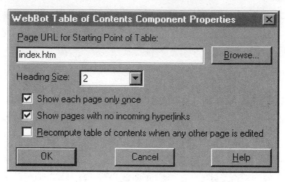

3. Enter the **page URL** of the page you want the TOC to begin with. The TOC will include all pages that have links that originate from the page you select. Specify the **home page** of your Web site if you want a full TOC. If you have a site open in the FrontPage Explorer, you can click the Browse button to see a list of pages in the site. If you do so, select a page in the Current Web dialog box, and then click OK.

4. From the Heading Size drop-down list, select a heading size for the first entry in your TOC. You can select a number from 1 (the largest size) to 6 (the smallest size), or select None if you want to use the default size.

5. You can select check boxes to have FrontPage do the following:

   **Show each page only once** Select this check box to allow each page to appear in the TOC only once. If a page in your site has multiple links that can be traced back to your starting page, it can appear more than once unless you check this option.

   **Show pages with no incoming hyperlinks** Select this check box to include orphan pages in your TOC. (These are pages that do not have any incoming links from other pages in the site.)

   **Recompute table of contents when any other page is edited** Select this check box to automatically recreate the TOC whenever pages are added, deleted, or edited in your site. If your site is large and if pages are edited often, having this option selected can slow down your work—for example, when saving. An alternative is to manually recreate the TOC by opening and saving the page containing the WebBot Table Of Contents Component.

6. When you finish entering your information in the dialog box, click OK. Your TOC appears on the page in the Editor. You cannot format the individual entries in the TOC, and the changes you can make to the formatting of the group of entries are limited. For example, you can't change the font style.

The following graphic shows the WebBot Table Of Contents Component as it appears in the Editor:

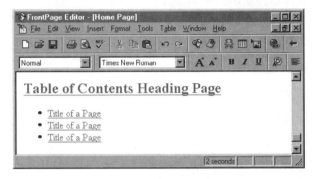

## Presenting One Page on Another Page

With the WebBot Include Component, you can present the entire contents of a page wherever you want on another page. The page you insert must be a page from the current Web site. The Include Component differs from the Scheduled Include Component (discussed later in this chapter) in that it presents a page on another page *at all times,* and not just at specified times.

Suppose you have a "Site in Summary" section in your company's Web site, which presents the most important pages in the site in one place, such as pages for urgent news and company information that your sales force needs to know. This kind of section might be good to include for those viewers who are "on the go" and who only need to see certain pages of your site. Plenty of business people don't even have the time to look at specific pages of your site one by one—if they're scanning the site for information in addition to their other daily tasks, you can understand how their time is limited. Your "Site in Summary" section can be a one-page section, in which you use several WebBot Include Components, one for each page you want to pull in from the rest of your site. The included pages can be presented in full, one after another, and all of the content will be scrollable as a single page.

WebBot Include Components are often used for including small pages, such as a page containing only a navigation bar. This is a great way to present a navigation bar throughout your site because you can create it once and use a WebBot Include Component to present it wherever you want in your site. Then, if you need to modify the navigation bar or change its links, you only have to change it in one location and it will automatically be updated throughout your site.

**Adding a WebBot Include Component** To insert the contents of a page on another page, do the following:

1. In the Editor, position your cursor at the place on the current page where you want the inserted page to appear.

2. From the Insert menu, choose WebBot Component. Then select Include in the Insert WebBot Component dialog box, and click OK. You'll see the WebBot Include Component Properties dialog box.

3. In the Page URL To Include text box, enter the page URL of the page you want to have appear. You can click the Browse button to see a list of pages in your site; if you do so, select a page and click OK.

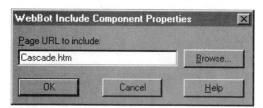

4. After you enter the page URL, click OK. The contents of that page are inserted on your page in the Editor.

The following graphic shows an example of another page included on the current page using a WebBot Include Component:

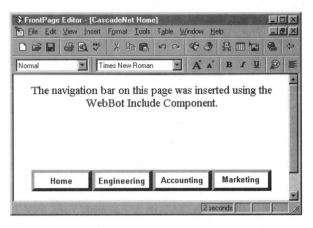

## Making Images Appear at a Certain Time

You can use the WebBot Scheduled Image Component to make an image available to users during a specified time period. The image is displayed on a page when the time period begins, and it's removed when the time has expired.

For example, suppose your human resources department is trying to increase employee enrollment in the company's 401K plan, and it's running a seven-day special sign-up event on its intranet pages. The pages will feature different "catchy" images each day. To avoid having to update the images manually every day, you can insert several Scheduled Image Components to make those images appear automatically when you want them to.

**Adding a WebBot Scheduled Image Component** To make an image appear during a specified time period, take the following steps.

**TIP**

To be certain that a Scheduled Image Component works on the day that the image is scheduled to appear or disappear, either make a change to your site or use the Recalculate Hyperlinks command in the Explorer on the same day to "refresh" the links and other information on the pages. These actions act as a reminder to FrontPage to update the information related to the WebBot components.

1. In the Editor, position your cursor at the place on your page where you want the image to appear.

2. From the Insert menu, choose WebBot Component. Then select Scheduled Image in the Insert WebBot Component dialog box, and click OK. You'll see the WebBot Scheduled Image Component Properties dialog box.

3. In the Image To Include text box, enter the name of the image you want to have appear. You can click the Browse button to see a list of images available in the currently open site in the Explorer; if you do so, select an image and then click OK.

4. Enter the starting date and time and the ending date and time for the period that you want the image to appear.

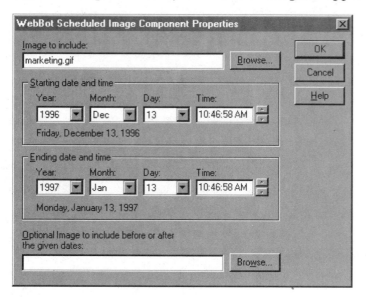

5. You can also specify a "placeholder" image that will appear in the same location before and after the scheduled image appears. If you want to do so, type the name of the image in the text box near the bottom of the dialog box, or click Browse to see a list of images available in the current site. This placeholder image will fill up the space when the scheduled image does not appear.

6. When you finish entering your information in the WebBot Scheduled Image Component Properties dialog box, click OK.

If you're within the time period you specified for the image to appear, the image will appear on the page. If you specified the image to appear at a future time (a more likely scenario) and did not specify a placeholder image, the words *Expired Scheduled Image* will appear in the WebBot component on the screen in the Editor (but not in a browser). If you see these words, don't worry—the image will appear at its scheduled time. If you specified a placeholder image to appear when the scheduled image does not appear, that image will appear in the Editor and in the browser when the scheduled image does not appear.

## Making Content Appear at a Certain Time

You can use the WebBot Scheduled Include Component to make specific content available to users in the same way that the Scheduled Image Component works with images. In fact, using the same 401K scenario discussed in the previous section, you can make an entire page of 401K information appear at a certain time. The Scheduled Include Component inserts an entire page at a time.

Like the Scheduled Image Component, the Scheduled Include Component works only if a change is made to the site or the Recalculate Hyperlinks command is executed on the day the content is scheduled to appear. For more information, see the tip on page 253.

**Adding a WebBot Scheduled Include Component** To make the contents of a page appear during a specified time period, do the following:

1. In the Editor, position your cursor at the place on your page where you want the content to appear.

2. From the Insert menu, choose WebBot Component. Then select Scheduled Include in the Insert WebBot Component dialog box, and click OK. You'll see the WebBot Scheduled Include Component Properties dialog box.

3. In the Page URL To Include text box, enter the page URL of the page you want to have appear. You can

click the Browse button to see a list of pages in your site; if you do so, select one and click OK.

4. Enter the starting date and time and the ending date and time for the period that you want the page to appear.

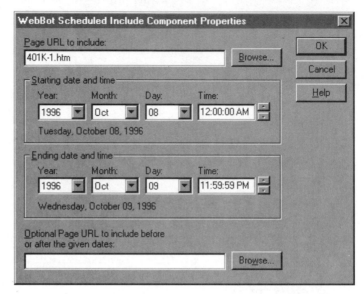

5. To present the contents of another page in the same location before and after the scheduled page appears, type the name of the page in the text box at the bottom of the dialog box, or click Browse to see a list of pages currently available in your site. You can specify that a simple placeholder page appear at these times, which fills up the space when the scheduled page does not appear.

6. When you finish entering your information in the WebBot Scheduled Include Component Properties dialog box, click OK.

The following graphic shows an example of a WebBot Scheduled Include Component being used in the Editor..

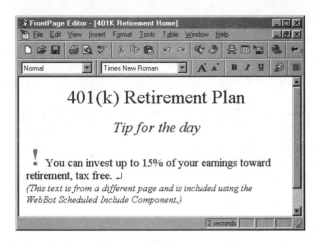

*(This text is from a different page and is included using the WebBot Scheduled Include Component.)*

# Confirming User-Entered Information

When you are using your site to collect information from users, you want to do everything you can to make sure that the information they provide is correct. In particular, you should give them an opportunity to review the text that they've submitted. Not only does this give them an opportunity to discover any typing errors, but it emphasizes that the information they provide is important. Maybe they'll read it a second time to make sure it really says what they want it to say.

If you've seen Web pages or other forums where information that you've entered is presented to you later for your confirmation, you've seen an example of this process. If you find that some of the information is incorrect, you can usually go back to the original page, change it, and resubmit it, and if all the information is correct, you can click a button to say so. The WebBot Confirmation

> ## TIP
>
> In FrontPage you can specify validation rules for a form field. For example, you can specify that numbers be within a certain range, or that a text field contain only certain characters. FrontPage automatically generates the JavaScript or VBScript directly onto the page so that the browser will enforce those validation rules. For more information on validation rules, see the section titled "Validating Form Fields" later in this chapter.

Field Component manages this process of presenting the information back to the viewer. (For more information on confirmation pages, see the section titled "Creating a Confirmation Page" later in this chapter.)

The Confirmation Field Component presents the contents of one form field—a single item such as name, age, or occupation—on a form **confirmation page**. (We'll discuss **forms** and **form fields** later in this chapter.) Each form field requires a separate Confirmation Field Component, but several such components can be combined on a single page. So if a user has entered lots of information in different form fields, you can use a page of Confirmation Field Components to replicate that information in one place for the user to confirm.

> ### T I P
>
> Confirmation Field Components are case sensitive. That means that *FirstName* is not the same as *firstname*.

**Adding a WebBot Confirmation Field Component** To present the contents of one form field on a confirmation page, do the following:

1. In the Editor, position your cursor at the place on the confirmation page where you want the WebBot Confirmation Field Component to appear.

2. From the Insert menu, choose WebBot Component. Then select Confirmation Field in the Insert WebBot Component dialog box, and click OK. You'll see the WebBot Confirmation Field Component Properties dialog box.

3. Enter the name of the form field whose contents you want to confirm.

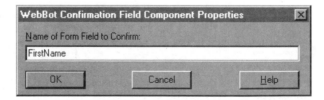

When you click OK, the Confirmation Field Component appears in the Editor as a set of brackets surrounding the name of the field you just typed in. In a browser, the field's contents are shown to the user in place of the Confirmation Field Component. It's a good idea to provide appropriate text on the page to make sure users know what information is being shown back to them.

## Inserting a Configuration Variable

You can insert the contents of a **configuration variable** (also called a *parameter*) on a page by using the WebBot Substitution Component. This is useful for many purposes, such as for noting who created or modified a page, or the page's URL. The Substitution Component can also be used to present text strings that you might want to modify later, such as a company's fax number.

**Adding a WebBot Substitution Component** Here's how to insert the value of a configuration variable on a page.

1. In the Editor, place your cursor on the page where you want to insert the WebBot Substitution Component.

2. From the Insert menu, choose WebBot Component. Then select Substitution in the Insert WebBot Component dialog box, and click OK. You'll see the WebBot Substitution Component Properties dialog box.

3. From the drop-down list, select a configuration variable. If you've added parameters to your site, they will appear in this drop-down list.

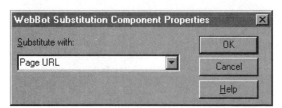

When you click OK, the WebBot Substitution Component appears on the page in the Editor, filled in with the value of the configuration variable.

**This use of the WebBot Substitution Component automatically substitutes the current page's URL where the component is inserted. The page URL will appear in the browser. The author typed** *Current page:* **on the page.**

For more information on adding configuration variables and setting their values, see Chapter 3.

## Editing a WebBot Component's Properties

If you want to modify a WebBot component's properties, you don't have to replace the entire component—you can change its properties instead. To edit a WebBot component's properties, simply right-click on the component (when you move your cursor over the component, the WebBot cursor will appear), and choose WebBot Component Properties from the pop-up menu. The Properties dialog box for the WebBot component appears; you can make your changes here. When you finish, click OK to exit the dialog box and return to your page in the Editor.

# Creating and Using Forms

A **form** is a collection of text and **form fields** that allows users to enter information. FrontPage form fields include one-line text boxes, scrolling text boxes, check boxes, option buttons (called *radio buttons* in FrontPage), and drop-down menus. In addition, you can add command buttons (known as *push buttons* in FrontPage) to your form to perform actions. The following graphic shows an example of the form fields in the Editor.

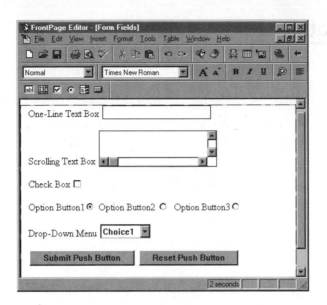

You use a combination of these form fields to collect the information you want from the user. For instance, in an intranet setting, forms can be used to gather and store employee identification information. Or perhaps you want to find out what users think of your Web site or the products showcased in your site. Users provide answers to your questions in the form fields.

You create a form whenever you add a form field to a page. Some templates (such as the User Registration, Feedback Form, and Survey Form templates) and some wizards (such as the Discussion Web Wizard) create pages that already contain forms.

Forms use applications called *handlers* on Web servers that take the data from the form fields and process it. The handler can also respond to the user when it receives the input, by presenting a confirmation page so that the user can confirm the information he or she submitted. So, in a sense, the handler is a go-between for the form and the Web server. A handler can be a WebBot Save Results Component; WebBot Discussion Component; WebBot Registration Component; custom ISAPI DLL, NSAPI module, or **CGI** script; or Internet Database Connector. (These handlers are discussed in the section titled "Assigning a Form Handler" later in this chapter.)

# Creating a Data-Collection Form

Once you know how to create a form, the process will seem fairly simple, but learning it can be a little tricky. We'll step through the process by modifying two pages created using FrontPage's Feedback Form and Confirmation Page templates. The templates already contain working examples of forms and confirmation pages; we'll create more examples on these pages so you can learn how to build them yourself.

Let's get going with some preliminaries:

**Creating a Feedback Form page**  We'll begin by creating a Feedback Form page in the Editor.

1. Choose New from the File menu, select Feedback Form from the list of templates and wizards in the New Page dialog box that appears, and click OK.

2. When the page appears in the Editor, save it with the title *Feedback Form* and give it the name within the current site, *feedback.htm*. We'll refer to this page from now on as the Feedback Form.

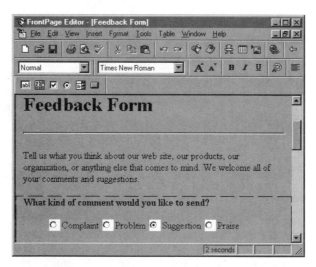

The Feedback Form includes several fields. In fact, it includes at least one of each of the five field types, plus two command buttons (push buttons):

**Option button** The buttons on the page under the line "What kind of comment would you like to send?" are option buttons (radio buttons). These buttons act as a group; you'll find out more about their group functions shortly. Each of the buttons was added to the form separately, and the text for each was typed next to that button. You use option buttons when you want the user to be able to select a single option from a group of options. (You can also use a drop-down menu for this purpose.)

**Drop-down list** The field below the line "What about us do you want to comment on?" is a drop-down list. You can customize the list choices when you modify the field properties. A drop-down list allows the user to select one or more items (which is why these form fields are often called drop-down menus).

**One-line text box** The text box next to the drop-down list is a one-line text box. Users can type text in this box. You set the width of this box as part of its properties.

**Scrolling text box** The large box under the line "Enter your comments in the space provided below:" is a scrolling text box. This type of text box allows users to type lengthy comments.

**Check box** The box near the bottom of the page next to the line "Please contact me as soon as possible regarding this matter" is a check box. When a user clicks a check box, a check mark appears in it. Use check boxes to offer the user a Yes/No choice.

**Command button** The two buttons at the bottom of the Feedback Form labeled *Submit Comments* and *Clear Form* are command buttons (push buttons). A user clicks these buttons to perform either of these tasks.

Now we'll replicate some of these fields and the buttons directly below them on the Feedback Form, to show you how to create them.

**Creating an option button group** Let's create a group of two option buttons that resembles the group of four on the Feedback Form.

1. Position your cursor following the option button labeled *Praise* below the line "What kind of comment would you like to send?" (The cursor should be blinking beside the *e* in *Praise*.) Hold down the Shift key and press Enter.

2. With the cursor on the blank line you just created, just below the Complaint option button, click the Radio Button button on the Forms toolbar. (Remember, Front-Page uses the term *radio button* rather than option button.) If the Forms toolbar is not visible, choose the Forms Toolbar command from the View menu. The button appears on the screen.

3. Right-click on the button you just inserted, and choose Form Field Properties from the pop-up menu. You'll see the Radio Button Properties dialog box.

4. Fill in the following information:

   *Group Name*—Enter the word *CommentType*. This is the name of the group of option buttons you'll be creating. You'll use this name later on the confirmation page. If you give the same group name to a series of buttons, only one of them can be selected by a user. Assigning the same group name is what actually creates a group of option buttons.

   *Value*—Enter the word *Compliment*. The word will appear on the confirmation page if the user selects this option while using the Feedback Form. You'll see how this works shortly.

*Initial State*—Select the Selected option. When the user sees the Feedback Form, this option will be selected as the default. Only one option button in a group can be initialized as Selected (because only one option in a group can ever be selected). FrontPage doesn't require you to initialize any option button as Selected; this is your choice.

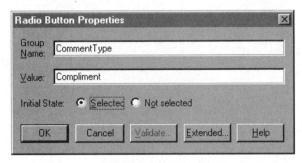

5. Click OK to exit the Radio Button Properties dialog box, and then click on the page next to the option button you just inserted and type the word *Compliment*. You've just created an option button that, when selected, indicates that the user is sending a compliment back to you.

6. Using the same procedure, create another option button immediately to the right of the Compliment button. (You might want to press the Spacebar to create a little space between the buttons.) In the Radio Button Properties dialog box, give the option button the same group name, *CommentType*, but give it the value of *Criticism*. Select the Not Selected option for its initial state. When you finish, click OK to exit the Radio Button Properties dialog box.

7. Type the word *Criticism* following the option button you just inserted. The option button is now complete. The following graphic shows a sample of how the option button section of your page should look.

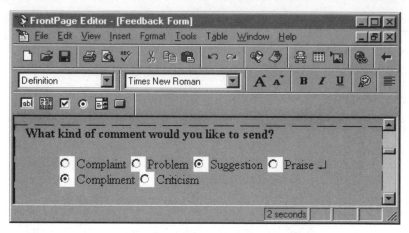

Make sure you save your changes as you go along.

You've just created a two-button group called Comment-Type. If you look at the properties for the buttons directly above (the Complaint, Problem, Suggestion, and Praise buttons), you'll see that their group name is MessageType. You've just created a similar group. You can create any option button group in the same way.

**Creating a drop-down list**   Next we'll create a four-element drop-down list (known as a drop-down menu in FrontPage) directly below the existing one.

1. Position the cursor following the one-line text box below the sentence "What about us do you want to comment on?"; hold down the Shift key and press Enter.

2. With the cursor just below the existing drop-down list, click the Drop-Down Menu toolbar button. A drop-down list appears on the page.

3. Right-click on the new drop-down list and choose Form Field Properties from the pop-up menu. You'll see the Drop-Down Menu Properties dialog box.

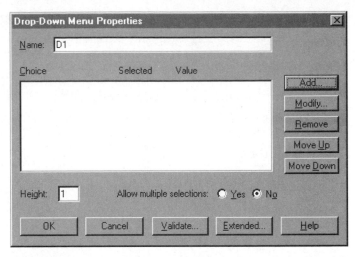

4. Enter the name *Topic* in the Name text box. You'll use this name later on when you configure the confirmation page.

5. Click the Add button to add an element to the box. You'll see the Add Choice dialog box:

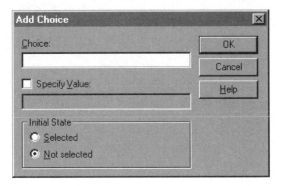

6. In the Choice text box, enter the word *Site*. By default, the value of this element is the same as its name; if you want the value to be different from the name, select the Specify Value check box, and then enter the value. In the Initial State section, select the Selected option. This sets the Site element as the item displayed in the drop-down list when the user first sees it in a browser.

Click OK when you finish entering information in the Add Choice Dialog box.

7. Add three more elements, named Technical Support, Prices, and Other, using the same procedure. For each one, select the Not Selected option in the Initial State section of the Add Choice dialog box. The width of the drop-down list will automatically expand to accommodate the widest element you add. The following graphic shows the Drop-Down Menu Properties dialog box after all the elements have been added.

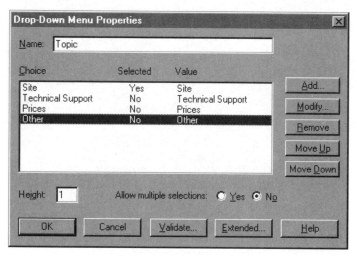

8. You can click the following buttons in the Drop-Down Menu Properties dialog box to perform some additional functions:

*Modify*—To modify any element in the list, select the element and click Modify. You'll see the Modify Choice dialog box for that element.

*Remove*—To remove any element from the list, select the element and click Remove.

*Move Up*—To move an element up in the list, select the element and click Move Up. (The elements will appear in the drop-down list in the order that they appear in this list.)

*Move Down*—To move an element down in the list, select the element and click Move Down.

In addition, you can enter the height of the list in the Height text box. Keep the height at 1 for now. The height of the list determines how the list is displayed.

In most browsers, if Height is set to 1, the drop-down list displays only one element and you can click on the down arrow button to view the rest of the elements. If Height is set to a value greater than 1, the list typically behaves like a scrollable text box, where the number of elements displayed at one time equals the Height.

Finally, for the Allow Multiple Selections option buttons, select the No option to disallow multiple selections. Clicking Yes allows the user to select more than one element from the list. This is useful in many situations, such as when offering the user choices of receiving information about multiple products that you can display in a drop-down list.

9. When you finish entering the information, click OK. The following graphic shows a sample of how the drop-down list section of your page should look.

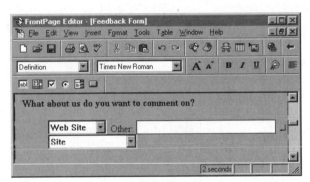

You've created a four-element drop-down list. You can create all drop-down lists in the same fashion.

**Creating a one-line text box** Next we'll create a one-line text box that appears next to the drop-down list, for users to enter an element if they selected (Other) from the drop-down list.

1. Position the cursor to the right of the drop-down list you just created. Press the Spacebar to create a little space between the drop-down list and the text box. Type *OTHER:*, and then press the Spacebar one more time.

2. Click the One-Line Text Box toolbar button. A one-line text box appears.

3. Right-click on the new one-line text box and choose Form Field Properties from the pop-up menu. You'll see the Text Box Properties dialog box:

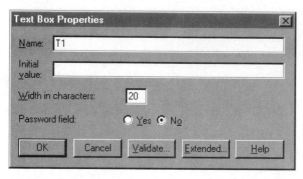

4. In the Name text box, enter *IfOther.* You'll use this name later on when configuring the confirmation page.

5. Do not enter anything in the Initial Value text box. In this instance, because the user will enter additional elements in the text box, there's no need to add an initial value. If you do enter an initial value, it appears in the text box when the user first views the form. The user can change the text if desired.

6. Type *20* in the Width In Characters text box if the current value is different. This sets the initial width of the text box to a rather wide 20 characters, giving it a user-friendly look. If you want to reset the size later, you can click and drag the text box's size handles in the Editor.

7. Select No in the Password Field section to specify that the text box will not be used as a password field in this instance.

8. You can click the Validate button if you want to set restrictions on the information that a user can enter in the one-line text box. For instance, you can set a maximum amount of characters that the user can enter in the text box, or restrict the entries to text or numbers only.

9. Click OK after you finish entering information in the Text Box Properties dialog box. The following graphic shows a sample of how the drop-down lists and the one-line text boxes should look on your page.

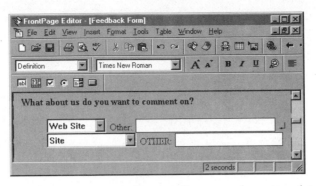

You've just created a one-line text box in which a user can enter additional comments.

**Creating a scrolling text box** Next we'll create a scrolling text box directly below the existing one on the Feedback Form.

1. Position the cursor to the right of the existing scrolling text box, below the line "Enter your comments in the space provided below:" Press Enter twice.

2. Click the Scrolling Text Box toolbar button, and a scrolling text box appears on the page.

3. Right-click on the new scrolling text box and choose Form Field Properties from the pop-up menu. You'll see the Scrolling Text Box Properties dialog box:

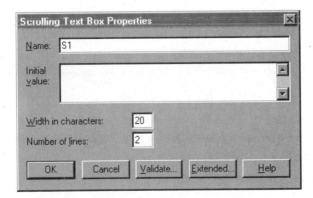

4. In the Name text box, enter *UserComments*. You'll use this name later on when configuring the confirmation page.

5. Do not enter anything in the Initial Value text box. In this instance, because the user will enter additional elements in the scrolling text box, there's no need to add an initial value.

6. Type *40* in the Width In Characters text box. This sets the initial width of the text box to a wide 40 characters, giving it a user-friendly look. If you want to reset the size later, you can click and drag the text box's size handles in the Editor.

7. Type *5* in the Number Of Lines text box. This sets the height of the scrolling text box in number of lines, and five is a good number to start with. Because the text box is scrollable, a user can enter more than five lines of text, and it's often unnecessary to set the initial height to more than five lines.

8. You can click the Validate button if you want to set restrictions on the information that a user can enter in the scrolling text box. For instance, you can set a maximum amount of characters that the user can enter in the text box, or restrict the entries to text or numbers only.

9. Click OK after you finish entering information in the Scrolling Text Box Properties dialog box. The following graphic shows a sample of how the scrolling text box should look on your page.

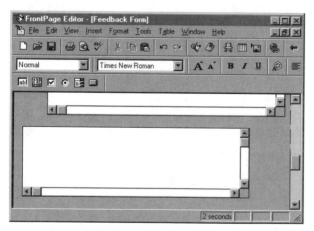

**Creating a check box** Next we'll create a check box below the existing check box at the bottom of the Feedback Form. The check box will allow the user to indicate that he or she wants more information sent via e-mail.

1. Position your cursor at the end of the line that reads "Please contact me as soon as possible regarding this matter." Hold down the Shift key and press Enter.

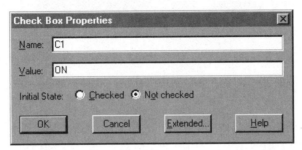

2. With the cursor underneath the check box, click the Check Box toolbar button. A new check box appears on the page.

3. Right-click on the new check box and choose Form Field Properties from the pop-up menu. You'll see the Check Box Properties dialog box:

| Check Box Properties | ☒ |
| --- | --- |

Name: `C1`

Value: `ON`

Initial State: ○ Checked  ● Not checked

| OK | Cancel | Extended... | Help |

4. In the Name text box, enter *RequestInfo*. You'll use this name later on when configuring the confirmation page.

5. In the Value text box, enter the same value, *Request-Info*. You'll see this value later when you're reviewing the information the user has sent to you with the Feedback Form. When you see this value, you'll know that the user wants more information sent.

6. In the Initial State section, select the Not Checked option. The check box will be deselected (unchecked) when the user sees it in a browser. In instances like this, it's wise to leave check boxes deselected so that you'll know for certain whether a user actually wants information sent.

7. Click OK after you finish entering information in the Check Box Properties dialog box.

8. Click to the right of the check box you just inserted, and press the Spacebar to create a little space between the check box and the text label you're about to add. Type the following sentence: *Please send me more information via e-mail.* The following graphic shows a sample of how the check box should look.

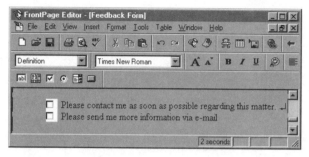

You've just created a simple check box and labeled it for users to indicate they want more information from you. You can create all your check boxes in FrontPage in the same way.

**Creating a command button** Next we'll create a command button (push button) for users to click when they finish entering information on the form and are ready to send it to you.

1. Position your cursor after the command button labeled *Clear Form* at the bottom of the screen, and then press Enter.

2. Click the Push Button toolbar button. A command button appears on the page.

3. Right-click on the new command button and choose Form Field Properties from the pop-up menu. You'll see the Push Button Properties dialog box:

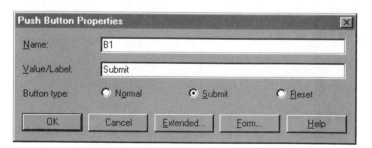

4. In the Name text box, leave the name as B1. If you supply your own handler by using a **CGI** script or other script, you can enter a name here and process the form based on the name. But for the purposes of this exercise, do not enter a name now.

5. In the Value/Label text box, enter the text that will appear on the command button: *Submit Now.*

6. In the Button Type section, select the Submit option. This allows the button to submit all information a user has entered in the form to the handler on the Web server. Selecting the Reset option turns the button into one that resets the form to its initial state when a user clicks the button in a browser. You'll select Normal when you want to assign a script to the button.

7. Click OK after you finish entering information in the Push Button Properties dialog box. The following graphic shows a sample of how the command button should look on your page.

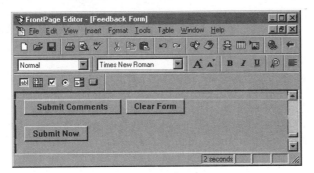

**Using alternative command buttons** FrontPage provides several additional styles of command buttons you can use on your pages, so you're not limited to the style of the standard command button. These buttons do not give you the same options as standard command buttons; for example, you cannot set them to reset or submit information. You can, however, assign your own scripts to these buttons. To reach the buttons, you must use a menu command. Here's how to add them to your page:

1. Position your cursor where you want the button to appear.

2. Choose Form Field from the Insert menu, and then choose Image from the submenu. The Image dialog box appears.

3. On the Clip Art tab, select Buttons from the Category drop-down list. You'll see a display of several buttons:

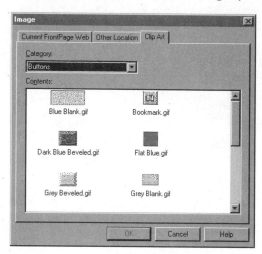

4. Select a button, and then click OK. The button appears on the page.

You can right-click on the button and choose Form Field Properties from the pop-up menu to display the Image Form Field Properties dialog box.

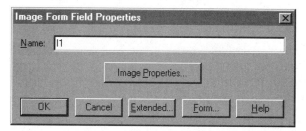

In the Image Form Field Properties dialog box, you can adjust the image properties by clicking the Image Properties button and making the appropriate settings in the Image Properties dialog box. In the Image Form Field Properties dialog box, you can also assign a handler by clicking the Form button and making the appropriate settings in the Form Properties dialog box.

## Validating Form Fields

FrontPage allows you to confirm that certain information you receive from users in form fields is the type of information you want, or that it's in the correct format. For instance, you can specify that a text box contain a minimum or maximum number of characters, or that a selection is made from a drop-down list or group of option buttons. This process is called *form field validation*.

To specify validation rules for a form field, right-click on the field and choose Form Field Validation from the pop-up menu. You'll see a dialog box specific to the form field you're validating, such as the Text Box Validation dialog box below.

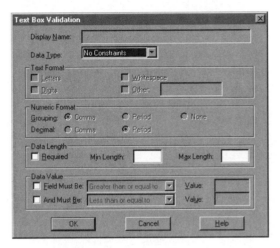

This is one of the most complicated Validation dialog boxes. It allows you to set validation rules for the type of data a user enters in the text box, as well as the format of text or numeric characters, minimum and maximum data length, and values for the data. When you finish specifying the rules you want for the form field, click OK to exit the Validation dialog box.

You can also reach the various Validation dialog boxes by clicking the Validate button in the Form Field Properties dialog box for the following form fields: text box, scrolling text box, option button, and drop-down list.

It's a good idea to explicitly tell users on the page (next to the form field, if possible) what you expect from them—for example, that a text field requires a value. If users submit information that does not fit within the rules you've specified for a particular form field, they will receive a validation error message in the browser notifying them that they must enter the correct type of information in the form.

How the validation error message is presented is based on a setting in the Explorer's FrontPage Web Settings dialog box. If you choose Web Settings from the Tools menu in the Explorer, the FrontPage Web Settings dialog box is displayed. On the Advanced tab, in the Validation Scripts section, you can select the language of the validation script. If you select VBScript or JavaScript, the validation error message will be displayed as a message box. If you select <None>, the validation error message will display as an HTML page. Here's an example of a validation error message with the validation script language set to VBScript. (A similar message would be displayed if the language were set to JavaScript.)

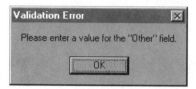

Here's an example of the same validation error message with the validation script language set to <None>:

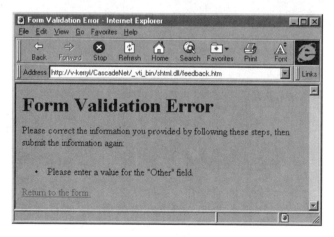

In either case, the user can click a button or link to return to the form to make corrections to the entered information.

Note: When a user receives a validation error message, the information from the form *has not yet been submitted* to the Web site; only when a user submits all information according to any specified validation rules does the information get sent to the site.

A neat technique with drop-down list validation is to specify that the first item be something like "Pick One," to remind users that they really do need to make a selection. This also helps you determine, after the information has been submitted, whether the user made a valid choice. To do this, make sure that "Pick One" is selected by default. Another technique is to display an error message if the user does not make a valid selection from the drop-down list. To do this, make "Pick One" the first item in the drop-down list and select the Disallow First Item check box in the Drop-Down Menu Validation dialog box. The user will see a validation error message if he or she tries to submit the information with the first item in the drop-down list still selected.

## Creating a Confirmation Page

A confirmation page displays information to a user confirming some action. For example, the user can receive confirmation that the information submitted in a form was received by the server. Users do make mistakes; the confirmation page can help them catch many mistakes and allow them to resubmit the form with the correct information. Also, a confirmation page can add a professional touch to your site.

Note that once a user submits a form to a Web site, that information is stored at the site (or wherever the site creator specifies) and cannot be changed. Confirmation pages simply allow the user to confirm that the information is what he or she wanted to submit. It's a good idea to advise users to review all information on a form before they submit it. You can take some steps to ensure that information is submitted correctly; see "Validating Form Fields" on page 276 for more details.

A confirmation page is just a standard page that can be specified in the Form Properties dialog box for a form. (You'll learn more about this in the section titled "Specifying Form Settings" later in this chapter.) A confirmation page typically uses WebBot Confirmation Field Components to present information back to the user for review. The following graphic shows an example of a confirmation page in Microsoft Internet Explorer.

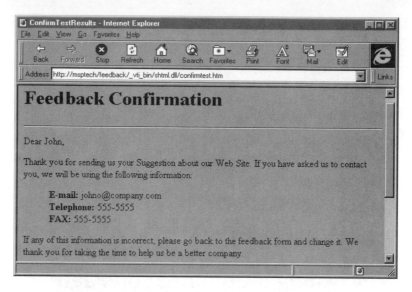

Let's step through the process of creating a confirmation page. For this example, we'll use the form fields we created earlier in this chapter. First we'll start the easy way—by using a template to create a confirmation page.

1. In the Editor, choose New from the File menu, select Confirmation Form from the list of templates and wizards in the New Page dialog box, and click OK.

2. When the page appears in the Editor, save it with the title *Confirmation Form* and give it the name within the current site, *confirmation.htm*. We'll refer to this page from now on as the Confirmation Form.

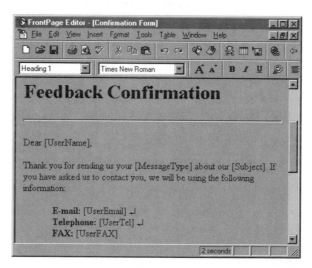

You'll see that the Confirmation Form is a template that's ready for you to customize. It's designed to be used with the Feedback Form template, and it includes many of the form field names used in that template. These names appear in brackets; they're actually individual WebBot Confirmation Field Components.

If you move your cursor over one of these WebBot components, such as the WebBot component labeled *[UserName]*, you'll see that the cursor turns into the cute little WebBot cursor. The value of the UserName field will replace the string *[UserName]* when the Confirmation Form appears to a user in a browser; whatever name the user entered will appear there. All WebBot Confirmation Field Components on the Confirmation Form work in the same manner.

The Confirmation Form also includes some introductory and concluding sentences that you can use; you can change any of this information if you want to.

**Inserting a WebBot Confirmation Field Component** When you know what information you want to present to the user for confirmation, you're ready to insert WebBot Confirmation Field Components on the page. Using the fields you created earlier, here's how you can do it:

1. First, you delete the WebBot component labeled *[Message-Type]* and replace it with the one you created earlier called *[CommentType]*. Position your cursor immediately to the right of the [MessageType] Confirmation Field Component and press the Backspace key. (This is an easy way to delete any WebBot component on a page.)

2. Next, you insert a Confirmation Field Component for the form field called *[CommentType]*. From the Insert menu, choose WebBot Component. In the Insert WebBot Component dialog box, select Confirmation Field, and then click OK.

The WebBot Confirmation Field Component Properties dialog box appears:

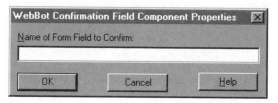

3. Enter the name of the form field whose information you want presented; in this case, enter *CommentType*. Then click OK.

You'll see that the Confirmation Field Component labeled *[CommentType]* has been inserted in the middle of the sentence. This example only shows how you can replace a WebBot component, but of course you can create original sentences and insert WebBot components in the same fashion for presenting form field information on a Confirmation Form. The following graphic shows a sample of how the Confirmation Form should look after the WebBot component has been added.

**TIP**

For option buttons only, the name you enter is the group name.

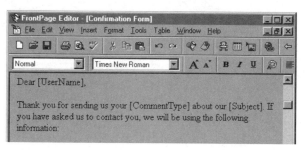

4. Using the same procedure, you can create original sentences or replace existing WebBot components for the other form fields you created earlier. Among these fields are the drop-down list named *Topic,* a one-line text box named *IfOther,* a scrolling text box named *User-Comments,* and a check box named *RequestInfo.*

It's a good idea to include a link at the end of the Confirmation Form that returns the user back to the Feedback Form if he or she needs to resubmit information. It's also wise to include other navigational links on this page, such as links to the site's home page, a Table of Contents page, or the major sections of the site, so the page doesn't seem like a dead end to the user.

Our form field and confirmation field examples end here. Read on to learn how to process the information in a form.

## Specifying Form Settings

Here's where it all comes together. You create forms by assembling a collection of form fields on one page, and you can present the information back to the user for confirmation on another page using a Confirmation Form. But in order for the two pages to work together, you must specify their relationship in the Forms Properties dialog box. You also specify the type of handler you want to use on the Web server for processing the information a user enters in a form.

FrontPage includes two forms in addition to the traditional data-collection forms: the discussion form and the registration form. Their handlers are specified in the Forms Properties dialog box. If you create a site using the Discussion Web Wizard, you're actually creating a form for users to "fill out" as the site is in use. When a user submits a message to the discussion group, the WebBot Discussion Component handler saves the information on the server so it can be accessed by others in the forum. You'll learn more about the discussion and registration form handlers later in this chapter.

## Assigning a Form Handler

A *handler* is an application on a Web server that communicates between the server and the user in relation to a form. Handlers can send messages to the user (via Confirmation Pages, for example), and they can process the information in a form that a user submits to the Web server. You assign and configure a form's handler in the Form Properties dialog box. Here's how:

1. You can open the Form Properties dialog box for the form you're assigning the handler to in one of two ways: You can right-click on any open space of the

form, and then choose Form Properties from the pop-up menu; or, if you're already in the Push Button Properties dialog box, you can click the Form button to reach the Form Properties dialog box.

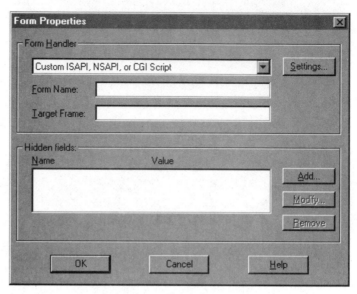

2. From the drop-down list in the Form Handler section, select a handler. You have five choices:

*WebBot Save Results Component*—A WebBot component that collects information from a form and stores it in the format of your choice. Stored information is appended to other information in the file you specify. Use this WebBot component for standard data-collection forms.

*WebBot Discussion Component*—A WebBot component that allows users to participate in an online discussion. FrontPage allows basic discussion group administration abilities. The WebBot Discussion Component gathers information from a form, formats it into an HTML page, stores the page on the Web server, and adds the page to a Table of Contents and a text index. It can also gather other information from the form and store it on the Web server. Note that it's much easier to use the Discussion Web Wizard than to configure settings here. The Discussion Web Wizard does all of this for you.

*WebBot Registration Component*—A WebBot component that allows users to register for a service offered in your site. It adds the user to the service's authentication database, and then collects other information from the form and stores it on the Web server in the file and format you specify.

*Custom ISAPI, NSAPI, or CGI Script*—In terms of forms, these are software components on a Web server that process the information submitted using a form. These software components can be written to add functionality to your Web site beyond what FrontPage's WebBot components can offer. For example, a company might want a handler that allows a user special access to certain areas of the site.

*Internet Database Connector*—A software component that allows users to access ODBC-compliant database information from a Web page. To use the Internet Database Connector, you must create an IDC file that typically contains the name of the ODBC data source, the name of the HTX or HTML template file, and the SQL statement.

3. After you select a handler, click the Settings button to the right of the drop-down list to configure it.

4. Each handler has its own Settings dialog box. Configure each handler accordingly, and then click OK to close the Settings dialog box. Then click OK to close the Form Properties dialog box. The following sections show how to configure each form handler.

## Configuring a WebBot Save Results Component

You configure a WebBot Save Results Component in the Settings For Saving Results Of Form dialog box, which you can reach in the following way:

1. Open the Form Properties dialog box for the form.

**TIP**

You can use the Save Results Component as the handler for pages created with the Feedback Form and Confirmation Form templates.

285

2. Select WebBot Save Results Component from the drop-down list in the Form Handler section, and then click Settings.

The Settings For Saving Results Of Form dialog box appears.

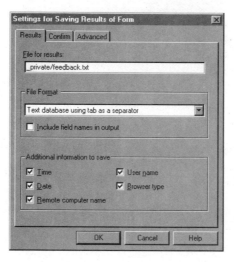

To configure the WebBot Save Results Component, do the following:

◆ On the Results tab, enter the name and location of the file you want the results saved to. The location can be either within or outside the current site. If it's in the current site, you might enter _private/feedback.txt. The results will be saved to the file called FEEDBACK.TXT in the _private folder in your Web site.

If a results file does not exist when the first results are saved, FrontPage creates the file. If a results file exists, the information is appended to the end of the file.

◆ Select the file format of the results file from the drop-down list in the File Format section. You have numerous choices:

*HTML*—Formats the file in HTML using normal text with line endings.

*HTML Definition List*—Formats the file using a **definition list** to format name-value pairs.

*HTML Bulleted List*—Formats the file using a bulleted list for name-value pairs.

*Formatted Text Within HTML*—Formats the file in HTML using formatted text with line endings.

*Formatted Text*—Formats the file in an easy-to-read text format.

*Text Database Using Comma as a Separator*—Formats the file in a text format with commas separating the elements. If the Include Field Names In Output check box is selected, names are listed on the first line, enclosed in quotes, and separated by commas. Values are listed on the second line, enclosed in quotes, and separated by commas. Use this format if you want to manipulate the information in a database or similar application.

*Text Database Using Tab as a Separator*—Formats the file in the same way as above, but using tabs instead of commas to separate elements.

*Text Database Using Space as a Separator*—Formats the file in the same way as above, but using spaces instead of commas to separate elements.

◆ Select the Include Field Names In Output check box to save the field name along with the field value in the results file.

◆ Select the check boxes in the Additional Information To Save section to include the corresponding information in the results file.

On the Confirm tab, you can specify an optional confirmation page and an optional validation failure page:

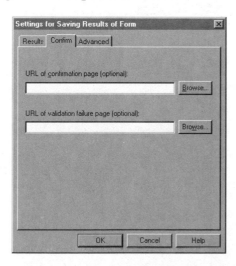

◆ If you've created a confirmation page for users to confirm the information they've entered, type its **page URL** in the URL Of Confirmation Page text box. This page will be displayed by the browser whenever the form is succesfully submitted to the Web server.

If you do not specify a confirmation page here, the WebBot Save Results Component will create and maintain one automatically.

◆ You can also specify a validation failure page in the URL Of Validation Failure Page text box. A field validation failure page is displayed when the form is submitted and it contains data that violates any defined form field validation. This page is typically used only when the validation script language in the Explorer's FrontPage Web Settings dialog box is set to <None>. Otherwise, if a validation failure occurs, a failure message is generated with either a VBScript or JavaScript message box. If you do not specify a field validation failure page here, FrontPage will create and maintain one automatically.

> ### TIP
>
> If the URL Of Validation Failure Page text box appears grayed out, you have not specified any validation for your form fields.

On the Advanced tab, you can specify a second results file and the form fields to include in the results:

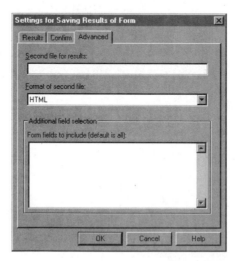

◆ If you wish, specify a second results file in the Second File For Results text box. Enter the location and the filename. You can use a second file if you want to use results files for more than one purpose, such as manipulating one in a database and printing the other for your review. If you enter a name for a file that does not exist, FrontPage creates the file the first time the form is submitted.

◆ Select a format for the second results file in the Format Of Second File drop-down list.

◆ In the Additional Field Selection section, you can specify which form fields and the order in which the form fields should be written to the results file. Separate multiple entries with spaces. Keep in mind that if you specify form fields in the Additional Field Selection section, they will be the only form fields included in the first results file (as well as in the second, if it is also specified).

After you finish entering all the information you need to configure the handler, click OK to close the Settings For Saving Results Of Form dialog box.

# Configuring a WebBot Discussion Component

You configure a WebBot Discussion Component in the Settings For Discussion Form Handler dialog box, which you can reach in the following way:

1. Open the Form Properties dialog box for the discussion form.

2. Select WebBot Discussion Component from the drop-down list in the Form Handler section, and then click Settings.

> **TIP**
>
> You can create a discussion Web site using the Discussion Web Wizard, and avoid having to configure the WebBot Discussion Component yourself. For more information, see Chapter 4.

The Settings For Discussion Form Handler dialog box appears, with three tabs.

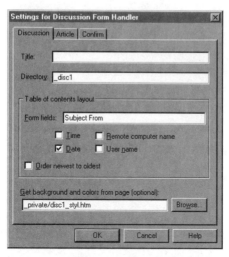

On the Discussion tab, you can enter the following information:

◆ Name the discussion group in the Title text box. The name will appear on pages containing articles.

◆ Enter the name of the discussion folder in the Directory text box. If you used the Discussion Web Wizard to create your discussion Web site, the folder you specified in the wizard will appear as the default. The folder name must be eight or fewer characters, one of which is a beginning underscore (_).

◆ In the Form Fields text box in the Table Of Contents Layout section, enter the names of the form field(s) you want displayed in the Table of Contents in the discussion group. If you enter multiple names, you must separate them with blank spaces.

◆ Select the appropriate check boxes if you want to display the time and/or date the article was submitted, the remote computer name the article came from, or the user name of the article's author.

◆ To place the most recently submitted articles first in the Table of Contents, select the Order Newest To Oldest check box.

◆ If you want to use the background and colors from another page in your site, you can do so by specifying the page in the Get Background And Colors From Page text box.

You specify the layout of each article in the discussion group on the Article tab:

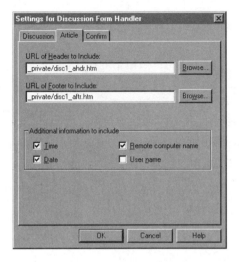

◆ To use a page as a header or footer of each article, you can specify the page in the URL Of Header To Include text box or the URL Of Footer To Include text box.

◆ In the Additional Information To Include section, select the appropriate check boxes if you want to include the time and/or date the article was submitted, the remote computer name the article came from, or the user name of the article's author.

On the Confirm tab, you can specify an optional configuration page and an optional validation failure page.

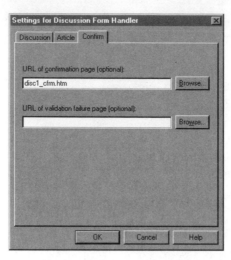

◆ If you've created a confirmation page for users to confirm the information they've entered, type its **page URL** in the URL Of Confirmation Page text box. This page will be displayed by the browser whenever the form is submitted to the Web server.

If you do not specify a confirmation page here, the WebBot Discussion Component will create and maintain one automatically.

◆ You can also specify a validation failure page in the URL Of Validation Failure Page text box. A field validation failure page displays information pertaining to fields with invalid data on a form. If you do not specify a field validation failure page here, FrontPage will create and maintain one automatically.

After you finish entering all the information you need to configure the Discussion Form handler, click OK to close the Settings For Discussion Form Handler dialog box.

## Configuring a WebBot Registration Component

You configure a WebBot Registration Component in the Settings For Registration Form Handler dialog box, which you can reach in the following way:

1. Open the Form Properties dialog box for the registration form. You can create your own form to use as a registration form, or you can use the User Registration template for this purpose. The registration form must be located in the **root Web site**. Be aware that registration forms do not work on the Microsoft Internet Information Server or the Microsoft Personal Web Server.

2. Select WebBot Registration Component from the dropdown list in the Form Handler section, and then click Settings.

   The Settings for Registration Form Handler dialog box appears, with four tabs. The first one is the Registration tab.

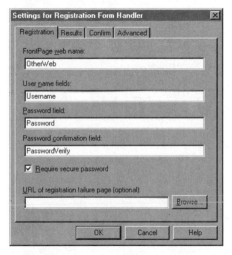

To configure the WebBot Registration Component, do the following:

◆ In the FrontPage Web Name text box, enter the name of the Web site you're allowing the user to register for.

◆ In the User Name Fields text box, enter the name(s) of the field or fields on the form, separated by commas or spaces, that the user inputs his or her name into. The user name is constructed from the contents of these fields.

◆ In the Password Field text box, enter the name of the field for the user's password.

◆ In the Password Confirmation Field text box, enter the name of the field for the user's confirmation password.

◆ If you want to require that the user supply a secure password (which consists of six or more characters and does not partially match the user name), select the Require Secure Password check box.

◆ You can also supply a failure page, which notifies the user that a registration attempt failed. Supply the page URL for this page in the text box at the bottom of the dialog box. This page is optional, but it's a good idea to include a page like this in your site.

The Settings For Registration Form Handler dialog box also includes Results, Confirm, and Advanced tabs. These are configured the same as described in "Configuring a WebBot Save Results Component" on page 285.

# Configuring a Custom ISAPI, NSAPI, or CGI Handler

You can also configure settings for a custom ISAPI, NSAPI, or CGI handler if you decide to use one in your Web site.

You configure the custom handler in the Settings For Custom Form Handler dialog box, which you can reach in the following way:

1. Open the Form Properties dialog box for the form.

2. Select Custom ISAPI, NSAPI, Or CGI Script from the drop-down list in the Form Handler section, and then click Settings.

The Settings For Custom Form Handler dialog box appears:

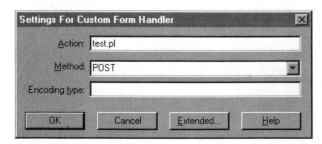

To configure the custom form handler, do the following:

◆ In the Action field, enter the **absolute URL** of the form handler.

◆ Use the Method drop-down list to select a method of submitting information to the handler—Post or Get. The Post method passes the name-value form field pair directly to the form handler as input, and the Get method encodes the form's name-value pairs and assigns the information to a server variable, QUERY_STRING.

◆ In the Encoding Type text box, enter the standard used to encode the form data that's passed to the handler. The default encoding method is *application/x-www-form-urlencoded;* leave this field blank to use the default.

## Configuring an Internet Database Connector Handler

You can also configure settings for an Internet Database Connector handler.

You configure the handler in the Settings For Database Connector dialog box, which you can reach in the following way:

1. Open the Form Properties dialog box for the form.

2. Select Internet Database Connector from the drop-down list in the Form Handler section, and then click Settings.

The Settings For Database Connector dialog box appears:

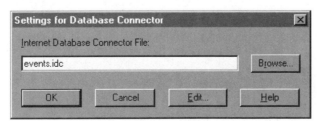

To configure the handler, do the following:

◆ Enter the name of the IDC file in the Internet Database Connector File text box.

◆ If you want to edit the IDC file, click Edit. The Internet Database Connector Wizard appears, allowing you to edit the file as you wish.

## Coming Up

You've now explored the big, amazing world of FrontPage WebBot components and forms. In the next chapter, you'll be introduced to some of FrontPage's more advanced features.

# Finishing Touches

# Chapter 10
# Advanced Features

## Getting Interactive

By now you pretty much know your way around FrontPage. You've learned about the Explorer and the Editor. You know how to build a Website, manage it, and work with it page by page. Maybe you're saying to yourself, "Geez, there has to be more than this. What about all of those cool features I keep hearing about? I want my ActiveX!" Well, this is your lucky day. FrontPage 97 directly supports advanced features—such as **ActiveX controls**; **Java applets**; **JavaScript**; Visual Basic, Scripting Edition (**VBScript**); Netscape **plug-ins**; the **Internet Database Connector**; and even Microsoft PowerPoint animations.

> ### TIP
> When you add a control, script, or applet to your pages in the Editor, FrontPage typically inserts an icon representing that feature. You can double-click or right-click on the icon and choose Properties from the pop-up menu to reach the Properties dialog box. With an icon selected, you can reach the Properties dialog box quickly by pressing Alt+Enter.

There are plenty of books specifically dedicated to these new features. You can hardly walk into the computer section of your favorite bookstore without bumping into a couple dozen books on Java alone. So, for the purpose of this chapter, we'll only discuss how FrontPage uses these features, and how you get them on your page and in your site. If you've installed Microsoft Internet Explorer on your system, you'll have several ActiveX controls already installed, but if you want to know how to create one from scratch, or how to create some of the other controls, you'll need to add another book to your library.

## The Advanced Toolbar

To get many advanced features onto your page, you use the Advanced toolbar. This toolbar is located on the menu bar of the Editor. If you don't see the toolbar in the Editor, choose Advanced Toolbar from the View menu. Likewise, to hide the toolbar, choose the same command. This toolbar floats, like the others in the Editor, which means you can move it anywhere on your screen, even outside the Editor. To move the toolbar, click inside the toolbar in an area not occupied by a button, and drag the toolbar to its destination. You can dock the toolbar by dragging and dropping it anywhere in the toolbar region of the Editor. Most of the advanced features can also be accessed by choosing the appropriate command from the Editor's Insert menu.

# Inserting HTML

Since HTML is a rapidly evolving language, new tags will be introduced that FrontPage might not directly support. Therefore, FrontPage allows you to insert any HTML directly, including new HTML. Be aware, however, that FrontPage will not check to see if the text you insert is valid HTML. To insert HTML, you use the Insert HTML button, the leftmost button on the Advanced toolbar. Clicking this button brings up the HTML Markup dialog box:

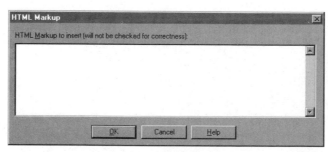

Enter your HTML, and then click OK to return to the Editor. The text you entered is shown in the Editor using the Unknown HTML placeholder icon (shown below). This icon reminds you that you created the HTML, not FrontPage. You can always edit the HTML in FrontPage. To learn how, see Chapter 7.

# Inserting an ActiveX Control

ActiveX controls are software components that add functionality to your page that can't be created using standard HTML. Examples of ActiveX controls include a label control that can display text at different sizes and angles, a timer control that can generate timed events, a stock ticker control that can display stock information, and an animation control that can display animations. ActiveX controls can be created with a variety of programming languages, including Visual C++ and Visual Basic 5.0. Be aware that some browsers do not recognize ActiveX controls on a Web page. For more information on ActiveX and ActiveX controls, as well as information on how to download free ActiveX controls, check out Microsoft's ActiveX site at //www.microsoft.com/activex/ on the World Wide Web.

 The second button from the left on the Advanced Toolbar is the Insert ActiveX Control button. Clicking the button brings up the ActiveX Control Properties dialog box.

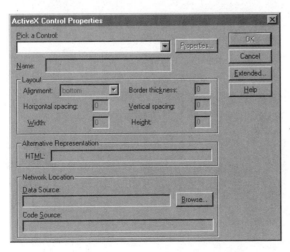

You use this dialog box to select and then configure an ActiveX control. Only the Pick A Control drop-down list is active at first, and the other areas are grayed out. When you select a control, the other areas of the dialog box become active.

**Pick a Control**  Select a control from this drop-down list, which displays all of the ActiveX controls currently installed on your computer.

To alter the properties for the control, click the Properties button. If the control you selected is installed on your computer, and if it takes advantage of local editing, you'll be presented with the Edit ActiveX Control dialog box as well as a Properties dialog box for that control.

The following graphic shows these dialog boxes for the ActiveX Microsoft Forms 2.0 TabStrip control.

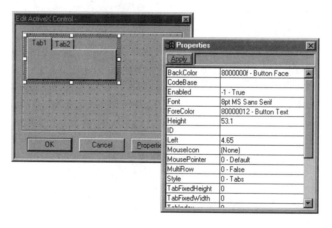

The Properties dialog box lists the current properties for the control. You can edit these options as needed.

If the control you selected is not loaded on your computer or does not support local editing, clicking the Properties button brings up the more generic Object Parameters dialog box. To use this dialog box, you need to know all of the properties for the control and their values.

```
Object Parameters                                           [X]

Additional parameters specified here will be available to the embedded object
in PARAM tags.

Attribute name          Value                    Type
                                                                    [ Add... ]

                                                                    [ Modify... ]

                                                                    [ Remove ]

 [    OK    ]        [    Cancel    ]        [    Help    ]
```

**Name**  The Name text box in the ActiveX Control Properties dialog box allows you to specify a name that represents the ActiveX control when it's used along with a script on the page.

**Layout**  In the layout section, you specify how the control will be placed on the page.

◆ *Alignment*—Specifies the type of alignment between the ActiveX control and the text around it.

◆ *Border Thickness*—Sets a black border around the control. The width of the border is measured in pixels.

◆ *Horizontal Spacing*—Sets a specified horizontal spacing (in pixels) from the control to the nearest object or text on the current line, on both sides of the control.

◆ *Vertical Spacing*—Sets a specified vertical spacing (in pixels) from the control to the nearest object or text on the line above and/or below the control.

◆ *Width*—Specifies the width of the control in pixels.

◆ *Height*—Specifies the height of the control in pixels.

**TIP**

You can adjust the size of an ActiveX control on a page by selecting it and then dragging its border controls with the mouse.

**Alternate Representation**  For browsers that do not support ActiveX controls, use this text box to enter text or HTML that will be displayed in place of the control. For example, typing *Pebbles* will cause that word to appear in the browser in place of the control. You can also type HTML to add font, size, and other attributes to the text. You can also enter HTML in this text box to show an image in place of the control, such as *<img src="images/Pebbles.gif">*. In this case, Pebbles.gif is in the Images folder of the Web site the page belongs to.

**Network Location** If the ActiveX control is not on the user's computer, you can specify a network location that the browser will search for the control or for data.

◆ *Data Source*—Use the Data Source text box to specify the network location or URL of the file containing the parameters, or use the Browse button to select a file. Certain ActiveX controls might take advantage of run-time parameters.

◆ *Code Source*—If the control is not on the user's computer, enter the network location or URL of the control in the Code Source text box to point the browser to that location when the page is opened. If necessary, this will allow the browser to download and install the control.

**Extended** Clicking the Extended button brings up the Extended Attributes dialog box, where you can insert additional attribute/value pairs for the ActiveX control. These attributes will be added to the <object> tag.

The two graphics that follow show a sample of an ActiveX Microsoft Forms 2.0 TabStrip control that has been inserted on a page. The first graphic shows the settings in the ActiveX Control Properties dialog box, and the second shows how the control appears in the Editor.

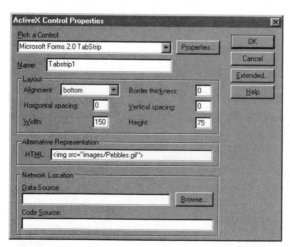

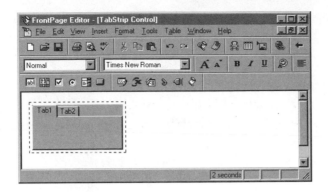

# Inserting a Java Applet

 The fourth button from the left on the Advanced toolbar is the Insert Java Applet button. Java applets are created in a programming language called **Java** and are very much like an ActiveX control in that they add dynamic functionality to your Web page. Clicking the Insert Java Applet button displays the Java Applet Properties dialog box.

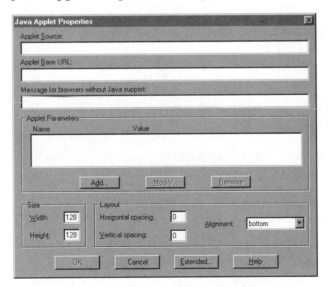

**Applet Source** Source files for Java applets typically have the file extension CLASS. Enter the name of the Java applet source file in the Applet Source text box. Keep in mind that Java is case sensitive, so using the correct uppercase and lowercase letters is important.

**Applet Base URL** In this text box, enter the URL of the folder that contains the Java applet source file.

**Message for browsers without Java support** For browsers that do not support Java applets, use this text box to enter text or HTML that will be displayed in place of the applet. For example, typing *BamBam* will cause that word to appear in the browser in place of the applet. You can also type HTML to add font, size, and other attributes to the text. You can also enter HTML in this text box to show an image in place of the applet, such as *<img src="images/BamBam.gif">*. In this case, BamBam.gif is in the Images folder of the Web site that the page belongs to.

**Applet Parameters** In this section, you specify parameter names and values for the applet. You must use the documentation that came with the Java applet to determine the names and values for the applet.

The text box lists the names and values of any parameters that have been added. You can use the Add, Modify, and Remove buttons to configure this list.

**Size** In this section, you can adjust the width and height (in pixels) of the Java applet.

**Layout** In this section, you specify the spacing and alignment of the applet on the page.

> **TIP**
>
> You can adjust the size of a Java applet on a page by selecting it and then dragging its border controls with the mouse.

- ◆ *Horizontal Spacing*—Sets a specified horizontal spacing (in pixels) from the applet to the nearest object or text on the current line, on both sides of the applet.

- ◆ *Vertical Spacing*—Sets a specified vertical spacing (in pixels) from the applet to the nearest object or text on the line above and/or below the applet.

- ◆ *Alignment*—Specifies a type of alignment between the Java applet and the text around it.

**Extended** Clicking the Extended button brings up the Extended Attributes dialog box. Here you can insert additional attribute/value pairs to the Java applet. These attributes will be added to the <applet> tag.

The two graphics that follow show a sample of a Java applet named First that has been inserted on a page. The first graphic shows the settings in the Java Applet Properties dialog box and the second shows how the applet appears in the Editor.

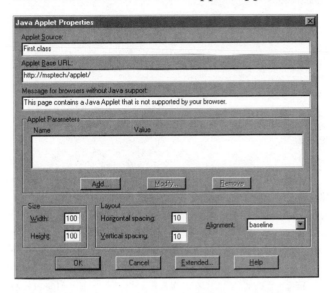

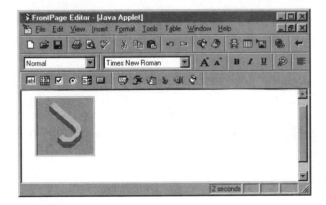

# Inserting a Plug-In

 Plug-ins were originally created for Netscape users, although they are now supported by Microsoft Internet Explorer version 3.0 and higher. Clicking the Insert Plug-In button, the fifth button on the Advanced toolbar, displays the Plug-In Properties dialog box.

**Plug-In Properties**

Data Source:

Browse...

Message for browsers without Plug-In support:

Size

Height: 128    Width: 128    ☐ Hide Plug-In

Layout

Alignment: bottom    Horizontal spacing: 0

Border thickness: 0    Vertical spacing: 0

OK    Cancel    Extended...    Help

**Data Source** In this text box, specify the file location or URL of the plug-in, or click the Browse button to select the plug-in.

**Message for browsers without Plug-in support** For browsers that do not support plug-ins, use this text box to enter HTML that determines what those browsers will display in place of the plug-in. For example, typing *Dino* will cause that word to appear in the browser in place of the plug-in. You can also type HTML to add font, size, and other attributes to the text. You can also enter HTML in this text box to show an image in place of the plug-in, such as *<img src="images/Dino.gif">*. In this case, Dino.gif is in the Images folder of the Web site the page belongs to.

**TIP**

You can adjust the size of a plug-in on a page by selecting it and then dragging its border controls with the mouse.

**Size** In this section, you can adjust the size of the plug-in by entering the height and width in pixels.

**Hide Plug-In** Select this check box if you don't want the plug-in to appear on the page.

**Layout** In the Layout section, you specify the position of the plug-in on the page.

◆ *Alignment*—Specifies a type of alignment between the plug-in and the text around it.

◆ *Border Thickness*—Sets a black border around the plug-in. The width of the border is measured in pixels.

◆ *Horizontal Spacing*—Sets a specified horizontal spacing (in pixels) from the plug-in to the nearest object or text on the current line, on both sides of the plug-in.

◆ *Vertical Spacing*—Sets a specified vertical spacing (in pixels) from the plug-in to the nearest object or text on the line above and/or below the plug-in.

**Extended** Clicking the Extended button displays the Extended Attributes dialog box. Here you can insert additional attribute/value pairs to the plug-in. These attributes will be added to the <embed> tag.

# Inserting PowerPoint Animations

As many Microsoft Office users know, PowerPoint easily creates slide-show animations, and now with FrontPage, you can just as easily add these animations to your Web page. A PowerPoint animation file is inserted onto your Web page as an ActiveX control or as a plug-in.

To view a PowerPoint animation on a Web page, you must have the PowerPoint Animation Player installed. (You can download it from Microsoft's PowerPoint Web site at //www.microsoft.com/powerpoint/.) When you install the PowerPoint Animation Player, it will detect the type of browser(s) you are using and install the ActiveX version, plug-in version, or both. The PowerPoint Animation Player can display standard PowerPoint animations, which have a PPT extension. The PowerPoint Animation Player for ActiveX can also display compressed PowerPoint animations, which have a PPZ extension. The advantage of using compressed PowerPoint animations is that they arc smaller files and can be downloaded more quickly. Compressed PowerPoint animations can be created using an add-in to PowerPoint called the PowerPoint Animation Publisher. For information on downloading, installing, and using the PowerPoint Animation Player and the PowerPoint Animation Publisher, visit Microsoft's PowerPoint Web site.

To add a PowerPoint animation to your page, choose Other Components from the Insert menu, and choose PowerPoint Animation from the submenu. This brings up the PowerPoint Animation dialog box.

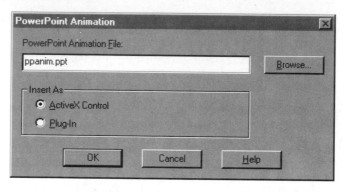

In the PowerPoint Animation File text box, enter the name of
the PowerPoint animation file you want placed on your page, or
use the Browse button to select a file.

In the Insert As section, select how you want the animation
to be inserted. The ActiveX Control option inserts the animation
as an ActiveX control; a graphic placeholder will display in
FrontPage when the animation is inserted as an ActiveX control.
The Plug-In option inserts the animation as a plug-in; a graphic
placeholder will display in FrontPage when the animation is inserted as a plug-in.

Once you have the PowerPoint Animation Player installed,
you can watch the animation play by previewing it in a browser.
The following graphic shows a PowerPoint animation displayed
in Internet Explorer.

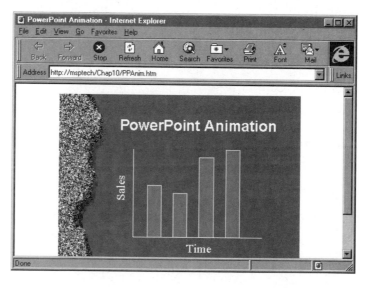

# Inserting VBScript or JavaScript

Using a scripting language, such as VBScript or JavaScript, in a Web page gives you a lot more capabilities. With the support of a script-enabled browser, you can use VBScript or JavaScript to read and modify form elements, perform event handling, interact with the browser, and manipulate objects. Writing VBScript or JavaScript is beyond the scope of this book, but this section will give you an introduction.

VBScript is a scripting language developed by Microsoft and is based on Visual Basic for Applications. JavaScript is a scripting language developed by Netscape and is based on the C programming language. Scripts are included in the HTML and can be understood by a browser that supports that particular scripting language.

 You can insert scripts, such as VBScript or JavaScript, by using the Insert Script button, the rightmost button on the Advanced toolbar. Clicking the Insert Script button displays the Script dialog box.

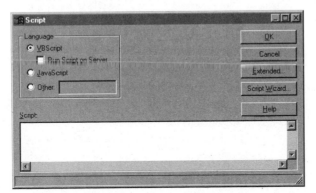

The language section allows you to specify the scripting language. Selecting the RunScript On Server check box causes the VBScript to run on the server and not the client. The Script scrolling text box allows you to actually insert a script. You can access the Script Wizard by clicking the Script Wizard button. The Script Wizard is a tool that helps you generate scripts. It contains a code view option that allows you to see the code that is being generated. The following graphic shows a sample from the Script Wizard.

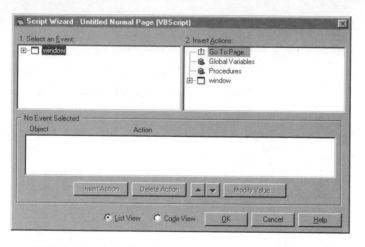

The basic methodology behind the wizard is that you select an object and an associated event, and then select an action to take place when the event is triggered. Once you are finished with the wizard, the VBScript or JavaScript code is inserted and an icon representing the script is placed onto the page.

The following graphics show a brief example of how the Script Wizard can be used to automate an ActiveX control. Specifically, it shows how VBScript code can be used to rotate a Label Object Control, named Label1, by 90 degrees when the user clicks on it. The following graphic shows the settings in the Script Wizard.

The following graphic shows the already inserted ActiveX control and the VBScript icon in the Editor.

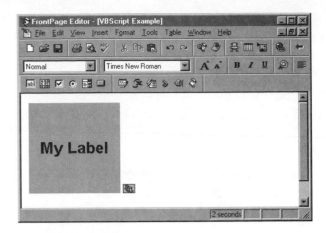

The following graphic shows the label control and VBScript in action in Internet Explorer.

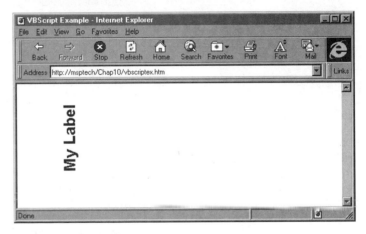

# Internet Database Connector

If you want to be able to access data in a database from a Web page, this section will help you get started.

One way that you can access information in an Open Database Connectivity (ODBC) database from a Web page is to use the Internet Database Connector (IDC), which allows you to insert, update, and delete information in an ODBC database. The Internet Database Connector is a standard feature of the Microsoft Internet Information Server (for Windows NT Server) and Microsoft Peer Web Services (for Windows NT Workstation). It's also available for the Microsoft Personal Web Server, but not for the FrontPage Personal Web Server. The FrontPage database features are not available for other Web servers. For more information on Web servers, see Chapter 11. For more information on the Internet Database Connector, review the online documentation for Internet Information Server (IIS), which is automatically installed with IIS.

The following diagram shows how the Internet Database Connector works:

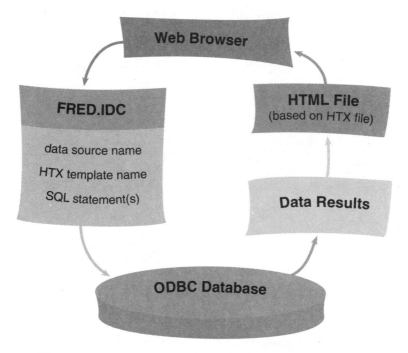

First, a message is sent from a browser to an IDC file (in this case, FRED.IDC) on the Web server. This is typically initiated by the user clicking on a link or a button. The IDC file is a text file that must contain at least the following information:

◆ ODBC data source name

◆ Query results template filename (HTX file)

◆ SQL query statement(s)

Based on the ODBC data source name and the SQL query statement, the Internet Database Connector communicates with the database and obtains the data results. Next, the Internet Database Connector merges the data results with the query results template file (HTX file) to create an HTML file. This new HTML file is then sent to the browser and displayed.

Therefore, in order for the Internet Database Connector to work properly, the following actions need to be performed:

- An ODBC database needs to be stored on the Web server.

- ODBC drivers need to be installed on the Web server and a system data source configured for your ODBC database using the ODBC administrator.

- An IDC file must be created and saved in an execute-enabled folder.

- A query results template file (HTX file) must be created.

- A Web page must be created that calls the IDC file.

FrontPage can help you create the IDC file, HTX file, and the initial Web page. You can start by using the Internet Database Connector Wizard.

## Internet Database Connector Wizard

The third button from the left on the Advanced toolbar starts the Internet Database Connector Wizard. This wizard helps you create an Internet Database Connector (IDC) file. You can also access the wizard by choosing New from the File menu in the Editor, and then selecting Database Connector Wizard in the New Page dialog box. The following shows the first screen of the wizard with information already entered.

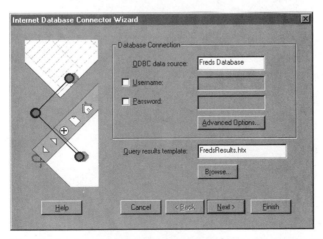

**The first screen of the Internet Database Connector Wizard configures connection to the ODBC database.**

**Database Connection** In this section you specify the ODBC data source, the user name, and the password, and you set any advanced options.

◆ *ODBC Data Source*—Enter the ODBC data source you want to connect to. This data source is defined using the ODBC Administrator and must be configured as a system data source. You must fill in this text box.

If the Web server runs on Windows 95 or Windows NT Server 4.0, and the database resides on the same server, you can create the named ODBC data source using the "32bit ODBC" or "ODBC" entry in the Windows Control Panel. For other ODBC configurations, consult the documentation for your database.

◆ *Username*—If the database system you're connecting to requires a user name, select the Username check box and enter the user name in the corresponding text box.

◆ *Password*—If the database system you're connecting to requires a password, select the Password check box and enter the password in the corresponding text box.

◆ *Advanced Options*—Clicking this button displays the Advanced Options dialog box. You can set various Query, Connection, Limits, and Driver Specific options here. These settings are optional.

**Query Results Template** A query results template file is a text file that typically has an HTX file extension. An HTX file is used to format the results of a database query into an HTML file that can be displayed by a browser. A FrontPage template named Database Results is available in the Editor for creating an HTX file. That template is discussed later in this chapter in the section titled "Creating a Query Results Template." In the text box, enter the name of the HTX file. As a practical matter, the HTX file should be in the same folder as the IDC file. If you haven't already created the HTX file, you can simply enter the name and location you will be using. This file is required.

To search the current Web site for a query results HTX file, click the Browse button.

Click the Next button to move to the next screen of the Internet Database Connector Wizard. Remember that you can always use the Back button to move backward through the wizard. The following graphic shows the second screen with a simple SQL query already entered.

### TIP

The minimum information required for the Internet Database Connector Wizard is the ODBC data source name, the query results template name, and the SQL query statement.

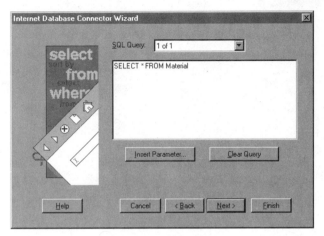

**In the second screen of the Internet Database Connector Wizard, you define SQL queries for the IDC file.**

This screen allows you to enter one or more SQL queries for the current IDC file. You enter a SQL query in the available text box. To enter additional queries, select Create Additional Query from the SQL Query drop-down list, which displays the Create Additional Query dialog box. In this dialog box, specify whether you want to create the additional query before or after the current query, and then click OK. You can switch between the queries by selecting them from the SQL Query drop-down list.

### TIP

If you don't know SQL, and you're setting up an IDC file to query a Microsoft Access database, you can easily create a SQL query for the Internet Database Connector Wizard in the following way: Create a query in Access, select the SQL view in Access, and then cut and paste that SQL query to the Internet Database Connector Wizard.

**Insert Parameter** Clicking this button brings up the Insert Parameter dialog box, where you can insert an IDC parameter value for the SQL query.

**Clear Query** Clicking this button clears the currently selected query from the list.

Click the Next button to move to the next screen of the wizard.

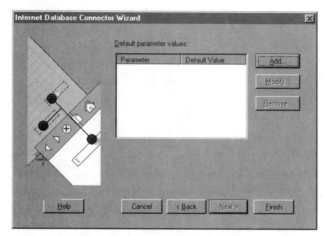

**In the third screen of the Internet Database Connector Wizard, you define default IDC parameter values.**

If the SQL query is run when a user follows a link to the IDC file, the default values defined in the third wizard screen will be used by themselves. If the SQL query is run when a user submits a form with the IDC file as the form's handler, the default values will be combined with those passed with the form.

The default names and values of the parameter appear in the list box. Click the Add button to add a parameter and a value to the list. Click the Modify button to change the parameter and value selected in the list. Click the Remove button to delete the parameter and value selected in the list.

When you finish entering information in the Internet Database Connector Wizard, click the Finish button.

This displays a dialog box that allows you to save the IDC file.

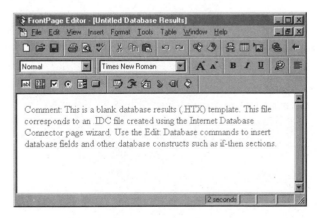

Name the file with an IDC file extension and save it in a folder that allows scripts or programs to be executed. You can check to see if a folder in the Explorer has this option selected, by right-clicking on the folder in the Explorer and selecting Properties from the drop-down list. The Properties dialog box will be displayed and will have a check box to allow scripts or programs to be run.

## Creating a Query Results Template

To create a query results template (HTX file), choose New from the File menu in the Editor. In the New Page dialog box, select Database Results and then click OK. The following page is displayed.

You can insert database fields and database constructs on this page by choosing the Database command from the Edit menu, and then choosing the items from the submenu.

◆ *Database Column Value*—Allows you to insert a field from the results data. This value must be inserted inside a Detail section.

◆ *IDC Parameter Value*—Allows you to insert a form field from the page that initiated the query or a default parameter specified in an IDC file.

◆ *Detail Section*—Since database queries typically return multiple records, this command allows you to define the region on your page where the database result set will be inserted.

◆ *If-Then Conditional Section*—Allows you to define an if-then structure.

◆ *Else Conditional Section*—Allows you to add an else to the if-then structure.

◆ *Remove Database Directive*—Allows you to remove all the database commands from a selected region.

After you complete the HTX file, be sure to save it with the name and location specified in the Internet Database Connector Wizard. The following graphic shows a sample of a query results template named FREDSRESULTS.HTX.

Next, you must create another page that calls the IDC file. This can be implemented with a link or a form with a submit button. The following graphic shows a page that calls the

FRED.IDC file with a link as well as a submit button. (This is just a simple example in which no form values are submitted.)

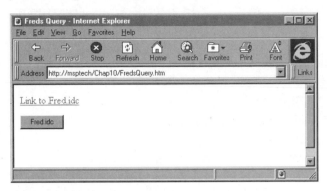

The following graphic shows the results of the database query.

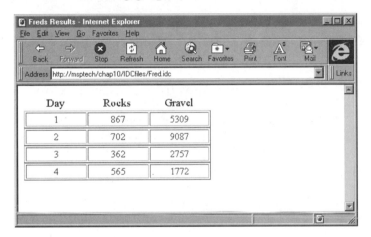

Here is the actual database as viewed in Access. It was set up with a system data source name of Freds Database using the ODBC Administrator. (Freds Database was specified in the first screen of the Internet Database Connector Wizard.)

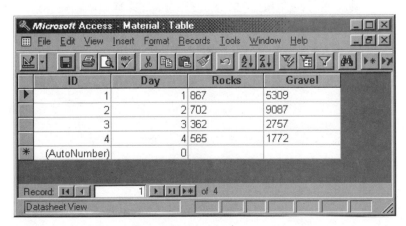

The ability to access information in a database from a Web page is a powerful feature. This section has given you an introduction to the feature, which you can explore further.

# Other Advanced Features

FrontPage includes other advanced features that you should know about but that are too technical to discuss at length in this book. For more information on these features, see the FrontPage Web site at //www.microsoft.com/frontpage/.

The following are two examples of the many FrontPage-related topics on the FrontPage Web site.

◆ The FrontPage 97 Software Developer's Kit (SDK), which can be downloaded from the Microsoft Web site. The FrontPage SDK allows you to create custom wizards and custom WebBot components, add custom menu commands, and create custom "Designer HTML" fragments that can be added to pages in the Editor using drag-and-drop.

◆ Integration with Microsoft Visual SourceSafe 5.0, to provide multi-user revision control on changes made to the Web site.

## Coming Up

Next we'll round out our tour of FrontPage by looking at FrontPage's server-related offerings, including the Microsoft Personal Web Server, the FrontPage Personal Web Server, and FrontPage Server Extensions.

# Chapter 11
# Web Servers

## FrontPage Knows Servers

All the wonderful Web sites you'll design and create with Front-Page will more than likely be stored on a Web server. A Web server is software or a computer that stores Web sites, scripts, databases, and other related files, and makes Web pages accessible from a browser. Since the term can refer to either software or a computer, you must look at the context to determine which it is referring to. The Web server market is becoming large and competitive, with versions of Web servers that meet various needs and run on different platforms.

This chapter discusses how FrontPage interacts with the numerous Web servers; it does not discuss the pros and cons of the servers themselves. For information on the advantages and disadvantages of major Web servers, look in Internet-related periodicals and on the server manufacturers' World Wide Web sites.

Once you make a choice of a Web server to use with Front-Page (perhaps you already have a server up and running), chances are that FrontPage will interact with it smoothly. FrontPage supports the most popular shareware and commercial Web servers in use today, via software programs and scripts known as the **FrontPage Server Extensions**, which are discussed later in this chapter. (You'll also find a list of the Web servers that Front Page supports later in the chapter.) The Server Extensions are the go-between from the FrontPage client to the Web server, helping both parties communicate behind the scenes.

If you're lucky, you might not need to buy a Web server at all; the FrontPage Bonus Pack includes the Microsoft Personal Web Server for Windows 95, and the FrontPage installation includes the FrontPage Personal Web Server.

## It's Server Time

The Microsoft Personal Web Server and the FrontPage Personal Web Server are ideal for working directly with FrontPage-created Web sites. They are best used for testing sites and for acting as the main server for a low-volume intranet at a small company or organization.

Many FrontPage Web-site developers create their sites locally, on a network or even on a single computer, and test them with the Personal Web Servers before moving the site to a higher-volume server within their company. The Personal Web Servers can help you test all aspects of a FrontPage site, including links to the Internet and the World Wide Web, the use of FrontPage's **WebBot components**, the **Internet Database Connector**, forms, and any other content that requires communication between the client and the server.

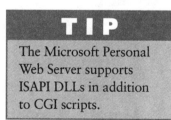

**TIP**

The Microsoft Personal Web Server supports ISAPI DLLs in addition to CGI scripts.

The servers fully support the Hypertext Transfer Protocol (HTTP) and Common Gateway Interface (**CGI**) standards. They are compatible with existing CGI scripts, so you don't need to be concerned with writing new scripts if you decide to use one of the Personal Web Servers.

The Personal Web Servers usually don't need to be configured; they're configured automatically when you install them. The Microsoft Personal Web Server can be installed from the Bonus Pack and the FrontPage Personal Web Server can be installed during the FrontPage installation. You can run the servers on a local computer or on a computer connected to a network.

If you create and edit sites using the Personal Web Servers over a network, you can often expect the communication between the FrontPage client and the Personal Web Servers (for example, when opening or saving a Web site) to be slower.

The Microsoft Personal Web Server is the preferred Web server for use with FrontPage. In fact, the FrontPage Setup program encourages you to install the Microsoft Personal Web Server rather than the FrontPage Personal Web Server. For more information on the Microsoft Personal Web Server, see the section titled "Microsoft Personal Web Server" later in this chapter.

Although the Personal Web Servers are excellent for testing and for use as low-volume Web servers, you might need a server that can handle higher traffic. For example, if you use the Microsoft Personal Web Server with Windows NT Workstation, the license permits only 10 simultaneous Web connections. If you need to support higher traffic, you can use Windows NT Server and Internet Information Server (IIS), or a UNIX Web server that can support FrontPage.

**The FrontPage Server Extensions** Suppose for a second that you're stranded in the Ukraine, but you speak only a wee bit of Ukrainian. Can you survive? Probably. Can you communicate? Sure, maybe a smidge. But can you communicate *well*? Probably not. You need a translator, or one of those English-to-Ukrainian pocket dictionaries, to make sure you come across the way you want to.

The FrontPage Server Extensions perform this kind of translation duty between your FrontPage site and a Web server. Each set of Server Extensions is software that lives on the Web server and gets involved whenever communication takes place between your site and the server. Since these extensions are available for a variety of Web servers, FrontPage can communicate with many different Web servers.

> **TIP**
>
> For the Microsoft Personal Web Server, Peer Web Services, and IIS, the many Server Extension components are implemented as ISAPI DLLs; for all other Web servers, they're implemented as CGI scripts.

The FrontPage Server Extensions are a good bargain for a number of reasons:

◆ They're free.

◆ They make uploading a site to a Web server fast and easy with FrontPage.

◆ They allow you to set author and end-user permissions for your Web sites.

◆ They ensure that FrontPage's WebBot components work the way they're intended to. For example, if you use a WebBot Search Component in your FrontPage site, the Server Extensions ensure that the component performs as it's supposed to. Without the Server Extensions installed, the WebBot component won't work.

The following four WebBot components won't work at run time without the Server Extensions: Search (for full-text searching), Discussion (for threaded discussion groups), Save Results (for saving form results to a file), and Registration (for requiring end-users to register before browsing your Web site). All others will work at run time without the Server Extensions.

**Web servers and platforms** As of this writing, FrontPage Server Extensions are available for the following Web servers.

*Commercial Web servers:*

◆ Microsoft Internet Information Server (for Windows NT Server 3.51 and 4.0)

◆ Microsoft Peer Web Services (for Windows NT Workstation 4.0)

◆ Microsoft Personal Web Server (for Windows 95; included with the FrontPage 97 Bonus Pack)

◆ FrontPage Personal Web Server (for Windows 95; included with FrontPage 97)

◆ Netscape Enterprise Server (for Windows NT and UNIX)

- ◆ Netscape FastTrack Server (for Windows 95, Windows NT, and UNIX)

- ◆ Netscape Commerce Server (for Windows NT and UNIX)

- ◆ Netscape Communications Server (for Windows NT and UNIX)

- ◆ O'Reilly WebSite and WebSite Professional (for Windows 95 and Windows NT)

*Noncommercial Web servers:*

- ◆ NCSA (for UNIX)

- ◆ Apache (for UNIX)

- ◆ CERN (for UNIX)

*Platforms:*

- ◆ Microsoft Windows 95

- ◆ Microsoft Windows NT Workstation and Windows NT Server

- ◆ UNIX (Solaris, SunOS, HP/UX, IRIX, BSDi, Linux, and Digital UNIX)

**Where to get 'em** The FrontPage Server Extensions for all Windows 95–based and Windows NT–based Web servers (including those from Microsoft, Netscape, and O'Reilly) are included with FrontPage 97 and are installed automatically when you install FrontPage. You can download the FrontPage Server Extensions for UNIX–based Web servers from the FrontPage Web site at //www.microsoft.com/frontpage/.

**Extracting the Server Extensions** Server Extensions are typically in the form of a self-extracting file or EXE file. Follow the specific instructions accompanying the Server Extensions to extract them on your Web server. Normally, you just double-click on the EXE file to begin the process.

The normal FrontPage Server Extensions setup process emphasizes ease of installation and is oriented toward a low-security intranet environment. However, Internet Service Providers that want to host the FrontPage Server Extensions, or customers who want a higher-security installation, should visit the Web Presence Providers section of the FrontPage Web site at //www.microsoft.com/frontpage/. Here you can download the documentation and software provided for Web Presence Providers.

# Server Administration

You can perform most everyday server management tasks in the FrontPage Explorer. For example, you can specify users; specify access rights for users; specify settings to work with a **proxy server**; and, based on the Web server, administer passwords via commands on the Explorer's menus. Most of these commands are related to site-specific tasks and are discussed in Chapters 3 and 5.

## The Server Administrator

**SHORTCUT**

You'll find a shortcut labeled *FrontPage Server Administrator* in the C:\Program Files\ Microsoft FrontPage folder or whatever folder you installed FrontPage in. You can launch the Windows version of the Server Administrator by double-clicking on that shortcut in the Windows Explorer.

The FrontPage Server Administrator is a program that helps you carry out numerous tasks related to installing and uninstalling Server Extensions and configuring various elements of the Web servers you use with FrontPage.

FrontPage comes with two flavors of the Server Administrator: a Windows version and a command-line version. Both are typically found in the Program Files\Microsoft FrontPage\bin folder on the drive or server that FrontPage is installed on. The Windows version is FPSRVWIN.EXE, and the command-line version is FPSRVADM.EXE. You can launch either application by double-clicking it in the Windows Explorer.

**The Windows version of the FrontPage Server Administrator.**

Below are step-by-step procedures for tasks you can perform with the Windows version of the FrontPage Server Administrator. Explicit directions for using the command-line version can be found in FrontPage's online help under the topic "FrontPage Server Administrator— Command Line Version."

**Installing the FrontPage Server Extensions** To install a set of FrontPage Server Extensions for an existing Web server, you must first install the Web server software—and it's a good idea to test it using a browser to ensure that it works properly. Also, the files required to install the Server Extensions on your Web server need to be copied to the server and extracted if necessary.

> **TIP**
>
> FrontPage supports multi-homing for all Web servers that offer this feature. Multi-homing is the ability of a single Web server to host sites for multiple domain names; for example, the domains *www.jeb.com*, *www.kathy.com*, and *www.eli.com* might actually reside on a single server. This option might be available to you during your Server Extensions configuration.

To install the Server Extensions, follow these steps:

1. Launch the FrontPage Server Administrator.

2. Click the Install button. In the Configure Server Type dialog box, from the Server Type drop-down list select your Web server type, and then click OK.

3. A dialog box or multiple dialog boxes will appear, depending on the server you're installing the Server Extensions for.

4. Follow the instructions, and enter the appropriate information when prompted.

5. When you return to the FrontPage Server Administrator dialog box, click Close.

**Uninstalling the FrontPage Server Extensions** To uninstall Server Extensions for a particular port, do the following:

1. Shut down the server.

2. Launch the FrontPage Server Administrator.

3. From the Select Port Number list, select the port for the Server Extensions you want to uninstall.

4. Click Uninstall. A Server Administrator dialog box appears, asking you to confirm the uninstall operation.

5. Click OK.

6. A message box is displayed indicating a successful uninstall; click OK.

7. In the FrontPage Server Administrator dialog box, click Close.

Uninstalling Server Extensions does not remove content files such as HTML files or image files.

**Changing a server's port number** To change a server's port number, you must first uninstall the Server Extensions on that port, change the port number, and then reinstall the Server Extensions.

To change the port number of a Web server that already has the Server Extensions running, do the following:

1. Shut down the server.

2. Launch the FrontPage Server Administrator.

3. From the Select Port Number list, select the port number you want to change.

4. Click Uninstall to remove the Server Extensions from the port. Click OK in the Server Administrator dialog box to accept your action, and when a dialog box appears indicating a succsssful uninstall, click OK.

5. Change the server's port number according to the directions supplied with the Web server. For example, for the FrontPage Personal Web Server, you would change the port number in the server configuration file (httpd.cnf).

6. Click Install in the FrontPage Server Administrator to reinstall the Server Extensions for the new port. Select the server type in the Configure Server Type dialog box and click OK. Follow the instructions, and enter the appropriate information when prompted.

7. If asked whether you want to restart the server, click Yes.

8. When you return to the FrontPage Server Administrator dialog box, click Close.

**Adding an administrator name and password** As described in Chapters 3 and 5, you can administer user names and possibly passwords in the Explorer using the Permissions command and the Change Password command. Depending on your Web server, you might also be able to add administrator names and passwords using the FrontPage Server Administrator. The advantage of using the FrontPage Server Administrator to add administrator names is that you don't have to have a site open in the Explorer, and in fact you can add administrator names and passwords for any site on any Web server you have access to. Simply follow these steps:

1. Launch the FrontPage Server Administrator.

2. Click the Security button. You'll see the Administrator Name And Password dialog box. (If you are using a Microsoft Web server, the Security button might be grayed out because passwords are handled at the system level. See the section titled "Passwords" in Chapter 5 for more information.)

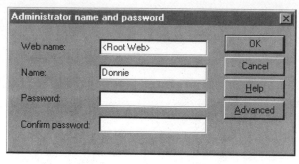

3. Enter the name of the site in the Web Name text box.

4. Enter the administrator's name and password in the next two text boxes, and then confirm the password in the last text box. If the name is already registered, the password will be changed to the password you enter.

## TIP

If you are using the Microsoft Personal Web Server, the Password text box, the Confirm Password text box, and the Advanced button will not be displayed in the Administrator Name And Password dialog box. Passwords for the Microsoft Personal Web Server are handled by a Web-based Internet Services Administrator. See the section titled "Microsoft Personal Web Server" later in this chapter for more information.

5. If you want to restrict administrative operations based on **IP addresses**, click the Advanced button to reach the Internet Address Restriction dialog box. Administrative operations will be limited to machines whose IP addresses fall within the restrictions you specify. For example, if you specify *200.130.\*.\**, only computers with IP addresses that begin with *200.130* will be allowed to perform administrative operations to the site. After you enter this information, click OK.

6. Click OK to close the Administrator Name And Password dialog box.

7. In the FrontPage Server Administrator dialog box, click Close.

**Enabling or disabling authoring on a selected port** Disabling authoring on a port means the Explorer and the Editor will not be able to access any sites on that port. So, if you want all your FrontPage sites on a particular port to be uneditable with FrontPage, you can do the following:

1. Launch the FrontPage Server Administrator.

2. From the Select Port Number list, select the port on which you want to enable or disable authoring.

3. Click the Authoring button. The Enable/Disable Authoring dialog box appears, indicating whether authoring is currently enabled or disabled on the port.

4. Make your selection to enable or disable authoring for the port.

5. If you want **Secure Sockets Layer** (SSL) authoring, select the Require SSL For Authoring check box. This ensures that all authoring operations on the port are performed with SSL security.

6. After you make your selections, click OK.

7. In the FrontPage Server Administrator dialog box, click Close.

**Upgrading older FrontPage sites when you install a new version of the FrontPage Server Extensions** When you install a new version of the FrontPage Server Extensions, you must upgrade sites created in the older version. This copies the necessary software to the content folders in the sites associated with the selected port. Content files or image files in the sites will not be changed.

Here's how to upgrade those old sites:

1. Launch the FrontPage Server Administrator.

2. Click the Upgrade button.

3. You'll see a Server Administrator dialog box telling you of the impending operation. Click OK. The Server Administrator upgrades the sites associated with the selected port. When the upgrade is finished, a dialog box is displayed confirming the operation. Click OK, and you are returned to the FrontPage Server Administrator dialog box.

4. Click Close to close the dialog box.

For more information on server administration and Server Extensions, consult FrontPage online help and the FrontPage Web site at //www.microsoft.com/frontpage/.

## Microsoft Personal Web Server

 The Microsoft Personal Web Server provides capabilities for administration and configuration. When you first install the Personal Web Server, it is automatically configured to run. You should see a new icon on your taskbar, as shown to the left, indicating this.

If you double-click on this icon, you see the Personal Web Server Properties dialog box, which has four tabs. You can also display this dialog box by clicking the Start button, choosing Control Panel from the Settings menu, and then double-clicking on the Personal Web Server icon.

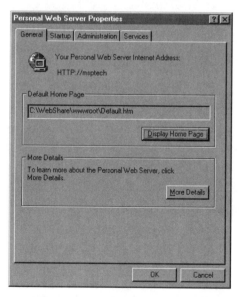

The General tab of the Personal Web Server Properties dialog box contains the server's Internet address, the home-page address, and a Display Home Page button. It also contains a More Details button, which when clicked displays information in your browser about the Personal Web Server such as getting started with the Personal Web Server, Personal Web Server Administration, and FTP Server Administration.

The Startup tab contains information about the Web server state and enables you to start or stop the server. The Options section allows you to specify whether the Web server should start every time you start up your computer, and whether to display the Web server icon on the taskbar.

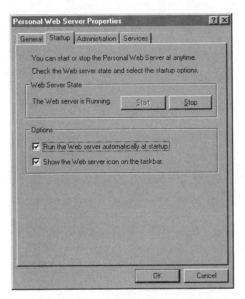

The Administration tab allows you to start the Web-based Personal Web Server administration tool. This lets you perform remote administration using a Web browser.

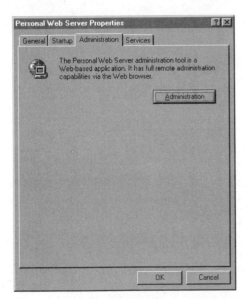

When you click the Administration button, the Internet Services Administrator page is displayed in your Web browser.

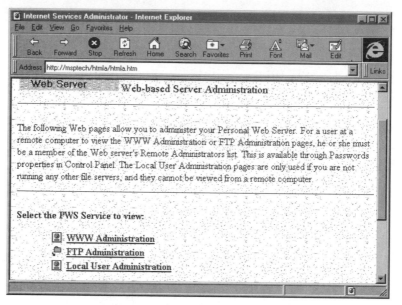

From here you can click on links for WWW, FTP, and Local User Administration. If you click on the WWW Administration link, the Internet Services Administrator -WWW page is displayed. From here you can click on the Service tab, which allows you to adjust password and other settings.

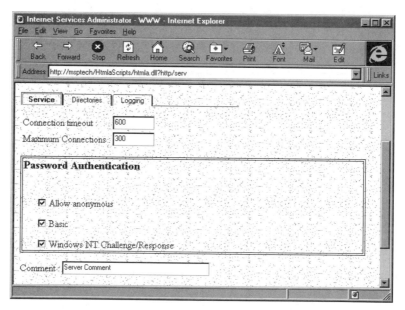

On the Directories tab, you can edit, add, or delete folders in your Web sites. The Logging tab allows you to configure your Web server log file, which by default is named InetServer-_Event.log and is stored in the Windows folder.

If you click on the Local User Administration link on the Internet Services Administrator page, the Internet Local User Administrator page is displayed. From here you can administer users and groups. These users and groups can then be added to sites using the Permissions command in the Explorer.

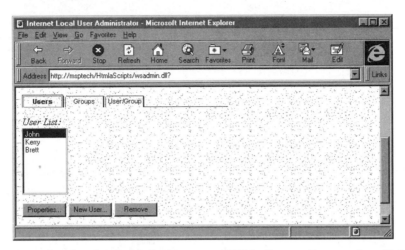

The final tab of the Personal Web Server Properties dialog box, Services, allows you to change the properties as well as start or stop the **FTP** or **HTTP** services. When you select a service and click the Properties button, the service's Properties dialog box is displayed. In this dialog box, you can set startup options and adjust home settings.

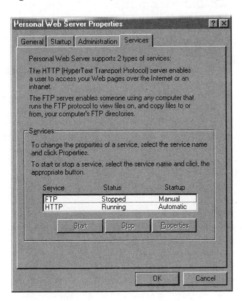

For more information on the Microsoft Personal Web Server, consult the documentation by clicking the More Details button on the General tab of the Personal Web Server Properties dialog box, or consult the FrontPage Web site, which is located at //www.microsoft.com/frontpage/.

## Internet Service Providers

You can always forgo the potential headaches of running your own Web server and let someone else take the aspirin for a change. Internet Service Providers (ISPs), also called Web hosts, are companies that house your site on their server and provide you with a variety of services—often for a very low fee when compared with the cost of hospitalizing those who suffer nervous breakdowns when their Web servers go on the fritz three times in the same week.

Most ISPs charge periodic fees (often monthly, biannually, or annually) to house your site; these fees generally increase with the size of your site. Some ISPs also charge according to the number of hits your site receives, or according to the bandwidth of information transferred between your site and those who view it.

The advantages of using the services of an ISP include not having to worry about maintaining a Web server in-house, and faster user access to your site. ISPs often have the fastest connections available on the Internet. In addition, you avoid the expense and hassle of having to install a **firewall** server to protect your company's computing resources if your site is on the World Wide Web.

The disadvantages are relatively few; among them is the fact that you're not the one in control. Nearly all business owners dream of having business go so well that their sites must expand to meet the growing consumer need for information; if these dreams come true for you, it might be easier (and ultimately less expensive) to manage a large site in-house instead of over a distance.

More than 100 ISPs nationwide have the FrontPage Server Extensions installed, and are specifically set up to host Front-Page sites. You can find a complete list at //www.microsoft.com/frontpage/.

If your Web site is already hosted by an ISP that does not support FrontPage, and you'd like to turn the site into a Front-Page site, refer the ISP to the FrontPage Web Presence Providers (WPP) information in the FrontPage Web site. In the meantime, you can still post your FrontPage site to your ISP as long as the ISP provides you with FTP access for posting your Web content. Whether or not your ISP supports FrontPage, you can use the Publish FrontPage Web command in the FrontPage Explorer to easily post your Web content. When you use this command, if FrontPage doesn't detect the FrontPage Server Extensions on your ISP's Web server, it will automatically launch the Web Pub-lishing Wizard, if it is installed. The wizard allows you to post your site to Web servers that do not have the FrontPage Server Extensions installed. (The wizard can be installed from the FrontPage Bonus Pack.)

For more information on the Web Publishing Wizard, see its online help. For more information on the Publish FrontPage Web command, see Chapter 3. For more information on Front-Page and ISPs, see the FrontPage Web site.

# Appendix
# Installing FrontPage

So you're ready to take the big step and install Microsoft Front-Page 97 with Bonus Pack. It's not such a big step, really; compared with installing some other applications, it's very easy. This appendix will step you through your installation of FrontPage 97, whether you're installing it for the first time or installing it over a previous version.

Before you install FrontPage, however, you should read the file README.TXT, which is on the FrontPage CD-ROM. It contains specific information on known problems with FrontPage, additional tips on running and troubleshooting FrontPage, technical support information and contacts, and more.

## System Requirements

To use Microsoft FrontPage 97 with Bonus Pack, you need:

◆ Personal or multimedia computer with 486 or higher processor

◆ Microsoft Windows 95 operating system or Windows NT Workstation version 3.51 Service Pack 5 or later

◆ 8 MB of memory for use on Windows 95, or 16 MB of memory for use on Windows NT Workstation; 16 MB recommended for Microsoft Personal Web Server

◆ 30 MB of available hard-disk space

◆ CD-ROM drive

◆ VGA or higher-resolution video adapter (Super VGA, 256-color recommended)

◆ Microsoft Mouse, Microsoft IntelliMouse, or compatible pointing device

The Internet features of FrontPage 97 require you to have Internet access; Internet and other online access might require payment of a separate fee to a service provider.

Other Bonus Pack components have separate hard-disk space requirements as follows:

◆ 11 MB for Microsoft Internet Explorer

◆ 1 MB for Microsoft Personal Web Server

◆ 1 MB for Microsoft Web Publishing Wizard

◆ 2 MB for Internet Mail and News Reader

To use Microsoft Image Composer, you need:

◆ 16 MB of memory (32 MB recommended)

◆ Hard-disk space required: 15 MB (compact); 30 MB (typical); or 300 MB (complete)

◆ VGA, 256-color (Super VGA TrueColor with 2 MB of video memory recommended)

## Installing FrontPage 97

Below are instructions for installing FrontPage 97. If you already have a previous version installed, consult the section titled "Upgrading to FrontPage 97 from FrontPage 1.1" later in this appendix before you install FrontPage 97.

1. Exit all Windows applications on your computer.

2. Insert the FrontPage 97 with Bonus Pack CD-ROM in your computer's CD-ROM drive.

3. After a moment, you should see the opening FrontPage 97 With Bonus Pack screen:

**The FrontPage97 installation screen. You'll be notified if a component is already installed on your computer, as in the case of Internet Explorer 3.0 above.**

If you don't see this screen, launch SETUP.EXE from the CD-ROM. In Windows 95 or Windows NT version 4.0, select the CD-ROM drive in the Windows Explorer and double-click SETUP.EXE. In Windows NT version 3.51, you can do this by opening a window to your CD-ROM drive in File Manager and double-clicking SETUP.EXE.

4. Click the FrontPage 97 Installation button.

5. If you do not have a Web server installed, you'll see a dialog box asking whether you want to install that component first. If you want to use the Microsoft Personal Web Server, you should install it at this stage. You can easily remove the server from your system later, so unless you know for certain you don't want to use the server, click Yes.

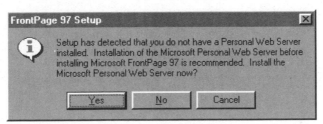

If you click No, you'll move to the Welcome screen of the Setup Wizard, described in step 7. If you click Yes, a License Agreement dialog box will be displayed for the Microsoft Personal Web Server. If, after reading the license agreement, you click the I Agree button, the Microsoft Personal Web Server will be installed on your computer. You'll then see a Personal Web Server dialog box asking whether you want to restart your computer.

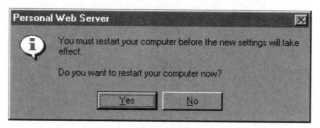

Click Yes, and this will restart your computer. Once your computer has restarted, return to the original FrontPage 97 installation screen as described earlier. Click the FrontPage 97 Installation button to continue with the installation.

6. If a Web server is running on your computer, a Question dialog box will appear, asking if you want to temporarily stop the server to continue the installation. Click Yes to continue.

7. In the Welcome screen of the Setup Wizard, you're asked to exit all Windows programs before proceeding with the installation. Do so, and then click Next.

8. In the FrontPage Registration screen, type your name and your company name in the appropriate text boxes, and then click Next.

9. FrontPage asks you to confirm that your name and company information is correct. Click Yes if it's correct, or click No to return to the previous screen to change the information.

10. In the Microsoft FrontPage 97 CD Key screen, enter your 11-digit CD Key (located on a sticker on the back of your CD case). Click OK to continue.

11. In the Destination Path screen, Setup tells you where it will install FrontPage. The Windows 95 default folder is C:\Program Files\Microsoft FrontPage, and the Windows NT default folder is C:\Microsoft FrontPage.

If you want to install FrontPage in a different folder, click the Browse button to locate and select the folder, and then click OK to return to the Destination Path screen. Click Next to continue.

> **T I P**
>
> If you want to quit Setup before it installs Front-Page, click Cancel in any screen that is displayed. No files will be copied to your hard drive.

12. In the Setup Type screen, you're asked to select either the Typical or the Custom installation. The differences are as follows.

> **T I P**
>
> Web sites created in FrontPage 1.1 are fully compatible with Front-Page 97. See page 351 for more information.

**Typical installation** Setup installs the FrontPage client software, the FrontPage Personal Web Server (if one is not already installed), and the FrontPage Server Extensions.

**Custom installation** You can select any available combination of the FrontPage client software, the FrontPage Personal Web Server, and/or the Server Extensions. In a network setting, you can select a Custom setup if you only want to install the FrontPage client software on a local computer.

Select either the Typical or Custom option, and then click Next. If you select Typical, skip to step 16. If you select Custom, proceed to step 13.

13. If you selected a Custom installation, the Select Components screen appears and allows you to select which portions of FrontPage to install.

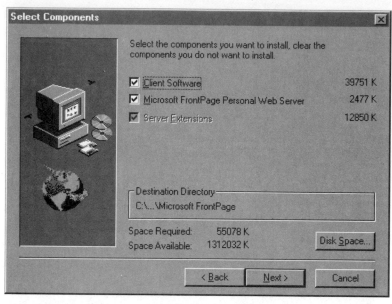

Select any available combination of the Client Software, FrontPage Personal Web Server, and Server Extensions check boxes. The Browse button allows you to specify a folder in which to install FrontPage. Based on your selections, the Space Required and Space Available values are updated. The Disk Space button allows you to see the space available on other drives. After you finish making your selections, click Next.

14. If you opted to install the FrontPage Personal Web Server, the Choose Microsoft FrontPage Personal Web Server Directory screen is displayed. Here you can specify a folder for the FrontPage Personal Web Server. The Default folder is C:\FrontPage Webs. If you want to install the FrontPage Personal Web Server in a different folder, click Browse, select the folder, and then click OK. Click Next to continue.

15. If you have an existing Web server installed and you are trying to install the FrontPage Personal Web Server, the FrontPage Personal Web Server screen will be displayed. It will contain information on how the FrontPage Personal Web Server will be configured. Write down this information, and click Next to continue.

16. If you have the Microsoft Personal Web Server, the FrontPage Personal Web Server, or another recognized Web server already installed on your computer, you'll see the Installed Servers Detected screen. Here you can select the servers for which you want to install the Server Extensions. Select the desired servers in the list box, and click Next.

17. If you are installing on a computer running Windows NT 3.51, the next screen is the Select Program Folder screen. Here you can select a program folder, which is by default Microsoft FrontPage, or enter a new one. After you select a program folder, click Next to continue.

18. Now you're just about done—you'll see the Start Copying Files screen, where you can confirm the information you entered in the wizard. Verify everything in the Current Settings list box.

    If you want to change any information that you've entered in the wizard, click the Back button until you reach the appropriate screen(s). Make the necessary changes, and then click Next until you once again reach the Start Copying Files screen. Click Next to have Setup begin copying files to your hard disk.

19. You might encounter some Server Administrator dialog boxes as the setup process nears completion. The following example is for the FrontPage Personal Web Server.

Enter the appropriate information in these dialog boxes, write down any necessary information, and then click OK to continue with the installation. If you see a dialog box asking you whether to restart the server to complete installation of the WWW Service of the Microsoft Personal Web Server, click Yes. You might also encounter a dialog box recommending that you restart Windows to complete the installation.

20. If you don't need to restart, you'll typically see the Setup Complete screen, which is the final wizard screen. You can start using FrontPage immediately by selecting the Start The FrontPage Explorer Now check box. Click Finish to complete your FrontPage installation.

## Upgrading to FrontPage 97 from FrontPage 1.1

This section describes some issues to consider when upgrading to FrontPage 97 from FrontPage 1.1.

**Installing FrontPage97 over FrontPage 1.1**   If you install FrontPage 97 in the same folder as FrontPage 1.1, it will be upgraded to FrontPage 97. If you do not want to overwrite FrontPage 1.1, you must install FrontPage 97 in a different folder.

**Upgrading the FrontPage Personal Web Server to the Microsoft Personal Web Server**   If you have the FrontPage Personal Web Server installed on the default port (80) and you try to install the Microsoft Personal Web Server, the following dialog box will appear, asking if you want instructions for switching to the Microsoft Personal Web Server:

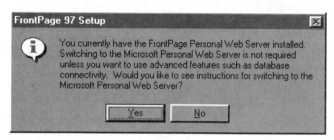

If you click Yes and you have a browser installed, an HTML file opens in your browser. (If you do not have a browser installed, you can install Microsoft Internet Explorer 3.0 from the Bonus Pack.) This HTML file (UPGRADE.HTM), which is on the FrontPage 97 CD-ROM, has information on the following topics:

◆ Upgrading your FrontPage 1.1 Personal Web Server and content to the new Microsoft Personal Web Server

◆ Using both the FrontPage Personal Web Server and the Microsoft Personal Web Server on the same machine

◆ Migrating existing content

**Importing preexisting FrontPage 1.1 sites into FrontPage 97** To import any preexisting FrontPage 1.1 sites, follow the steps below:

1. Launch the FrontPage Explorer.

2. Choose Import from the File menu. Since a site isn't open, this starts the Import Web Wizard.

3. Enter a name for the site in the Name Of New Front-Page Web text box, and click OK.

4. Enter the location of the FrontPage 1.1 site folder in the Source Directory text box in the Choose Directory screen. You can also click Browse to search for it. FrontPage 1.1 typically saves sites in the location C:\FrontPage Webs\Content\<Site Name>. Select the Include Subdirectories check box and then click Next.

5. Edit the file list if necessary in the Edit File List screen. Click Next.

6. In the Finish screen, click Finish to import the site.

For more information on the Import Web Wizard, see Chapter 4. For another method of importing your existing FrontPage 1.1 Web sites—using the Publish FrontPage Webs command—see the HTML file named UPGRADE.HTM on the FrontPage 97 CD_ROM (described above).

## Uninstalling FrontPage 97

If by some freak of nature you lose control of your mind by drinking seven triple grande almond mochas in the space of an hour and decide you want to uninstall FrontPage 97, here's all you have to do:

**In Windows 95 or Windows NT 4.0** In the Windows Control Panel, double-click the Add/Remove Programs icon, select Microsoft FrontPage 97 from the list box on the Install/Uninstall tab, and click Add/Remove. A dialog box will appear, asking you to confirm the removal. Click Yes to begin the uninstall process. The UnInstallShield program will display a screen with the status of the uninstall. Address any dialog boxes that might appear. When the UnInstallShield program is done, read any messages that it displays and click the OK button to complete the process.

**In Windows NT 3.51** The procedure is the same as with Windows 95 or Windows NT 4.0, but instead of using Add/Remove Programs, you double-click the Uninstall FrontPage icon in the Microsoft FrontPage program group.

## Uninstalling the Microsoft Personal Web Server

**In Windows 95** In the Windows Control Panel, double-click the Add/Remove Programs icon, select Personal Web Server from the list box on the Intall/Uninstall tab, and click Add/Remove. A dialog box will appear, asking you to confirm the removal. Click Yes to begin the uninstall process. When it's done, a message box will be displayed indicating that you must restart your computer to complete the removal. Click OK.

# Glossary

**absolute URL** The Internet address of a page or other World Wide Web resource that includes the protocol and complete network location of the page or file. The absolute URL includes a protocol, such as "http," network location, and optional path and file name. For example, `http://www.acme.com/welcome.html` is an absolute URL.

**active hyperlink** A hyperlink that is currently selected in a Web browser. Some Web browsers indicate the active hyperlink by changing its color.

**active page** The page currently being edited in the FrontPage Editor.

**ActiveX control** A component that can be inserted in a page to provide functionality not directly available in HTML, such as animation sequences, credit-card transactions, or spreadsheet calculations. ActiveX controls can be implemented in a variety of programming languages from Microsoft and third parties.

**address** A paragraph style usually used to render addresses on a page or to supply signatures or other indications of authorship. Address paragraphs are usually displayed in italics and are sometimes indented.

**anonymous FTP** A file transfer (FTP) service in which any user can copy files by logging on with the name "anonymous." See also *FTP*.

**applet** See *Java applet*.

**article** A single entry in a discussion group. An article can be a response to a previous article.

**ASCII** (American Standard Code for Information Interchange) The predominant method for encoding 7-bit characters on a personal computer. HTML tags and URLs must be in ASCII. The FrontPage Editor generates these elements automatically.

**authentication database** A database on a server that matches user names to passwords.

**background sound** A sound file that you associate with a page. When the page is displayed in a Web browser, the sound file repeats the number of times that you specify.

**base URL** An optional URL that you assign to a page to convert relative URLs on the page into absolute URLs. A base URL should end with a document name part, such as `http://sample/sample.htm`, or a trailing slash, such as `http://sample/subdir/`.

**BMP** A resolution-dependent file format for images created by Windows Paint, PaintBrush, and other applications.

**bookmark** A named set of zero or more characters in a paragraph that can be the target of a hyperlink. In a URL, a bookmark is preceded by a number sign character.

**broken hyperlink** In the FrontPage Explorer, a hyperlink that does not correctly point to a page or other Internet file. A broken hyperlink either indicates an incorrect URL or a missing page or file.

**browser** See *Web browser*.

**bulleted list** A paragraph style that creates a single list element, usually indicated by a bullet character. Also called an *unordered list*.

**bulletin board** An Internet service that makes multiple discussion groups available.

**cell** The smallest component of a table. In a table, a row contains one or more cells.

**cell padding** The space between the contents and inside edges of a table cell.

**cell spacing** The amount of space between cells in a table. Cell spacing is the thickness, in pixels, of the walls of each cell.

**CERN image map dispatcher** The program HTIMAGE.EXE, which handles server-side image maps in the Personal Web Server when the image map style is set to "CERN" in the FrontPage Explorer **Web Settings** dialog box.

**CGI** (Common Gateway Interface) A standard mechanism for extending Web server functionality by executing programs or scripts on the Web server in response to Web browser requests. A common use of CGI is in form processing, where the browser sends the form data to a CGI script on the server, and the script integrates the data with a database and sends back a results page as HTML.

**change style dropdown** A dropdown control on the FrontPage Editor toolbar in which you can choose the format of the currently selected paragraphs.

**check box** A form field that presents the user with a selection that can be chosen by clicking on a box. When the box is selected, it is usually displayed with a check mark or X. Check boxes can represent a set of non-exclusive choices.

**client** On the Internet, a program that requests files or services from a server.

**client-side image map** An image map that encodes the destination URL of each hotspot directly in the page. Client-side image maps do not require processing from your server to respond to clicks on the image map, so they are more efficient. However, not all browsers support client-side image maps.

**client-side program** On the Internet, a program that is run on the client machine rather than on the server machine. Client-side programs do not communicate over the Internet.

**clip art** A collection of icons, buttons, and other generally useful graphics files that can be inserted into pages.

**clipboard** A temporary storage area on the computer for cut or copied items.

**comment** Text that you can view in the FrontPage Editor but that will not be displayed by a Web browser. Comment text is displayed in purple and retains the character-size and other attributes of the current paragraph style.

**column** In a table, a vertical collection of cells.

**configuration variable** Information about a FrontPage web or page that can be displayed by WebBot form results components or WebBot **Substitution** components when the page is browsed. FrontPage includes standard web configuration and page configuration variables. You can define new configuration variables by editing the **Parameters** tab of the FrontPage Explorer **Web Settings** dialog box.

**confirmation page** A page that is displayed in the browser after a form has been submitted by a user. The confirmation page usually echoes the user's name and other data from the form. You specify a form's confirmation page in the form handler's dialog box.

**converter** A tool that converts a file, or a portion of a file, from one format to another. For example, FrontPage includes a Microsoft Word to HTML converter.

**current FrontPage web** The FrontPage web currently opened in the FrontPage Explorer.

**custom dictionary** A dictionary of words that are not in the standard dictionary but that should be accepted by the spelling checker as correct. The custom dictionary is built by the spelling checker Microsoft FrontPage\data\ Fpcustom.dic. You can edit this file with a text editor.

**default hyperlink** In an image map, the hyperlink to follow when the user clicks outside of any hotspots on the image. You set the default hyperlink by editing the **Default Hyperlink** field in the **Image Properties** dialog box.

**definition** The style of the second of a pair of paragraphs composing a definition list entry. The first paragraph in the pair is the term.

**definition list** A list of alternating term and definition paragraphs. Definition lists are often used to implement dictionaries in FrontPage webs. See also *term* and *definition*.

**discussion group** A FrontPage web that supports interactive discussions by users. Users submit topics by entering text in a form, and they can search the group using a search form or access articles using a table of contents.

**discussion group directory** A directory in a FrontPage web containing all of the articles in a discussion group. The name of a discussion group directory begins with an underscore character and is created automatically by FrontPage. Discussion group directories are not normally visible from the FrontPage Explorer. However, they can be searched by a WebBot **Search** component.

**domain name** See *network location*.

**drop-down menu field** A form field that presents a list of selections in drop-down menu style. A drop-down menu form field can be configured to permit the selection of many fields or a single field.

**editor** An interactive program that can create and modify files of a particular type. For example, the FrontPage Editor is an HTML editor.

**e-mail** (electronic mail) A service for sending messages electronically, over a computer network.

**emphasis text** The HTML character style used for mild emphasis. Certain browsers display emphasized text as italic.

**EPS** (Encapsulated PostScript) An extension of the PostScript graphics file format developed by Adobe Systems. EPS lets PostScript graphics files be incorporated into other documents. FrontPage supports importing EPS files.

**Ethernet** A commonly used local area network (LAN) technology.

**extended attribute** An HTML attribute not directly supported in FrontPage. In FrontPage, extended attributes are assigned to an object such as a page or image using the **Extended** button in the object's properties dialog box.

**external hyperlink** A hyperlink to any file that is outside the current FrontPage web.

**FAQ** (Frequently Asked Questions) A common type of document on the Internet that contains a list of questions and answers on a common theme. On the World Wide Web, questions are often hyperlinks to the answers.

**file** A named collection of information that is stored on a computer disk. Also, an Internet protocol that refers to files on the local disk. You can create file hyperlinks (file://) in the FrontPage Editor using the **Hyperlink** command.

**file server** A program running on a network that stores files and provide access to them. Also called *server*.

**file type** The format of a file, usually indicated by its filename extension. Editors usually work on a limited set of file types. Use the **Options** command in the FrontPage Explorer to select the application with which to edit different file types in FrontPage.

**finger** An Internet program that displays information about the users currently logged on to a computer.

**firewall** A method of protecting one network from another network. A firewall blocks unwanted access to the protected network while giving the protected network access to networks outside of the firewall. A company will typically install a firewall to give users access to the Internet while protecting their internal information. FrontPage works with firewalls.

**folder** In a URL, a single part of the path to a page. A folder is a named storage area on the computer containing files and other folders. In `http://my.web.site/sample/test.htm`, `sample/` is a folder.

**Folder View** In the FrontPage Explorer, the view of a FrontPage web that shows the containment relationship between folders in the FrontPage web. You can create, delete, copy, and move folders in the **Folder View**.

**form** A set of data entry fields on a page that are processed on the server. The data is sent to the server when the user submits the form by clicking on a button or, in some cases, by clicking on an image.

**form field** A data-entry field on a page. A user supplies information in a field either by typing text or by selecting the field.

**form handler** A program on a server that executes when a user submits a form. A FrontPage form is associated with a form handler in the Form Properties dialog box.

**formatted text** A mono-spaced paragraph style in which all white space (such as tabs and spaces) is displayed by the browser. In other text styles, extra white space may be ignored by the browser.

**formatting toolbar** The FrontPage Editor toolbar containing commands that reformat selected paragraphs or text.

**forms toolbar** The FrontPage Editor toolbar containing commands that create form fields.

**frame** A named element of a frame set. A frame appears in a Web browser as a scrollable window in which pages can be displayed. You assign a page to a frame when you create a hyperlink to the page.

**frame set** A page that defines a set of named scrollable windows in which other pages can be displayed. Use a frame set when you want the contents of one part of the page to remain unchanged while the contents of other parts of the page change based on hyperlinks that the user selects. To create a frame set in FrontPage, from the FrontPage Editor **File** menu, choose **New** and choose the Frames wizard.

**FrontPage Editor** The FrontPage tool for creating, editing, and testing Web pages.

**FrontPage Explorer** The FrontPage program that lets you create, view, modify, and administer FrontPage webs.

**FrontPage Server Extensions** A set of programs and scripts that support FrontPage and extend the functionality of the Web server. The FrontPage Server Extensions are available for the Microsoft Internet Information Server and other popular Windows NT and UNIX Web servers. If you are not sure if your Web server is supported, visit /www.microsoft.com/frontpage/.

**FrontPage web** A home page and its associated pages, images, documents, multimedia, and other files that is stored on a World Wide Web server or on a computer's hard drive. A FrontPage web also contains files that support FrontPage functionality such as WebBot components, and that allow the web to be opened, copied, edited, and administered in the FrontPage Explorer.

**FrontPage web name** The name of the FrontPage web. A FrontPage web name corresponds to a directory name on a Web server and is subject to the length, character restrictions, and case sensitivity of that server.

**FrontPage web title** A descriptive name for a FrontPage web. The FrontPage web title is displayed in the title bar of the FrontPage Explorer window when the FrontPage web is open. A FrontPage web title must start with a letter and can have a maximum of 31 characters.

**FTP** (File Transfer Protocol) The Internet service that transfers files from one computer to another. You can create ftp hyperlinks (ftp://) in the FrontPage Editor.

**gateway script** See *CGI*.

**GIF** (Graphics Interchange Format) A commonly used method of encoding images that contain up to 256 colors.

**gopher** The Internet protocol in which files are displayed in a hierarchical menu and are retrieved based on user input. You can create gopher hyperlinks (gopher://) in the FrontPage Editor.

**heading** A paragraph type that is displayed in a large, bold typeface. The size of a heading is related to its level: **Heading 1** is the largest, **Heading 2**, the next largest, and so on. Use headings to name pages and parts of pages.

**hidden field** A form field that is invisible to the user but that supplies data to the form handler. Each hidden field is implemented as a name-value pair. When the form is submitted by the user, its hidden fields are passed to the form-handler along with name-value pairs for each visible form field. You add hidden fields to FrontPage by clicking **Add** in the **Form Properties** dialog box.

**hidden folder** A folder in a FrontPage web with a name beginning with an underscore character, as in _hidden. By default, pages and files in hidden folders cannot be viewed from the FrontPage Explorer.

**home page** The starting point on a Web server. It is the page that is retrieved and displayed by default when a user visits the Web server. The default home-page name for a server depends on the server's configuration. On most Web servers, it is index.html or index.htm. Some servers support multiple home pages.

**horizontal line** A horizontal graphic element on a World Wide Web page often used to separate sections of the page.

**host** See *server*.

**host name** See *network location*.

**hotspot** A graphically defined area in an image that contains a hyperlink. An image with hotspots is called an image map. In browsers, hotspots are invisible. Users can tell that a hotspot is present by the changing appearance of the pointer.

**HTIMAGE.EXE** The CERN image map dispatcher. This program handles server-side image maps when the image map style is "CERN".

**HTML** (HyperText Markup Language). The standard language for describing the contents and structure of pages on the World Wide Web. The FrontPage Page Editor reads and writes HTML files. You do not need to know anything about HTML syntax to use FrontPage.

**HTML attribute** A name-value pair used within an HTML tag to assign additional properties to the object being defined. FrontPage assigns some attributes automatically when you create an object such as a paragraph or image map. You can assign other attributes by editing the Properties dialog box.

**HTML character encoding** A table which associates a numeric index with each character in a character set. The table is used when you create a Web page for use in a specific language.

**HTML tag** A symbol used in HTML to identify a page element's type, format, and structure. The FrontPage Editor automatically creates HTML tags to represent each element on the page.

**HTTP** (HyperText Transport Protocol) The Internet protocol that allows World Wide Web browsers to retrieve information from servers.

**hyperlink** A jump from text or from an image map to a page or other type of file on the World Wide Web. In World Wide Web pages, hyperlinks are the primary way to navigate between pages and among Web sites.

**Hyperlink View** A view in the FrontPage Explorer that graphically shows the hyperlinks among pages and other files in your FrontPage web along with the hyperlinks from your FrontPage web to other World Wide Web sites.

**hypertext** Originally, any textual information on a computer containing jumps to other information. The hypertext jumps are called hyperlinks. In World Wide Web pages hypertext is the primary way to navigate between pages and among Web sites. Hypertext on World Wide Web pages has been expanded to include hyperlinks from text and hyperlinks from image maps.

**IIS** (Internet Information Server) Microsoft's high-performance, secure, and extensible Internet server based on Windows NT Server. IIS supports the World Wide Web, FTP, and gopher.

**image** A graphic in GIF or JPEG file format that can be inserted in a World Wide Web page. FrontPage lets you import images in the following formats and insert them as GIF or JPEG: GIF, JPEG, BMP (Windows and OS/2), TIFF, TAG, PCD, RAS, EPS, PCX, and WMF.

**image alignment** In FrontPage, the specification of how images and text are aligned with each other on the page. You specify image alignment in FrontPage by editing the **Image Properties** dialog box.

**image form field** A form field that displays an image in a form. By clicking the image, the user either submits or clears the form.

**image map** An image containing one or more invisible regions, called hotspots, which are assigned hyperlinks. Typically, an image map gives users visual cues about the information made available by clicking on each part of the image. For example, a geographical map could be made into an image map by assigning hotspots to each region of interest on the map.

**image toolbar** The FrontPage Editor toolbar that contains commands that operate on images. You use the image toolbar to create hotspots, for example.

**IMAGEMAP.EXE** The NCSA image map dispatcher. This program handles server-side image maps when the image map style is "NCSA" and you are using the FrontPage Personal Web Server.

**inline image** An image that is embedded in a line of text rather than in its own window. In FrontPage, images are inline by default.

**interlaced image** A GIF image that is displayed full-sized at low resolution while it is being loaded, and at increasingly higher resolutions until it is fully loaded and has a normal appearance.

**internal hyperlink** A hyperlink to any file that is inside the current FrontPage web.

**internal web** A World Wide Web site created within an organization and accessible only to members of that organization on an intranet.

**Internet** The global computer network, composed of thousands of Wide Area Networks (WANs) and Local Area Networks (LANs), that uses TCP\IP to provide world-wide communications to homes, schools, businesses, and governments. The World Wide Web runs on the Internet.

**Internet address** See *network location*.

**Internet database connector** A Microsoft IIS feature that allows your World Wide Web site to access databases.

**IP** (Internet Protocol) Internet software that divides data into packets for transmission over the Internet. Computers must run IP to communicate across the Internet. See also *TCP*.

**IP address** (Internet Protocol address) The standard way of identifying a computer that is connected to the Internet, much the way a telephone number identifies a telephone on a telephone network. The IP address is four numbers separated by periods, and each number is less than 256, for example, 192.200.44.69. Your system administrator or Internet service provider will assign your machine an IP address.

**IP address mask** (Internet Protocol address mask) A range of IP addresses defined so that only machines with IP addresses within the range are allowed access to an Internet service. To mask a portion of the IP address, replace it with the asterisk wild card character (*). For example, 192.44.*.* represents every computer on the Internet with an IP address beginning with 192.44.

**ISAPI** (Internet Server Application Programming Interface) A high-performance Web server application development interface, developed by Process Software and Microsoft Corporation, that can be used in place of CGI.

**Java** A general-purpose programming language created by Sun Microsystems. Java can be used to create Java applets. A Java program is downloaded from the Web server and interpreted by a program running on the machine containing the Web browser.

**Java applet** A short program written in Java that is attached to a World Wide Web page and executed by the browser machine.

**JavaScript** A cross-platform, World Wide Web scripting language developed by Netscape Communications. JavaScript code is inserted directly into the HTML page.

**JPEG** (Joint Photographic Expert Group) A color image format with excellent compression for most kinds of images. JPEG is commonly used on the World Wide Web for 24-bit color images.

**LAN** (Local Area Network) A computer network technology that is designed to connect computers that are separated by a short distance. A LAN can be connected to the Internet and can also be configured as an intranet.

**line break** A special character that forces a new line on the page without creating a new paragraph.

**link** See *hyperlink*.

**list** A group of paragraphs formatted to indicate membership in a set or in a sequence of steps. In the FrontPage Editor you can create numbered lists or bulleted lists, menus, directories, or definitions.

**MAC** The Macintosh Paint image format.

**mailto** The Internet protocol that is used to send electronic mail. You can create mailto hyperlinks (mailto://) in the FrontPage Editor.

**marquee** A region on a page that displays a horizontally scrolling message.

**menu list** A list of short paragraph entries formatted with little white space between them.

**meta tag** An HTML tag that must appear in the <head> portion of the page. Meta tags supply information about the page but do not effect its display. A standard meta tag, "generator," is used to supply the type of editor that created the HTML page.

**Microsoft Image Composer** A powerful image composing and editing application that is integrated with FrontPage.

**MIME type** (Multipurpose Internet Mail Extensions type) A method used by Web browsers to associate files of a certain type with helper applications that display files of that type.

**MSP** Microsoft Paint image format.

**multihosting** The ability of a Web server to support more than one Internet address and more than one home page on a single server. Also called *multihoming*.

**name-value pair** The name of a form field and the value of the field at the time the form is submitted. Each field in a form can have one or more name-value pairs, and the form itself can have one or more name-value pairs.

**NCSA image map dispatcher** The program IMAGEMAP.EXE, which handles server-side image maps when the image map style is "NCSA" and you are using the FrontPage Personal Web Server.

**nested list** A list that is contained within a member of another list. Nesting is indicated by indentation in most Web browsers. When you create one list element within another list element in FrontPage, the new list element is automatically nested.

**network location** In a URL, the unique name that identifies an Internet server. A network location has two or more parts, separated by periods, as in my.network.location. Also called host name and Internet address.

**news** The Internet protocol for retrieving files from an Internet news service. You can create news hyperlinks (news://) in the FrontPage Editor.

**normal text** The default paragraph style of the FrontPage Editor, intended for use in text paragraphs.

**NSAPI** (Netscape Server Application Programming Interface) A Netscape-only Web server application development interface, developed by Netscape Communications Corporation.

**numbered list** The World Wide Web page paragraph style that presents an ordered list of items.

**OLE** (Object Linking and Embedding) An object system created by Microsoft. OLE lets the author invoke different editor components to create a compound document.

**one-line text box** A labeled, single-line form field in which users can type text.

**page** A single document in a World Wide Web site written using the HTML language. You use the FrontPage Editor to create, modify, and test pages, without having to learn HTML.

**page title** A text string identifying a page. The page title is displayed in the FrontPage Explorer and is used by many FrontPage Editor and FrontPage Explorer commands.

**paragraph style** A label for a FrontPage Editor paragraph-type. Paragraph style specifies the type of font to use in a paragraph, along with the font's size, and other attributes. Paragraph style also specifies whether to use bullets and numbering, and controls indentation and line spacing.

**password** A text string that allows a user access to an Internet service, if the service requires it.

**path** The portion of a URL that identifies the folders containing a file. For example, in the URL http://my.web.site/hello/world /greetings.htm, the path is /hello/world/.

**PCT** (Personal Communications Technology) An enhanced version of Secure Socket Layer. See also *SSL*.

**PCX** A file format that compresses its image data with RLE-type compression, used by early versions of Windows PaintBrush. FrontPage can import PCX files.

**plug-in** One of a set of software modules that integrate into Web browsers to offer a range of interactive and multimedia capabilities.

**port** One of the network input/output channels of a computer running TCP/IP. In the World Wide Web, port usually refers to the port number a server is running on. A single computer can have many Web servers running on it, but only one server can be running on each port. The default port for World Wide Web servers is 80.

**properties** The settings and values that characterize an item in a FrontPage web, such as the title and URL of a web, the file name and path of a file, or the name and initial value of a form field.

**protocol** A method of accessing a document or service over the Internet, such as File Transfer Protocol (FTP) or HyperText Transfer Protocol (HTTP). Also called *type*.

**proxy server** An Internet server that acts as a firewall, mediating traffic between a protected network and the Internet.

**push button** A form field that lets the user submit the form or that resets the form to its initial state.

**radio button** A form field that presents the user with a selection that can be chosen by clicking on a button. Radio buttons are presented in a list, one of which is selected by default. Selecting a new member of the list deselects the currently selected item.

**RAS** Sun Raster Image File image format.

**registered user** A user of a Web site with a recorded name and password. In a FrontPage web, you can register users with a WebBot **Registration** component.

**relative URL** The Internet address of a page or other World Wide Web resource with respect to the Internet address of the current page. A relative URL gives the path from the current location of the page to the location of the destination page or resource. A relative URL can

optionally include a protocol. For example, the relative URL `doc/sample.htm` refers to the page sample.htm in the directory doc, below the current directory.

**root web** The FrontPage web that is provided by the server by default. To access the root web, you supply the URL of the server without specifying a page name. FrontPage is installed with a default root web named <root web>. All FrontPage webs are contained by the root FrontPage web.

**row** In a table, a horizontal collection of cells.

**RTF** (Rich Text Format) A method of encoding text formatting and document structure using the ASCII character set. By convention, RTF files have an RTF filename extension. You can open RTF files in the FrontPage Editor and have them converted to HTML.

**script** A type of computer code than can be directly executed by a program that understands the language in which the script is written. Scripts do not need to be compiled into object code to be executed.

**scrolling text box** A labeled, multiple-line form field in which users can type one or more lines of text.

**search form** See *WebBot Search component*.

**Secure Socket Layer** (SSL) A low-level protocol that enables secure communications between a server and FrontPage or a browser.

**selection bar** An unmarked column along the left edge of the FrontPage Editor window that is used to select text with the mouse.

**server** A computer that offers services on a network. On the World Wide Web, the server is the computer that runs the Web server program that responds to HTTP protocol requests by providing Web pages. Also called host.

**server name** See *network location*.

**server-side image map** An image map that passes the coordinates of the cursor to a CGI handler routine on the server. Server-side image maps require your server to compute the target URL of the hyperlink based on the cursor coordinates.

**server-side include** A feature provided by some Web servers that automatically inserts text onto pages when they are given to the browser.

**SGML** An ISO (International Standards Organization) markup language for representing documents on computers. HTML is based on SGML concepts.

**size handle** The black rectangle displayed on a selected form field or hotspot. When you select a size handle, the cursor becomes a bi-directional arrow. Click and drag a size handle to reshape the field or hotspot.

**special character** A character not in the standard 7-bit ASCII character set, such as the copyright mark (©). In FrontPage, you add special characters in the FrontPage Editor using the **Symbol** command on the **Insert** menu.

**standard toolbar** The FrontPage Editor toolbar containing the most commonly used menu commands.

**status bar** The area at the bottom of the FrontPage Editor or FrontPage Explorer that displays information about the currently selected command or about an operation in progress.

**strong text** The HTML character style used for strong emphasis. Certain browsers display this style as bold.

**table** One or more rows of cells on a page used to organize the layout of a page or arrange data systematically. In FrontPage, you can place anything in a table cell, including text, images, forms, and WebBot components.

**table cell** See *cell*.

**tag** See *HTML tag*.

**tag selection** In the FrontPage Editor, a method of selecting a group of paragraphs and other objects on a page. Use tag selection to select the members of a list, an entire form, or a WebBot component. To tag select a set of objects, move the cursor to the left of the objects until the cursor becomes the tag selection cursor (an arrow pointing to the upper-right), and then double-click.

**task** An item on a FrontPage To Do List representing one action you need to perform to complete a FrontPage web. Some tasks are

automatically generated by FrontPage Wizards. You can also add your own tasks to the To Do list.

**TCP** (Transmission Control Protocol) Internet networking software that controls the transmission of packets of data over the Internet. Among its tasks, TCP checks for lost packets, puts the data from multiple packets into the correct order, and requests that missing or damaged packets be resent. Computers must run TCP to communicate with World Wide Web servers.

**template** A set of designed formats for text and images on which pages and FrontPage webs can be based. After a page or FrontPage web is created using a template, you can modify the page or FrontPage web.

**term** The first of a pair of paragraphs formatted as a definition list entry. The second paragraph is the definition.

**thumbnail** A small version of an image on a World Wide Web page, often containing a hyperlink to a full-size version of the image.

**TIFF** (Tagged Image File Format) A tag-based image format. TIFF is designed to promote universal interchanges of digital images.

**To Do List** The FrontPage tool that maintains a list of the tasks required to complete a FrontPage web. To complete a task on the list, click on it; the program required to do the task starts up with the correct file opened.

**type** See *protocol*.

**typewriter font** The text style that emulates fixed pitch typewritten text. Every character in this font is the same width. Typewriter font is useful for computer code examples and for presenting sample input from the user.

**UNIX** An operating system typically used on proprietary workstations and computers. Some World Wide Web servers run on UNIX systems.

**unordered list** See *bulleted list*.

**URL** (Uniform Resource Locator) A string that supplies the Internet address of a resource on the World Wide Web, along with the protocol by which the resource is accessed. The most common URL type is "http," which gives the

Internet address of a World Wide Web page. Some other URL types are "gopher," which gives the Internet address of a Gopher directory, and "ftp," which gives the address of an FTP resource.

**VBScript** A subset of the Microsoft Visual Basic programming system. Microsoft Internet Explorer version 3.0, along with other browsers, can read VBScript programs embedded in HTML pages. VBScript programs can be executed either on the browser machine or the World Wide Web server. In the FrontPage Editor you can insert and edit VBScripts.

**veronica** An automated Internet search service available through gopher. See also *gopher*.

**video clip** A short video sequence that can be embedded into a World Wide Web page. Video clips can be inserted into FrontPage using ActiveX Controls, VBScripts, Java applets, or plug-ins.

**visited hyperlink** A hyperlink on a page that has been activated. Visited hyperlinks are usually displayed in a unique color by the browser.

**Visual SourceSafe** A document source-control system developed by Microsoft. FrontPage integrates with Visual SourceSafe if you have it installed.

**WAIS** (Wide Area Information Service) Supports searching over the Internet.

**WAN** (Wide Area Network) A computer network that spans a long distance and that uses specialized computers to connect smaller networks.

**watermark** An image that appears on the backgrounds of pages in a Web site to decorate and identify the pages, but which does not scroll as the page scrolls.

**Web browser** A client program that retrieves World Wide Web pages and displays them to the user.

**Web Wizard** The FrontPage interactive tool that guides the author through the creation of a FrontPage web.

**WebBot component** A dynamic object on a page that is evaluated and executed when the author saves the page or, in some cases, when the user browses to the page. Most WebBot components generate HTML.

**WebBot component cursor** The robot-shaped cursor that appears when you move the FrontPage cursor over an area of the page containing a WebBot component.

**WebBot Confirmation Field component** A FrontPage WebBot component that is replaced with the contents of a form field. It is useful on a form confirmation page, where it can echo the user's name or any other data entered into a field.

**WebBot Discussion component** A FrontPage form handler that allows users to participate in an online discussion. The WebBot **Discussion** component collects information from a form, formats it into an HTML page, and adds the page to a table of contents and to a text index. In addition, the WebBot **Discussion** component gathers information from the form and stores it in one of a selection of formats.

**WebBot form component** A FrontPage WebBot component that supplies processing of a form.

**WebBot HTML Markup component** A FrontPage WebBot component that is replaced with any arbitrary text you supply when you create the WebBot component. This text is substituted for the WebBot component when the page is saved to the server as HTML. Use this WebBot component to add non-standard HTML commands to a page.

**WebBot Include component** A FrontPage WebBot component that is replaced with the contents of another page in the FrontPage web. This lets you update parts of many pages in one step.

**WebBot Registration component** A WebBot form component that allows users to automatically register themselves for access to a service implemented as a World Wide Web site. The WebBot **Registration** component adds the user to the service's authentication database, then optionally gathers information from the form and stores it in one of many available formats.

**WebBot Save Results component** A WebBot form component that gathers information from a form and stores it in one of a selection of formats. When a user submits the form, the WebBot **Save Results** component appends the form information to a file on the server in a specified format.

**WebBot Scheduled Image component** A Front-Page WebBot component that is replaced on the page by an image during a specified time period. When the time period has expired, the image is no longer displayed. This is useful for displaying graphical information that has a limited lifetime, such as the announcement of a new product.

**WebBot Scheduled Include component** A FrontPage WebBot component that is replaced with the contents of a file in the FrontPage web during a specified time period. When the time period has expired, the contents of the file are no longer displayed. This is useful for displaying textual information that has a limited lifetime.

**WebBot Search component** A FrontPage WebBot component that creates a form that provides full text-searching capability in your FrontPage web when the FrontPage web is browsed. When the user submits a form containing words to locate, the WebBot **Search** component returns a list of hyperlinks to the pages in your FrontPage web containing matches for the words.

**WebBot Substitution component** A FrontPage WebBot component that is replaced by the value of a selected page configuration or web configuration variable.

**WebBot Table of Contents component** A FrontPage WebBot component that creates an outline of your FrontPage web, with hyperlinks to each page. The WebBot **Table of Contents** component updates this outline each time the FrontPage web's contents change.

**WebBot Timestamp component** A FrontPage WebBot component that is replaced by the date and time the page was last edited or updated.

**Wizard** A FrontPage program that creates FrontPage webs and pages based on interaction with the author.

**WMF** (Windows MetaFile) A device-independent method of representing an image.

**World Wide Web** The graphical Internet hypertext service that uses the HTTP protocol to retrieve World Wide Web pages and other data from World Wide Web servers. Pages on the World Wide Web usually contain hyperlinks to other pages or to multimedia files.

**WPG** An image format used by WordPerfect.

**WYSIWYG** (What You See Is What You Get). An editing interface in which the file being created is displayed as it will appear to the end-user. The FrontPage Editor is a WYSIWYG editor.

# INDEX

# About the Authors

**Kerry A. Lehto** is still in Geek Denial although he can't seem to stop taking on projects with Microsoft. His work history intertwines various interests, including writing and editing in journalism, archaeology, and computing. He has also taught college-level English grammar, coauthored the first corporate archaeological style guide, and worked "Grasshopper Patrol" for the USDA in Wyoming. He has a BA in journalism from the University of Wyoming (go Pokes) and an MA in journalism from the University of Oregon (go Ducks). He spends his spare time getting away to the Cascades, growing his collection of Peanuts books, and racking up as many frequent flyer miles as he can.

From his home in Kirkland, Washington, he writes for Microsoft's Enterprise Customer Unit intranet and Internet sites and offers professional intranet, Internet, and business-writing seminars through his business, KL Communications. For further information, e-mail Kerry at tigerpaw@accessone.com.

**W. Brett Polonsky** has more than 10 years of experience in award-winning graphic design and art direction. Self-taught in computers, he learned on early Macintosh computers and PageMaker 1.0, and has climbed the ladder to high-end Web development, incorporating site planning, structure, UI and design. He currently contracts as a Web producer at Microsoft, creating intranet and Internet sites. He lives in Kirkland, Washington, with his wife, Janell, and his two children, Gage, 5, and Emma, 1.

Brett's other business interests include Polonsky Design, a firm specializing in online and print graphic design. He is also co-founder of Skywards Consulting, Inc., a consulting firm offering services that include an intricate blend of design, layout, information flow, and content structure for the Web, intranets, and the Internet. Visit the Skywards site at //www.skywards.com, or e-mail brett@skywards.com.

Together, the authors offer comprehensive FrontPage training via Skywards Consulting. For more information about their various training options, including general and customized training for your company, e-mail info@skywards.com.

The manuscript for this book was prepared and submitted to Microsoft Press in electronic form. Galleys were prepared using Microsoft Word for Windows 95. Pages were composed using PageMaker 6.01 for Windows, with text type in Sabon and display type in Syntax. Composed pages were delivered to the printer as electronic prepress files.

Cover Graphic Designer
**Greg Erickson**

Cover Illustrator
**Scott Baker**

Interior Graphic Design & Photography
**Polonsky Design**

Illustrator
**David Holter**

Composition and Layout
**Frog Mountain Productions—Katherine Erickson**

Proofreader
**Frog Mountain Productions—Sam Ferriss**

Indexer
**Leslie Leland Frank**

All-Around Great Guy
**Kerry A. Lehto**

# Want to: Find a job? Buy a car? Raise ants? Find you uncle? Study paleontology? Learn about bats? Meet casting directors? Look at pictures through the Virtual Magnifying Glass? **Well, be our guest!**

**Includes CD-ROM version with direct links to thousands of Internet sites! A simple double click of the mouse takes you *immediately* wherever you want to go!**

**T**he MICROSOFT® BOOKSHELF® INTERNET DIRECTORY is your host for thousands of Internet sites—an amazing spectrum that covers everything from activism to zoology. Unlike most other Internet directories, this book brings you only the best—the hand-picked crème de la crème, complete with descriptions of and comments on the most useful and entertaining Web sites and ftp sites (locations for down-loading files) on the Internet. The wonders of the Internet await you, and the MICROSOFT BOOKSHELF INTERNET DIRECTORY is your magic carpet to a vast world of information resources.

**So what are you waiting for? Get the MICROSOFT BOOKSHELF INTERNET DIRECTORY!**

| | |
|---|---|
| **U.S.A.** | **$35.00** |
| U.K. | £32.99 [V.A.T. included] |
| Canada | $47.95 |
| ISBN 1-55615-947-1 | |

**Microsoft**®*Press*

# Take productivity in stride.

Microsoft Press® *Step by Step* books provide quick and easy self-paced training that will help you learn to use the powerful word processor, spreadsheet, database, desktop information manager and presentation applications of Microsoft® Office 97, both individually and together. In approximately eight hours of instruction prepared by the professional trainers at Catapult, Inc. and Perspection, Inc., the easy-to-follow lessons in each book present clear objectives and real-world business examples, with numerous screen shots and illustrations. Put Microsoft's Office 97 applications to work today, *Step by Step*.

Microsoft Press® products are available worldwide wherever quality computer books are sold. For more information, contact your book retailer, computer reseller, or local Microsoft Sales Office.

To locate your nearest source for Microsoft Press products, reach us at www.microsoft.com/mspress/, or call 1-800-MSPRESS in the U.S. (in Canada: 1-800-667-1115 or 416-293-8464).

To order Microsoft Press products, call 1-800-MSPRESS in the U.S. (in Canada: 1-800-667-1115 or 416-293-8464).

Prices and availability dates are subject to change.

**Microsoft® Excel 97 Step by Step**
**U.S.A.   $29.95**   ($39.95 Canada)
ISBN 1-57231-314-5

**Microsoft® Word 97 Step by Step**
**U.S.A.   $29.95**   ($39.95 Canada)
ISBN 1-57231-313-7

**Microsoft® PowerPoint® 97 Step by Step**
**U.S.A.   $29.95**   ($39.95 Canada)
ISBN 1-57231-315-3

**Microsoft® Outlook™ 97 Step by Step**
**U.S.A.   $29.99**   ($39.99 Canada)
ISBN 1-57231-382-X

**Microsoft® Access 97 Step by Step**
**U.S.A.   $29.95**   ($39.95 Canada)
ISBN 1-57231-316-1

**Microsoft® Office 97 Integration Step by Step**
**U.S.A.   $29.95**   ($39.95 Canada)
ISBN 1-57231-317-X

***Microsoft*®*Press***

# Register Today!

## Return this
### *Introducing Microsoft® FrontPage™ 97*
## registration card for
## a Microsoft Press® catalog

U.S. and Canada addresses only. Fill in information below and mail postage-free.  Please mail only the bottom half of this page.

1-57231-571-2A                              *INTRODUCING MICROSOFT ®*               *Owner Registration Card*
                                               *FRONTPAGE™ 97*

_____

NAME

_____

INSTITUTION OR COMPANY NAME

_____

ADDRESS

_____

_____

CITY                                                       STATE           ZIP

# **Microsoft** Press
## *Quality Computer Books*

**For a free catalog of
Microsoft Press® products, call
1-800-MSPRESS**

**MICROSOFT PRESS REGISTRATION**
INTRODUCING MICROSOFT®
FRONTPAGE™ 97
PO BOX 3019
BOTHELL  WA    98041-9946